MW01076825

SALONS, SINGERS AND SONGS

In memory of Jean Maillard (1926–1985)
man and musicologist *par excellence*

Salons, Singers and Songs

A background to romantic French song 1830–1870

David Tunley

John Michael Cooper
28 April 2005
Georgetown, Texas

Ashgate

Published by
Ashgate Publishing Limited
Gower House
Croft Road
Aldershot
Hants GU11 3HR
England

Ashgate Publishing Company
131 Main Street
Burlington, VT 05401–5600 USA

Ashgate website: http://www.ashgate.com

British Library Cataloguing-in-Publication data

Tunley, David
  Salons, singers and songs:a background to romantic French song, 1830–1870:David Tunley
  1. Songs, French – 19th century – History and criticism
  2. Love songs – France – History and criticism
  I. Title
  782.4'2'0944'09034

Library of Congress Cataloging-in-Publication data

Tunley, David
  Salons, singers, and songs:a background to romantic French song 1830–1870/David Tunley.
    p. cm.
  Includes bibliographical references and index.
    1. Songs, French – France – Paris – 19th century – History and criticism. 2. Singers – France – Paris – History – 19th century. 3. Romanticism in music – France – Paris. 4. Salons – France – Paris – History – 19th century. 5. Paris (France) – Social life and customs – 19th century. I. Title.

  ML2527.8.P37 T86 2002
  782.42164'0944'361 – dc21   2001046037

ISBN 0 7546 0491 8

Printed on acid-free paper

Typeset in Times by Express Typesetters, Farnham, Surrey and printed in England by MPG Books Ltd, Bodmin, Cornwall

Contents

Introduction

No other society wrote about itself so fervently, and often so wittily, as did that of nineteenth-century Paris. Through diaries, letters, memoirs and, above all, the music periodicals of the day we can gain a glimpse of the ebullient musical life of the capital, even entering the doors of private salons, many of which included musical performances that were reported on by critics of the day. Performances in these fashionable salons, which almost invariably included songs, provided musicians with many professional opportunities. Some singers, for example, were to make their careers in the salons. An intimate alliance between salons, singers and songs – particularly in the first half of the century – may be observed in the development of the nineteenth-century romance and mélodie.

Although often mentioned in general terms, details about music in the private Parisian salons are not readily available in the literature. Appendix A lists in chronological order (1834–1870) all those cited in the *Revue et Gazette musicale* (including its predecessors the *Revue musicale* and the *Gazette musicale de Paris*), *Le Ménestrel* and *Le Monde musical*. Strange to say, their reporters were often invited to these gatherings – even in the most aristocratic homes – and we are thus able to glimpse what went on behind otherwise closed doors. Such salons, for which an invitation was essential, ranged from very intimate gatherings to those to which a thousand guests might throng, host and hostess belonging to the aristocracy, the government, the wealthy middle class or from the music profession (particularly teachers) and the artistic community generally. Music critics and reporters were hard-pressed enough to cover as many of the commercial recitals, concerts and opera performances as they could at a time when music was burgeoning in Paris (by 1865 it was estimated that over 400 public concerts took place in Paris in the first six months of that year) and therefore accounts of private events are relatively few in comparison. The nearly one thousand recitals listed in Appendix A amounted to probably far less than a quarter of those actually given in private homes and at receptions. There were many salons that offered their guests music every week, yet only one such recital might be reported during the concert season, and sometimes we learn from a single report that a particular salon had been the centre of fine performances for some years. Thus Appendix A must remain incomplete. Furthermore, because the terminology 'matinée musicale' and 'soirée' and even 'salon' was common to both private and commercial music making, there is sometimes a blurred line between public and private. However, only those in which it is clear that the event was in someone's home or at a private reception have been included in the list, which also excludes recitals by the students in the homes of music teachers and those organized for charitable purposes. Because of the nature of the present study Appendix A also excludes the names of instrumentalists and the music they played; otherwise the list would have become impossibly overloaded. In Chapter Two there are sufficient descriptions of some salons to enable the reader to gain a good idea of all the music that was performed on some of those occasions. Unfortunately, many of the reviews of salon recitals are frustratingly incomplete and inconsistent. For example there were many salons at which some of the finest professional singers (like Pauline Viardot) appeared, yet all we learn is that some unnamed romances were sung; yet, on the other hand, in February 1862, an entire column of the *Revue et Gazette musicale* was devoted to the performance of an opéra comique composed by a young aristocratic officer whose only claim to fame was that he had fought gallantly in the Crimea and in Italy! (The review was masterfully noncommital.) It must also be said that some of the salons were visited by the music critic or reporter because the works of a colleague were being performed there. The value of the list might therefore be questioned. The fact is, however, that – incomplete and sometimes skewed as the reports may be – except for some information in diaries and letters, they provide the only hard evidence we have of what went on in many of those often sumptuous surroundings which have given the cachet to fashionable Paris. We can trace in them the names and popularity of performers and composers and understand more fully what Parisian music lovers wanted and were given. We can recognize musical trends and fashions and note the contribution given to musical life in the capital by those who devoted much energy, wealth and, often, knowledge to their private salons.

Yet the private salons were, of course, only a small part of the scene. For example, in the musical seasons of 1845 and 1846 there were reports of fourteen public recitals or concerts that included songs by Victor Massé (in the Salle Herz, Salle Pleyel, Salle Erard and other venues); yet, in the same period his name is mentioned only twice in accounts of private salons. Thus, the latter must be placed in the larger context of musical Paris, which, in turn, needs to be placed in the wider frame of those events that shaped French society in one of the most turbulent centuries in its long history. This wider background has been lightly sketched throughout this study, the cut-off point of which is the

Franco-Prussian War and the civil strife that followed it. These last events and the role that music was called upon to play in them – not least in song – have been briefly described in a 'postscript' to the study indebted to a series of hitherto-neglected articles in *Le Ménestrel* by the musician and writer Arthur Pougin. Pougin was in Paris during both the Siege and the Commune, and his articles give us a glimpse of musical life there during those terrible times which brought to an end a period of extraordinary panache (see Chapter 9).

It may be questioned as to why 1870 is the cut-off point of the present study. Saint-Saëns and Massenet, for example, continued their output until the early years of the next century – and without discernible changes to their style – and we can be quite sure that if the Franco-Prussian War and Commune had never happened Fauré, Duparc and Debussy would have followed the same paths of originality in their songs as they did. Thus, it does not do to make too much of the impact of 1870 upon the future course of French song. Yet by then nearly all the repertoire which had established the characteristic style of romantic French song had been composed, this being the starting point for the songs of those who imbued it with their distinctive originality and whose achievements in bringing French mélodie to its final stage are well known and written about. So much so, that the earlier repertoire has been cast into shadow – indeed, in most cases, into oblivion. Yet there are many fine songs from this era which deserve to be heard – even the earliest, many of which display a touching naïveté that is missing from the later ones. (The publication of the six volume facsimile edition *Romantic French Song 1830–1870*, Garland Press, 1995, now allows a wider acquaintance with some of the best of that repertoire.) Moreover, during the Third Republic the salon tradition was beginning to weaken, these fashionable private gatherings no longer having the same importance in Parisian musical life that they once held.

For those readers who prefer the flavour and character of the French language, quotations appear (when appropriate) in their original form in the Notes, sometimes in a slightly more expanded way than in the translations or paraphrases that are in the body of the text. Any study of nineteenth-century French song is indebted to Frits Noske's *French Song from Berlioz to Duparc* (1970). The present study is by no means an attempt to re-write that magisterial book. Rather, it is meant to complement it, exploring aspects largely left alone by Noske, although some overlap is inevitable. The present book provides no roll-call either of works or composers, for its purpose is to place romantic French song in the framework of the society which nurtured it.

Some of the material concerning the salons was presented at the University of New England (Australia) for the 1997 Gordon Athol Anderson Memorial Lecture and published by that university which has given me permission to use it here. The research leading to this study was greatly assisted by a grant from the Australian Research Committee in 1992 which funded the purchase of many of the sources on microfilm and the provision of a part-time assistant in the early years of the research, Dr Lorraine Richards, to whom I am most indebted. A period as The Fowler Hamilton Visiting Research Fellow at Christ Church, Oxford in 1993 and later as a Visiting Scholar at Wolfson College, Oxford gave me the benefit of a scholarly environment in which to carry out the research and writing leading to both the Garland anthology and the present study. I am indebted, as always, to the School of Music at The University of Western Australia which, since my retirement from the Chair of Music in 1994, has appointed me an Honorary Senior Research Fellow. My customary deep thanks go to Miss Jennifer Wildy, Music Librarian at the Wigmore Library in the School of Music for her untiring efforts to help me in ways that would be too long to list here and also to Ms Lucy Peachey in the University's Fine Arts Library. Professor Hugh Macdonald at Washington University, St Louis, offered the kind of encouragement in the early stages of the research that led to its completion. Others who have helped me are Mrs Elisabeth Redfern, Dr Roland Hähnel, Mr Richard Hewison and Professor Virginia Spate. I should like to thank Ms Valerie Langfield especially for help in various and essential ways, and whose keen eye for detail and perceptive comments contributed much to the final version of the manuscript. To my wife Paula go my usual heartfelt thanks for the help she has provided in all ways during the course of the research and writing.

David Tunley
The University of Western Australia

Abbreviations

DS	*Le Dilettante des salons*
GM	*Gazette musicale de Paris*
M	*Le Ménestrel*
MM	*Le Monde musical*
RGM	*Revue et Gazette musicale*
RM	*Revue musicale*
SM	*La Semaine musicale*

CHAPTER ONE

Musical Paris

'Music! it is the great pleasure of this city, the great occupation of the drawing-rooms, which have banished politics, and which have renounced literature, from ennui.', observed the American in Paris in Jules Janin's book of the same name written in the early 1840s.[1] It was not a description likely to please Janin's fellow writers who, on the whole, considered music to be a barrier to conversation and who tended to exclude it from their own salons. According to Daudet, most literary people held music in horror, citing Gautier, for example, who was supposed to have described it as the most disagreeable of all the noises.[2]

About the same time, in a derisive article about the plethora of uninformed musical journals then appearing in Paris, Henri Blanchard suggested that the reason for music's popularity was because politics had gone off the boil, religion interested few people and literature was no longer an essential nourishment for lively minds, having degenerated into serialized novels and into vaudevilles. Thus it was, he claimed, that music now preoccupied all classes of society.[3]

The 'invasion of music' into the salons of the fashionable world, banishing dance (which it was claimed had once been the primary amusement) was the topic for the first editorial of the journal *Le Dilettante des salons*,[4] which first appeared in 1838. It ascribed several causes to this.

> ... first of all the real or affected seriousness of most of our young people, who find the pleasure of dancing ill-befitting the ideas of progress and regeneration which are hovering, they say, over modern societies; but such change is attributable above all to the taste for music, which is spreading daily throughout all classes, and which is becoming almost a necessity, by virtue of the charm that it exerts and the reward that it gives to those who cultivate it successfully.[5]

It is clear from reviews, diaries and letters that the Parisian salons were contributing to the revival of Paris as the centre of musical Europe, regaining the reputation that the capital had once enjoyed before the French Revolution. If their contribution was modest in the overall scene, the salons nevertheless mirrored the musical ferment that followed the accession of Louis-Philippe.

A few months before the revolution that brought Louis-Philippe to the

throne in 1830, François-Joseph Fétis had contemplated the musical scene
around him.

> It is a recognized fact, which would be unnecessary to prove, that each year
> music in France is making rapid and noticeable progress. New schools and
> philharmonic societies are being established everywhere, taste is being formed,
> and appreciation of music is acquiring that perfection which only habit can
> bring. What for so long opposed the development of music was the attitude of
> men occupied with public affairs who believed that cultivation of the arts was
> little needed by the State, while those who were still imbued with the prejudices
> of the *ancien régime* maintained that such activities should be left to the
> professionals. But since a new generation has arisen and a universal thirst for
> knowledge has spread throughout society, music has taken up its rights again
> and has accordingly become an indispensable part, or at least, a useful accessory
> of education. And if anyone doubts this, he would find material proof of it in the
> growth of schools [of music], and in the manufacture of instruments which are
> multiplying in every part of France. Finally, there is a crowd of teachers who can
> scarcely cope with the enormous number of students.[6]

Some forty years earlier it had not only been the dismantling of the social
system and its tradition of musical patronage that had created a crisis for
musicians during the early years of the Revolution; it was also the attitude of
the new political leaders who saw music primarily as a vehicle for propaganda.
No matter their personal inclinations, poet and composer alike had been
harnessed to writing for the 'public-good', resulting in a plethora of rousing,
large-scale odes in praise of liberty or the pagan goddess of agriculture. As for
Napoleon Bonaparte, his musical tastes were so decidedly towards Italian
opera that a distinctively French school had little encouragement during his
reign as the first Emperor of France. It had a greater chance with the
Restoration of the monarchy following Napoleon's downfall in 1815.

Nevertheless, as Jean Mongrédien has shown, during the troubled early
years music lovers were not denied opportunities to hear music, even if public
concerts were primarily, as he suggests, occasions to see and be seen, and
where individual programmes depended for their success upon a variety of
music and performers, the ranks of whom almost always included some
singers.[7] Mongrédien has pointed to the extraordinarily large number of
orchestras that are tantalizingly glimpsed in the documents in the early years
of the Revolution, but about which little is known. From the Restoration
onwards, however, were to be sown the strong seeds of the later growth, most
notably the revival of the Concerts des Amateurs (1825) and the establishment
of the Société des Concerts du Conservatoire (1828).

Amongst these seeds was the revival of the Parisian salon tradition, which,
because of its previous association with rank and wealth (although not
exclusively so), had been broken in the early years of the Revolution. For so

long an intrinsic part of French intellectual and artistic life, salons in Paris and elsewhere soon re-emerged following the death of Robespierre, many of them opening their doors to music for their guests. In examining the documents of the period Mongrédien has concluded that the list of salons that offered music during the time of the First Empire would be far longer than usually imagined. Although the quality of their offerings may often have been questionable, in some the presence of musicians of the calibre of the violinist Pierre Baillot (who, amongst other things, instituted a subscription series of chamber music from 1814 onwards) was sufficient guarantee of high standard.[8] Twenty years later his chamber music recitals – lasting two-and-a-half hours – were attracting six to seven hundred people, a situation that Fétis declared would have been impossible ten years before.[9] The significance of the salons to music in Paris in the years leading up to 1830 may be gauged by the *Revue musicale* where it claimed in one of its issues that salon recitals had become so fashionable as to substitute for regular recitals.[10] Such a fashion was not to last for long, but nevertheless the salons were to remain an important element in Parisian musical life throughout the century. However, it was the proliferation of professional performances in the theatres and commercial concert rooms that provided the real marker of progress, and Fétis had good cause for optimism about the future of music in the capital as he contemplated the musical scene unfolding in Paris during the 1830 season.[11]

The 1830 Season

Now in their third year, the programmes presented by the Société des Concerts du Conservatoire, founded by the violinist/conductor François Habeneck, continued to be the most important orchestral events in Paris. They were devoted primarily to the works of Beethoven, and during the 1830 season, beginning on 21 February, Habeneck conducted eight of the nine symphonies, the 'Choral' symphony waiting for its Paris première until the following season. As well as its six 'regular' events the Société des Concerts presented three 'concerts spirituels' during Easter, and a 'royal command' performance. Usually including a symphony and an overture by Beethoven, the 'regular' concerts, which took place on Sunday from 2.00 p.m., always included a variety of other items. The programme presented on Sunday 25 April is typical. It started with a Haydn Symphony and concluded with Beethoven's Symphony no. 2. In between were choral works: *Ave verum* (Mozart) and *Gloria* (Beethoven), and three solos: one for bassoon, one for violin and one for voice.

For those whose tastes inclined towards sacred choral music, especially from earlier periods, there were the programmes presented by another major organization, the Institution royale de musique religieuse de France founded in 1817 by Alexandre Choron. He had set himself against the prevailing taste for Italian opera, and as a teaching establishment his school was the only rival to the Conservatoire. Far more limited in its activities than the Conservatoire, the Institution trained a number of musicians featured in this book, including the celebrated tenor Gilbert Duprez. During the 1829/30 season the Institution royale presented some 13 concerts, given by professionals and advanced students. Although some of these concerts involved repeat performances the solid choral repertoire, given over a period of just a few months, is impressive by any standards. Handel was strongly represented: *Alessandro*, *Judas Maccabeus*, *Alexander's Feast* and *Samson*. Performances of these and works by C. P. E. Bach, Mozart, Haydn and Graun, as well as by sixteenth-century composers such as Palestrina and Jannequin clearly established Choron's school as an organization of prime musical and educational importance. Its closure soon after this season was a great blow to the artistic life of the city, and its demise was mourned for many years.

That winter season also saw the appearance of a new series of monthly concerts. These were given by the recently formed Athénée musicale which met in the Salle de Saint-Jean of the Hôtel-de-Ville under the auspices of the Prefect of the Seine. The organization had been founded in 1829 both for pedagogy and performance and was a star for some years in the musical firmament. Like many concerts at this time the programmes were immensely long. The third concert in their series was typical:

> Scène (Elwart) on the subject of *L'exilé*, sung by Cambon
> Symphonie concertante (Tulou) for flute, oboe, horn & bassoon
>   soloists: Coche, Biters, Callant, Rickmans
> Fantaisie for piano (Payer), played by Rickmans
> Variations for alto bassoon, (no composer given), played by Rickmans,
>   accompanied by his son aged 8
> Unnamed work, played by Ourry, lst Violin of the Italian Opera, London
> Romance (Panseron), sung by Cambon
> Italian aria (Raoul), sung by Mlle. Beck
> Overture for orchestra (Rigel)
> Fantaisie for harpe (Bochsa), arr. for orchestra [and harp], by
>   Barbiguier, played by Mme Barbiguier
> Aria from *Le barbier de Seville* (Rossini), sung by Mlle. Olivier of the
>   Théâtre des Nouveautés
> Aria, '*Mon enfant, plus de tendres fleurettes*' from *Les noces de
>   Figaro* (Mozart), sung by Heurteaux
> Hate scene from *Armide* (Lully) sung by Mme Kretschmer
> Underworld scene from *Armide* (Gluck) sung by Mlle. Bolard, with
>   orchestra
> Aria from *Armida* (Rossini) sung by Mlle. Kunzé with orchestra[12]

It can be seen that there were some items of exceptional interest, such as the three extracts from settings of the opera *Armide* by Lully, Gluck and Rossini. At the next month's concert two songs from Berlioz' recently composed *Mélodies irlandais* were to be performed.

Other organizations active during that winter season were the Gymnase musicale, the Société musicale des amateurs, the Société libre des Beaux-Arts and the Société Académique des Enfants d'Apollon. With the exception of the Société Académique des Enfants d'Apollon, which had been founded in the first half of the previous century, others had been in existence for only a year or two.

But above all, Paris was a city of theatres. Of some 26 that were active at the beginning of the nineteenth century Napoleon Bonaparte had allowed only a few to remain open, ostensibly to 'protect literary taste' (as Fétis scornfully described this action in his the *Revue musicale* of 1829).[13] The five surviving major theatres were the Comédie-Française, Théâtre de l'Odéon and, for operas, the Opéra, Opéra-Comique and the Théâtre-Italien. Others, which often staged works that required music, were the Théâtre de l'Ambigu, Gaîté, Variétés and Vaudeville. After the fall of Napoleon's Empire new theatres were opened and by the 1830s 17 theatres operated in Paris alone. This, of course, increased as the years went by, a picture mirrored throughout France.

At the beginning of 1830 a Parisian could have turned to the Opéra, the Opéra-Comique or the Théâtre-Italien for the pleasures of either opera or ballet. The Opéra and the Théâtre-Italien each played three nights of the week on alternate nights while the Opéra-Comique, with an enormous repertoire, played every night of the week during its season. From January to June 1830, however, this gave way to a season of German opera given by visiting soloists and chorus. It included Weber's *Der Freischütz* and *Oberon* and Beethoven's *Fidelio*. What with Grand Opera and those in a lighter vein, orchestral and choral concerts, chamber music and other intimate recitals, there was more than enough to exhaust the most avid music lover. It would be hard not to share Fétis' admiration of the musical scene developing so well by the first half of 1830.

*   *   *

Ironically, music got off to a bad start at the beginning of Louis-Philippe's reign. Faced with a severe financial recession and in order to cut government expenditure he used depressingly familiar ways: reduction or removal of subsidies to the arts, and privatization of some institutions.[14] In the case of the Opéra, privatization was an outstanding success. Louis-Philippe appointed as Director a man of great managerial skill and entrepreneurial flair – Louis Véron, who during the five years of his directorship brought the Opéra into a period of greater brilliance than it had ever known. The first work, produced at the beginning of 1831 – and at enormous expense – was the première of Meyerbeer's spectacular *Robert le diable*, the stage effects made even more sensational by the introduction of gas lighting. But in addition to the brilliance on stage was the brilliance of the audience itself which now flocked to the Opéra as never before. One of the reasons for this was that as the Opéra was now formally disassociated from the court, it was seen as 'neutral' territory where political antagonisms could be forgotten in the elegant parade that was fashionable Paris.[15]

Most of the theatres survived their financial crises following Louis-Philippe's economies, but it was the end of Choron's fine school. He attempted various ways to continue, such as restricting the choir to women's voices only, and organizing benefit concerts which, despite being put on in the centre of Paris (at the Salle Taitbout) instead of its own premises in rue Vaugirard, failed to attract large audiences. Its days were numbered and in 1834 its founder died.

*   *   *

This left a large gap in the performance of sacred (and secular) choral masterpieces from the past, but ten years later this was filled, at least temporarily, through the efforts of a remarkable aristocrat: Prince Moskowa.

Prince Joséph Napoléon Ney de la Moskowa (1803–1857), son of the unfortunate Marshal Ney, was an outstanding French statesman who contributed richly to both political and musical life. He became a member of the Chamber of Peers in 1831, and as well as involving himself in the affairs of state, he also indulged in his greatest passion – music. Trained in music from childhood, he showed great natural aptitude, his interests were in composition and in the music of the past. He was responsible, for example, for publishing a body of vocal music from Renaissance to classical times. Amongst his compositions were two operas and some masses, one of which was performed on 19 February 1831 by students of Choron's school who formed the choir to sing with the orchestra of the Théâtre-Italien under the direction of Girard. The Mass created an excellent impression. 'An amateur, a prince moreover, who composes a mass with full orchestra, filled with fugues and counterpoint, is a rare enough phenomenon; but the situation is even stranger, for title of Prince apart, the mass is very good, and its effect is remarkable' wrote Fétis.[16] In 1831 Prince Moskowa, together with the composer Louis Niedermeyer, was admitted to associate membership of the Academy of Santa Cecilia in Rome.

Some ten years later, inspired by Choron's example of performing sacred music from the past, Prince Moskowa and the composer Adolphe Adam formed the Société des concerts de musique vocale, religieuse et classique, enlisting into its ranks of performers notable members of the aristocracy, many of whom – the women in particular – were good musicians. A long account of the second concert was given in *Le Monde musical* part of which is reproduced below. A number of the personalities mentioned in it will re-appear in later pages.

Choron's death seemed to extinguish with him the spirit of musical proselytism and of discovery. The Conservatoire, which appears to have the gift of dogmatic immobility, falls back immediately into its majestic disdain for all new research. [Instead] this is developing in the salons ... The prince de la Moskowa conceived the plan of taking up again the work of Choron; and not only that, to take it up with only the best talents that Parisian society has. A group was formed forthwith, under a patronage so illustrious, that one considers oneself almost indiscreet to deliver up the names to the publicity of a journal: Marquise Duchess d'Albuféra, Duchess de Coigny, Duchess de Gramont, Duchess de Massa, Princess de la Moskowa, Duchess de Poix, Duchess de Talleyrand, Princess Ch. de Beauveau, Princess de Craon, Grand Countess de Lobau, Countess Merlin, Viscountess de Noailles, Countess de Sandwich, whom you see in this double row of armchairs placed before the stage. And on the stage, which singers? Prince de Belgiojoso, Count Eugène Ney, Count Etienne de Byron, Baron de Varaigne, Countess de Murat, Countess de Sparre, Countess de Bordesoulle, Countess Merlin, Countess Rodolphe Apponyi, Mlle Alice Thorn, Mme Dubignon, Mlle Eudoxie de Chancourtois. ... And as for the performance, if sometimes the singers betrayed a little timidity, if here and there was a moment of hesitation, it must be said that they are still superior to the choirs of our theatres, in taste, in intelligence, in the delicate feeling for the nuances, in the precise emphasis of the *forte*, and above all in the expressive softness of the *piano*.[17]

The programme included music largely from Renaissance and baroque times – Palestrina, Arcadelt, Lassus, Victoria, Marcello, J. S. Bach, Handel, Scarlatti – Haydn being the only representative of the classical school. It had been eleven years since Fétis had begun to champion the cause of 'early' music through articles in the *Revue et Gazette musicale* and through his celebrated 'concerts historiques'. As Katharine Ellis has pointed out, Fétis had been almost a lone voice in campaigning for the public performance of Renaissance and baroque music.[18] Returning from the first of these 'concerts historiques', Count Rodolphe Apponyi (whose wife is listed in the above review of Moskowa's concert), elated by what he had heard, spoke glowingly of Fétis' lecture illustrated by music from the sixteenth century (performed where possible on instruments of the period), declaring that only in Paris could one expect to be instructed and entertained at the same time.[19]

Fétis returned to live in Belgium in 1833 when he was offered the Foundation Directorship of the Brussels Conservatoire and the *Revue musicale* was left in the hands of his son Édouard. Another musical journal, under the editorship of Maurice Schlesinger, the *Gazette musicale de Paris* had already started up and in 1835 the two merged to create the long-lived *Revue et Gazette musicale*. It boasted an international editorial committee to bring news from other musical centres of the world and to which Fétis *père* continued to provide articles for the new journal over many years.[20]

The *Revue musicale* started a fashion for music journals in Paris. By 1842 there were fourteen (admittedly a small number of the total of 493 journals which the *Journal des débats* estimated were in circulation in Paris at the end of that year). Many were short-lived – *La Mélodie* seems to have survived only a few issues in 1843 – but some, like the *Revue et Gazette musicale, Le Ménestrel* and *La France musicale,* became permanent fixtures of nineteenth-century musical life. Long-lived or not, the large number of journals circulating in Paris in the nineteenth century is further indication of the hold that music had gained over Paris[21] – and over all classes of society it would seem.

For example, in 1836 free classes in choral singing for workers were offered by the polytechnic association, resulting in a choir of four hundred voices which in August that year, with the support of a large orchestra, gave an impressive concert for which a special cantata had been composed. The celebrated tenor Adolphe Nourrit lent his support to this gathering, singing the solos of a cantata *La destinée* (specially written for the occasion by an unnamed composer to words by Lamartine) and joining with the choir, which was said to be of 'colossal power and majesty'.[22] It was reviewed by Berlioz. Three years later an exhausted critic, Henri Blanchard, admitted that there was at least a little more variety than usual because all classes of society seemed to be initiating themselves into 'the mysteries of musical art' and everyone, right through to the youngest and simplest workman to Countess Merlin ... and other 'amateurs of the musical aristocracy', were now singing in Paris.[23] The demand for musical scores was such that nearly 5000 musical works were published in Paris during the twelve months from September 1864, a quarter of which were songs and arias far outnumbering publications in any other category of music.[24]

Even before the half-century was out Paris had resounded not only with music, but also with a chorus of writers proclaiming, usually with mock horror, that the city was being overwhelmed with concerts. Thus wrote Mme Delphine de Girardin in 1841:

> For the last eight days, how many songs, symphonies, sounds, melodies, chords, accents! It's a veritable flood of harmony; flood is the word. Ah, how much music, and what's so awful, what beautiful and excellent music! One wouldn't want to lose a note, and that's the difficulty: you could get drunk on it, passing every day just listening to it. It's worth nothing in some quarters. To form the

bad habit of listening when by profession you're a talker, that's very dangerous; lawyers know very well what they should do: they never listen to anyone and this is not through indifference, but so as not to lose their speciality.[25]

Three years later a letter appeared in *Le Monde musical*:

In Paris, concerts are following one upon the other without respite, morning, noon, evening and night. During four months of the year, it's raining, blowing, snowing and hailing concerts. It's a veritable downpour, a cataclysm, a deluge. There are such concert halls, like the Salle Herz, the Salle Pleyel and the Salle Erard, for example, where the seats don't have time to go cold; the stalls are always kept at a temperature of forty-five degrees, to the point that one is often in need of iced water between two fiery cavatinas. The Parisian people must love music passionately![26]

In summer as well as winter, it would seem, for although 'the season' was from December to April, entrepreneurs began also to present concerts in the warmer months to fill a gap in musical life caused through the closure of the salons and the departure of artists who toured in summer. Those months in Paris encouraged concerts out of doors, particularly in beautiful garden settings – the Champs-Elysées, Jardin Turc and the gardens of the Tuileries, to name the best known. These concerts usually featured light classical music, which was also heard at the Concerts Valentino and at the Casino Paganini. The more serious recitals and concerts were, of course, held indoors, and music lovers, performers and entrepreneurs were constantly seeking new and better concert rooms.

In one of the earliest issues of his *Revue musicale* Fétis was complaining that Paris did not have a true concert hall. During the first half of the nineteenth century there were concert and recital rooms associated with instrument makers: Petzold, Pleyel, Erard, Dietz, and Henri Herz (who combined a career as pianist and composer with that of piano manufacturer). Other salons at this time, and not associated with instrument makers, were the Taitbout, Wauxhall, Chantereine, Saint-Honoré and the Salle Vivienne which held an immensely popular series of orchestral concerts during the 1830s and 1840s. In the summer of 1841 when most of the concert rooms were closed and the salons were silent while their owners enjoyed their country estates and while the best artists were on tour, the Salle Vivienne – to entice music-lovers – was decorated to look like a garden. Its patrons could listen to orchestral music by Hérold, Auber, Meyerbeer and Halévy, sitting on rustic benches, surrounded by perfumed lemon trees, flowers and shrubs in profusion, and with little cascades spilling out here and there to add to the illusion.[27]

In 1848 the instrument maker Adolphe Saxe opened what was to be a very popular recital room. Next year the opening of Salle Saint-Cécile in rue Chaussée-d'Antin was rapturously welcomed by the *Revue et Gazette musicale:* 'Paris possesses a concert-room !!! an excellent hall, perfect sound, sufficiently big, situated in the best area of Paris, moderate rental charges, suitable for all kinds of music from quartets to oratorios and to the largest orchestra with choirs.'[28]

Yet even this was overtaken three years later by the opening of a concert hall which all Paris had been anticipating since the announcement of its construction a few years before – the Salle Barthélemy. Constructed in the boulevard du Temple, it seated 3000 people with room on the stage for a large orchestra and choir. Built in an elliptical form, its acoustics were pronounced perfect (perhaps a little too resonant, complained one), and a major innovation was that the auditorium was lit by electricity instead of gas.[29]

Haussmann's reconstruction of Paris offered new venues. A handsome new one, for example, was built in the recently constructed rue Scribe (opposite the present Paris Opéra) by a philanthropist, Bischoffsheim, a rich banker whose daughter had married a nephew of Meyerbeer. Meyerbeer, himself, was involved in the venture the profits of which were to go to the needy and to supporting a professional school of young workers.[30]

Yet the political events that had led to the rebuilding of Paris, changing it to its present day appearance also led initially to the same kind of problems that had faced musicians in 1830. In 1848 musicians had not been tardy in celebrating the birth of the short-lived Republic before it gave way to Napoléon III's Second Empire three years later. The first two months of the Republic saw a rash of nationalistic songs, including Elwart's *Hymne à la Fraternité* and *Te Deum républicain* (both performed in front of the National Assembly) and patriotic songs from the 1789 Revolution. A de-luxe edition of *Chants patriotiques de la France* offered Méhul's *Le chant du départ*, Halévy's *Guerre aux tyrans* and three songs by Rouget de Lisle, including – predictably – *La Marseillaise*. In April there was advertised a cantata called *La jeune République* composed by the young singer Pauline Viardot whose career was soon to blossom. Some envisaged the Republic as a utopia in which music would be one of its finest glories and, as in the Revolution of 1789, one of its most powerful incitements to action. 'It will call, it will encourage artists; it will open their careers as widely as possible, and it is thus that it will accomplish, we firmly believe, one of the highest and most important missions of a government founded *by the people*, and *for the people!*' prophesied the *Revue et Gazette musicale* in February that year.[31] It told a very different story six months later.

> Theatres closed, some for a while, others never to open again. In March the Opéra National disappeared following a final order to close, previously demanded with much authority, granted after much trouble, carried at the price of much sacrifice, indisputably necessary and struck, however, by a fatal curse,

which seems to pursue it even after its ruin. In May, the Opéra-Comique itself, this stage so eminently French, closed its doors for a long time while waiting for administrative questions to be resolved. Its notices were only replaced after a change of Director. On the other side, the cloud of concerts that each year would rain down on Paris, vanished as if by magic. Virtuosi, singers, the public, all vanished like a dream. The Société des concerts itself had to cut short its programmes formerly so rich. Indeed, the only kind of concert possible was in the streets, reduced, it is true, to a very modest programme: *La Marseillaise, Les Girondins, Le chant du départ, Le chant du départ, Les Girondins, La Marseillaise*; but the enthusiasm and the volume of gigantic sound made up for lack of variety. During two months, the place de l'Hôtel-de-Ville, the surroundings of the Luxembourg Palace, the Champs-de-Mars, the boulevards – all lined with patriotic processions – were transformed into immense 'concert-halls', vast arenas where the populace was both singer and audience.[32]

Euphoria amongst musicians had thus been brief, for, as usual, artists were amongst the first to suffer in the grip of social turmoil and economic depression. It was in the salons that the musical flame was kept alight during those difficult months – such as in the home of the pianist Lambert Massart, who every Thursday evening gathered together fellow musicians to perform works by Beethoven, Chopin, Liszt, Thalberg and others – an example, hoped the *Revue et Gazette musicale*, that others would follow.[33]

Yet, despite the problems of economy and unemployment, the dark storm eventually receded and France experienced a revitalization under Napoleon III as Emperor (1852–70) – at least in the early years. A great deal of the music characteristic of the Second Empire reflected that era's determination to enjoy itself. Amongst the ways to do this was to go to one of the many theatres.

The number of theatres, many of which required musical performance, increased considerably. Using figures provided by *La Semaine musicale*, we can compare how France's theatres (for all artistic forms) fared with those of other leading European countries during the Second Empire.[34] By 1866 there were 1581 theatres operating throughout Europe: France 337, Italy, including Venice 346, Spain 168, Great Britain 150, Austria 150, Germany 191, Russia and Poland 41, Belgium 34, Holland 23, Switzerland 20, Sweden and Norway 18, Denmark 15, Portugal 16, Turkey 4, Greece 4, Rumania 3, Serbia 1. Clearly, France and Italy outstripped all other countries in their love of theatre. Opera, operetta and ballet were amongst the most popular entertainments. Indeed, the speed with which music recovered from the shock and violent turmoil of the 1848 Revolution is vividly illustrated by the fact that during the following year ten new operas were staged at the Opéra and Opéra-Comique including Meyerbeer's *Le prophète* in which Pauline Viardot made her sensational appearance. Public concerts and recitals soon revived, a number of them taking advantage of some new venues which had opened just before the revolution. The beauty of reconstructed Paris and the facilities it offered its citizens was further encouragement to an already ebullient musical life. *La Semaine musicale* lists 16 lyric theatres operating in 1865 (not including Garnier's new Opera House which was still under construction), and in the first six months of the same year the *Almanach de la musique* lists 408 concerts. Amongst them were the 'permanent' concerts of the long-lived Société des Concerts, of the revived Sociéte Sainte-Cécile and of Pasdeloup's Concerts populaires de musique classique held in the immense Cirque Napoléon named in honour of the new Emperor and opened soon after his reign began. In 1857 Berlioz spoke highly of the standard achieved by the orchestra of the Concerts de Paris.

Amongst other notable developments at this time were the outdoor concerts in the settings of the Champs-Elysées and the Bois de Boulogne, the latter once a wild and remote forest that few visited but now within easy coach ride. There had been some concerts in 1839 near the entrance of the Champs-Elysées but these had not prospered. In the Second Empire, however, the building of the Cirque des Champs-Elysées (where a rival to Pasdeloup's concerts, the Société Philharmonique, offered its programmes) and the general allure of the area with its cafe and band concerts, its throng of elegant promenaders at night strolling under brilliant gaslight, made this one of the centres of Parisian life.

Only an eye-witness account can do justice to the setting of concerts in the Pré-Catalan in the Bois de Boulogne in the August of 1856:

> The Administration of the Pré-Catalan yesterday gave the second *grande fête de nuit*. Nothing had been neglected to attract the attention of the large public, and its expectation was not misplaced. The crowd admired the splendours of this magical illumination which made the great lawn look like a lake of greensward with chequered islands of light. These new lighting effects, the pantomime by Paul Legrand in this natural theatre, the ballets, the blaze from the coloured fires reflected by the banks, the concerts, the fanfares, pastimes of all kinds, continued to be offered until three in the morning – all the most varied pleasures, favoured by fine weather.[35]

The Pré-Catalan concerts were not necessarily lightweight in their programmes, featuring, amongst other works, those by Haydn, Handel, Beethoven, Gluck and Weber. But as well, the passion for dancing, which had held sway from the earliest years of the century gained new momentum when the Parisian ballrooms of the 1840s were conquered by the waltz and the polka, when Musard's baton and bow shed enchantment over his orchestra and over all those who danced or listened to his music. For those with the financial means and the zest for pleasure la vie parisienne must have seemed the only life worth living.

Thus, in Paris during the nineteenth century there was a seemingly unquenchable thirst for music. That a vast amount of this music was merely ephemeral can be said about music in most societies in any age. Vocal music was the staple diet of the salons and drawing-rooms, and a number of excellent singers made their livelihood in the fashionable quarters by singing not only excerpts from the best-loved operas of the day, but also the latest romance or, as the century progressed, the more developed form known as mélodie. In any history of French song, the salons must be accounted for, as they must also be when studying the overall development of music in Paris during the nineteenth century. In a comment inspired by the recitals offered in the home of the pianist Zimmerman the *Revue et Gazette musicale* claimed in 1840 that it was in salons such as his that the taste for fine music was being spread in Paris,[36] a comment equally applicable to the homes of some other leading Parisian musicians and in the salons of the many musically-gifted women of the aristocracy whose position precluded them from pursuing a performance career, although they frequently appeared in public to participate in the many charitable concerts to help the victims of poverty and natural disaster. These women were the great patrons of music in Paris. At the other end of the social scale or – more accurately – in the middle of it were gatherings where one was more likely to hear the daughter of the house perform one of the 'romances' doing the rounds of the salons, for, as Anne Martin-Fugier has pointed out, the social nature of the salon was not the sole prerogative of the fashionable world; it served as a model for the middle class.[37] Yet there was also what has been described as the 'aristocratie bourgeoise'[38] whose magnificent homes were the scene for many a fine salon recital.

Notes

1. Jules-Gabriel Jain, *An American in Paris* (London, 1843), 217. This is an English translation of the writer's *L'été à Paris* and *L'hiver à Paris* (Paris, 1843), 217. A far more extensive quotation is found in Appendix E.
2. 'En général, les gens de lettres ont la musique en horreur. On connaît l'opinion de Gautier sur "le plus désagréable de tous les bruits"; Leconte de Lisle, Banville, la partagent. Dès qu'on ouvre un piano Goncourt fronce le nez. Zola se souvient vaguement d'avoir joué de quelque chose dans sa jeunesse; il ne sait plus bien ce que c'était', Alphonse Daudet, *Trente ans de Paris* (1888), 290.
3. 'La matière politique n'est pas en suffisante ébullition, en l'absence des chambres, pour arriver à l'effet dramatique recherché par la plupart des lecteurs de nos grands journaux; malgré les fréquents tentatives des gens intéressés à la chose, les questions religieuses passionnent fort peu de personnes, et l'on en est toujours en France à l'indifférentisme que M de Lamennais a si éloquemment combattu dans son premier ouvrage; la littérature n'est plus un aliment de première nécessité pour les esprits; les classiques et les romantiques l'ont tuée, ou du moins l'ont fait dégénérer en romans feuilletonisés et en vaudevilles: c'est la

musique qui préoccupe toutes les classes de la société.' *RGM*, 4 December, 1842.

4. The term 'dilettante' had not yet acquired the contemptuous connotation that it has today. The *Dictionnaire de musique* (1854) edited by the Escudier brothers makes the further distinction between 'dilettante' and 'amateur de musique', in that while both mean 'music lover', the second also may mean those who can perform well while not being members of the musical profession.

5. 'C'est un fait remarquable que la musique a depuis ces dernières années envahi presque tous les salons du monde fashionable, et qu'elle en a pour ainsi dire banni la danse. La danse n'est plus qu'un plaisir accessoire là où elle était l'amusement principal. On pourrait assigner plusieurs causes à ce changement; c'est d'abord la gravité vraie ou affectée de la plupart de nos jeunes gens, qui trouvent le plaisir de la danse bien peu digne des idées de progrès et de régénération qui planent, disent-ils, sur les sociétés modernes; mais c'est surtout le goût de la musique, qui se répand chaque jour davantage dans toutes les classes, et qui devient presque un besoin, par le charme qu'elle exerce et par le relief qu'elle donne à ceux qui la cultivent avec succès.' *DS*, ed. Romagnesi, January, 1838.

6. 'C'est une chose reconnue, et qu'il serait inutile de démontrer, que chaque année la musique fait en France de rapides et sensibles progrès. Des écoles nouvelles et des sociétés philharmoniques s'établissent partout; le goût se forme, et la sensibilité musicale acquiert une perfection qu'il n'appartient qu'à l'habitude de donner. Ce qui s'était opposé si long-temps aux progrès de la musique, c'est qu'il était convenue parmi les hommes qui s'occupaient des affaires publiques, que la culture des arts est peu nécessaire dans un état, tandis que ceux qui étaient imbus des préjugés de l'ancien régime, disaient qu'il fallait laisser de telles études aux individus dont c'est le métier. Mais depuis qu'une génération nouvelle s'est élevée et qu'un soif universelle de connaissances s'est répandue dans la société, la musique a repris ses droits, et elle est devenue sinon une partie indispensable, du moins un accessoire utile de l'éducation; et si quelqu'un se refusait à cette évidence, il en trouverait des preuves matérielles dans l'accroissement que prennent les écoles et les fabriques d'instruments qui se multiplient sur tous les points de la France; enfin, dans cette foule de professeurs, qui peut à peine suffire à l'énorme quantité des élèves.' *RM*, 8 May, 1830, vol. 2, 86.

7. Jean Mongrédien, *La musique en France des lumières au romantisme* (1986), 200.

8. Mongrédien, 233.

9. *RM*, 1833, 7.

10. 'Les soirées de salon que la mode a substituée aux concerts d'apparat ont commencé leurs cours jeudi 29, *RM*, (undated), 453.

11. For full details of that season see François Lesure (ed.), *La musique à Paris en 1830–31* (1988).

12. Programme details from Lesure.

13. *RM*, 1829, 75.

14. A year later Fétis, a vehement critic of Louis-Philippe's attitude to the arts, wryly pointed out that it was the musicians who were called upon to celebrate the anniversary of the new reign: 'La musique, si maltraitée par le gouvernement né des journées, a été cependant appelée à fêter l'anniversaire de ces fameuses journées; ces pauvres artistes, qui, dans le noble langage des bureaux du ministère des arts, sont appelés par dérision les *crins-crins* ['die-hard Republicans'] de l'Opéra, sont venus payer leur dette au Panthéon, et prêter le secours de leur

archet aux émotions simulées.' *RM*, July, 1831.

15.   Vicomte de Beaumont-Vassy, *Les salons de Paris et la société parisienne sous Louis-Philippe I* (1866), 98.

16.   'Un amateur, et de plus un *prince*, qui compose une messe à grande orchestra, rempli de fugues et de contrepoint, est un phénomène assez rare; mais ici la chose est encore plus singulière, car, principauté à part, la messe est fort bonne, et l'effet en est remarquable.' *RM*, February, 1831, 21.

17.   'La mort de Choron parut éteindre avec lui l'esprit de prosélytisme musical et de découverte. Le Conservatoire, qui semble doué de l'immobilité du dogme, retombe aussitôt dans son majestueux dédain de toute recherche nouvelle. ... Il se développe dans les salons ... M le prince de la Moskowa a conçu le projet de reprendre avec les seuls beaux talens que renferme la société parisienne. Aussitôt une réunion s'est formée, sous un patronage tellement illustre, que l'on se trouve presque indiscret d'en livrer le nom à la publicité d'un journal: la marquise duchesse d'Albuféra. ... Et pour l'exécution, si quelquefois les chœurs trahissent un peu de timidité, s'il se rencontre ici et là un moment d'hésitation, il faut dire qu'ils sont encore supérieurs aux chœurs de nos théâtres, par le goût, par l'intelligence, par le sentiment délicat des nuances, par l'accentuation précise du fort, surtout par la douceur expressive du piano.' *MM*, 25 May, 1843.

18.   Katharine Ellis, *Music Criticism in Nineteenth-Century France* (1995), 57.

19.   'Je rentre dans ce moment du concert historique que M Fétis a donné ce matin au Conservatoire de musique, j'en suis dans l'enchantement. C'était non seulement délicieux à entendre, mais en même temps instructif. On voyait passer devant ses yeux tout le seizième siècle avec ses habitudes, ses goûts, ses mœurs. Les discours prononcés par M Fétis étaient un véritable cours de musique raisonné, offrant le plus haut intérêt et appuyé par des exemples de composition de musique ancienne exécuté avec une rare perfection et en grande partie sur des instruments du douzième siècle. Les cantiques chantés par les confrères à Rome au seizième siècle sont d'une rare beauté; je n'ai jamais rien entendu dans ce genre qui ait réuni plus de grâce, plus d'effet. Il n'y a vraiment que Paris dans le monde où l'on s'instruit en s'amusant.' Rodolphe Apponyi, *Vingt-cinq ans à Paris 1826–1850* (1913), entry for 16 December, 1832, vol. I, 299.

20.   For a study of the significance of the *Revue et Gazette musicale*, see Ellis above.

21.   In 1866 the *Almanach de la musique* (Anon [A. Pougin],) listed the following musical journals that were then in circulation, with the year of their initial appearance in parenthesis: *Le Ménestrel* (1833), *Revue et Gazette musicale de Paris* (1834), *La France musicale* (1837), *La Presse théâtrale et musicale* (1854), *L'Orphéon* (1855), *La Réforme musicale* (1857), *L'Art musical* (1860), *L'Écho des Orphéons* (1861), *La France chorale* (1861), *Revue de musique sacrée* (1861), *L'Union chorale de Paris* (1862), *La Musique populaire* (1863), *La Chronique musicale* (1865), *L'Orphéon illustré* (1865), *La Semaine musicale* (1865), *La Voix de l'Orphéon* (1865).

22.   *RGM*, 7 August, 1836.

23.   'Cela vient sans doute de ce que toutes les classes de la société s'initient aux mystères de l'art musical, et que depuis le plus simple comme le plus jeune ouvrier jusqu'à la comtesse Merlin, MM de Bongars, de Bourdesoulle, de Sousay, et autres amateurs de l'aristocratie, tout chante maintenant à Paris.' *RM*, 2 May, 1839.

24.   A breakdown of the total: romances, chansons, arias and duets (1,580); choral

works (196); military music (219); piano solos and duets (831); violin, cello, clarinet etc. (534); pieces for harmonium (144) piano dance music (904); orchestral dance music (288); methods (38); string chamber music (22); orchestral (21) arrangements of opera (64); Anon [A. Pougin], *Almanach de la musique*, 1866.

25. 'Depuis huit jours, que de mélodies, que de symphonies, que de sons, que de chants, que d'accords, que d'accents! Ce sont de véritables torrents d'harmonie; torrents est le mot! Ah! que de musique, et, ce qu'il y a de plus affreux, quelle bonne et excellente musique! On n'en veut pas perdre une note et voilà le malheur: on se laisse enivrer par elle, et l'on passe ses jours à écouter. Cela ne vaut rien du tout dans certains états. Prendre la mauvaise habitude d'écouter quand on a une profession de bavard, c'est très dangereux; les avocats savent bien ce qu'ils font: ils n'écoutent jamais personne, et ce n'est point par indifférence, c'est pour ne pas perdre leur spécialité.' Mme. de Girardin, *Lettres parisiennes* (1986), vol. II, 47–50 (letter dated 6 March, 1841).

26. A Paris, les concerts se succèdent sans relâche, le matin, à midi, le soir et dans la nuit. Durant quatre mois de l'année, il en pleut, il en ventre, et en neige et il en grêle; c'est une averse, un cataclysme, un déluge. Il y a telles salles de concert, comme la Salle Herz, la Salle Pleyel et la Salle Erard, par exemple, où les banquettes n'ont pas le temps de refroidir; les stalles y sont toujours entretenues à un chaleur de quarante-cinq degrés Réumur a ce point qu'on est souvent obliger d'eau glacée entre deux brûlants cavatines … Il faut que le peuple parisien aime furieusement la musique.' *MM*, 24 April, 1844.

27. 'La Salle Vivienne a inauguré d'une manière brillante ses concerts d'été. Elle a ainsi comblé la lacune laissée dans nos habitudes musicales par la clôture des salons et le départ des artistes. D'heureuses dispositions on été prises pour ménager au public un refuge contre les rigueurs de la chaude saison. La salle a été transformée en jardin; les couleurs ont fait place à des citronniers odorants; les chaises ont été remplacées par des sièges rustiques; les fleurs et les arbustes ont été semés avec une large profusion. Pour ajouter encore à l'illusion, de nombreuses cascatelles sont répandues çà et là. Ceci n'est que le côté pittoresque. Au point de vue de l'art musical la sollicitude des chefs de l'établissement n'est pas moins méritoire. L'orchestre présente un ensemble recommandable de jeunes talents, et se distingue par une précision et une vigueur remarquable. Grâce à ces louables qualités, les œuvres d'Hérold, d'Auber, de Meyerbeer, d'Halévy, etc., les compositions pleines de fraîcheur et d'originalité de Strauss, de Musard, ont trouvé des interprètes dignes d'elles. Dès l'ouverture des concerts Viviennes le public a répondu à l'appel qui lui était fait, et aujourd'hui ce délicieux jardin offre une piquante physionomie et une réunion des plus élégantes.' *RGM*, 5 June, 1841.

28. 'Paris possède un salle de concert!!! une salle excellente, d'une sonorité parfaite, d'une grandeur suffisante, située dans le meilleur quartier de Paris d'un prix de location modéré, et propre à tous les genres de musique depuis le quatuor jusqu'à la plus vaste symphonie avec chœurs.' *RGM*, 28 January, 1849.

29. A detailed description of Salle Barthélemy is given in *RGM*, 29 January, 1851.

30. *SM*, 30 August, 1866.

31. 'Elle appellera, elle encouragera les artistes; elle leur ouvrira la carrière aussi large que possible, et c'est ainsi qu'elle accomplira, nous le croyons fermement, une des missions les plus hautes et les plus importantes d'un gouvernement fondé *par le peuple* et *pour le peuple*.' *RGM*, 27 February, 1848.

32. 'Les théâtres fermèrent, les uns pour un temps, d'autres pour ne se plus rouvrir. En mars, une clôture définitive fit disparaître l'Opéra-National, demandé naguère avec tant d'instance, obtenu après tant de peines, soutenu au prix de tant de sacrifices, incontestablement nécessaire et frappé cependant d'une fatale malédiction, qui semble le poursuivre même après sa ruine. En mai, l'Opéra-Comique lui-même, cette scène éminemment française, laissa longtemps ses portes closes, en attendant que les questions administratives fussent résolues. Il ne replaça ses affiches qu'après avoir changé de directeur. D'autre part, la nuée de concerts, qui chaque année venait s'abattre sur Paris, s'était évanoui comme par enchantement. Virtuoses, chanteurs, public, tout s'était dissipé ainsi qu'un rêve. La Société des concerts elle-même dut couper court à ses séances naguère si recherchées. Au fait, le seul concert possible courait alors les rues, réduit, il vrai, à un programme bien restreint: *La Marseillaise, les Girondins, le Chant du Départ; le Chant du Départ, les Girondins, la Marseillaise*; mais l'enthousiasme et le volume de sonorité gigantesque suppléaient la variété. Deux mois durant, la place de l'Hôtel-de-Ville, les abords du Luxembourg, le Champ-de-Mars, les boulevards, sillonnés de processions patriotiques furent transformés en salles immenses de concert, vastes arènes, où le peuple était à la fois chanteur et auditeur.' *RGM*, 3 September, 1848.
33. *RGM*, 5 November, 1848.
34. *SM*, 8 November, 1866.
35. 'L'administration du pré Catelan donné hier sa seconde grande fête de nuit. Rien n'avait été négligé pour y attirer un nombreux public, et l'attente de la direction n'a pas été trompée. La foule a admiré les splendeurs de cette magique illumination qui faisait ressembler la grande pelouse à un lac de verdure accidenté d'îles de lumière. Ces nouveaux effets d'éclairage, la pantomime exécutée par Paul Legrand au théâtre-nature, les ballets, l'embrasement réitéré des massifs par des feux de couleur, les concerts, les fanfares, les jeux de toute espèce n'ont cessé d'offrir, jusqu'à trois heures du matin, les plaisirs les plus variés, favorisés par un admirable temps. *RGM* 17 August, 1856.
36. 'Si les auditeurs de la *Société des concerts* au Conservatoire forment un public tout spécial, habituel, compté d'avance; si la fureur d'entendre des quadrilles a duré si long-temps; si trois ou quatre ouvrages suffisent pour la saison aux dilettanti peu difficiles du Théâtre-Italien, on est forcé de convenir cependant que le goût de la bonne musique se répand dans les salons de Paris, et qu'un noyau de connaisseurs et de critiques compétents en très petit nombre, à la vérité, aide à propager ce mouvement artistique.' *RGM*, 5 January, 1840.
37. Anne Martin-Fugier, *La vie élégante ou la formation de Tout-Paris 1815–1848* (1990), 94.
38. Adeline Daumard, *La bourgeoisie parisienne de 1815 à 1848* (1963), 650.

CHAPTER TWO

The Salons and their Music

The salons of the fashionable and artistic world were in four areas of Paris inhabited by members of the French aristocracy of ancient lineage as well as those more recently elevated to titles, financiers, politicians, wealthy industrialists and other members of the wealthy middle class, as well as successful musicians and other artists. These four areas were the faubourg Saint-Germain, the faubourg Saint-Honoré, the Marais and the Chaussée-d'Antin. It was, however, less the address and more the style of person admitted to their salons, the most exclusive being the faubourg Saint-Germain,[1] which, according to Viscount Beaumont-Vassy, divided itself into two further cliques – the 'small' and the 'large' although he confesses that it was difficult to explain the line of demarcation.[2]

The faubourg Saint-Germain was the only fashionable quarter on the Left Bank and stretched roughly from Invalides to the church of Saint-Germain-des-Prés taking in, near its northern edge, the rue de Grenelle. In the second half of the century its very long rue Saint-Dominique was to form the basis of the present boulevard Saint-Germain. The houses in this area were largely owned by aristocrats who had for long been associated with the power and privilege of the monarchy and the faubourg Saint-Germain, connected to the Palace of the Tuileries by the Pont Royal, was in a sense an extension of the court. The Marais, on the right Bank, was another area of old, but faded aristocracy, for although the Marais had once been an exclusive part of Paris, by the nineteenth century fashionable society had moved elsewhere and much of the area was left in decay and dilapidation. The only salon in that area mentioned in the musical journals was that of a wealthy Jewish family of music lovers: the Lévi-Alverès.

The faubourg Saint-Honoré, stretching from the southern side of the Champs-Elysées along the rue faubourg Saint-Honoré and rue Saint-Honoré past the Place Vendôme and up to the boulevard de la Madeleine, though still essentially wealthy and aristocratic, was considered to be more liberal in its style and in its thinking than both faubourg Saint-Germain and the Marais. But the most liberal and therefore the most frowned upon by the other three coteries was the Chaussée-d'Antin. Because of its close association with leading artists, writers and musicians we shall examine it in more detail.

Newest of the fashionable residential quarters the Chaussée-d'Antin, which took in far more than just the new street of the same name, was part of a mid-eighteenth-century urban development that took up areas of land outside what had been the old city walls. On one side was the Chaussée-d'Antin which ran along what was eventually to be known as the boulevard des Italiens and the boulevard des Capucines (these built upon the foundations of the old wall) and on the other was the new rue Saint-Lazare. It was an area that in the late eighteenth century had housed quite a number of artists and musicians.

In the early nineteenth century the Chaussée-d'Antin began to take on a new character when bankers and financiers – the new elite – built fine mansions in the area, but something of the style of earlier times remained, and to the stern eyes of those living in the other fashionable quarters, the Chaussée-d'Antin presented, for all its wealth, a rakish air – certainly 'not a place for cardinals', declared Napoleon, chiding his nephew Cardinal Flesch who had bought a mansion there in 1800.[3] It is not surprising that in the area of the Chaussée-d'Antin at one time lived George Sand and Chopin, Grétry, Berlioz, Boieldieu, Félicien David, Liszt, Gounod, Halévy, the singers Pauline Viardot, Duprez and Roger, the painters Delacroix, Géricault and Millet, the sculptor Clodion, the young Sarah Bernhardt, and various writers, including Balzac. When Rossini returned to Paris in 1855, exhausted and depressed, he rented out the first floor of no. 2 rue de la Chaussée-d'Antin where he lived out a rejuvenated retirement.

The image of this area as rather 'flashy' was undoubtedly coloured by its proximity to the heart of pleasure-loving Paris, that great thoroughfare built upon the foundations of the old walls: the Boulevard. It was also the area in which lived a number of very wealthy financiers and bankers, and where were situated the Théâtre Feydeau and the Casino Paganini, the latter a popular house over many years for gambling, concerts and balls. In the Hôtel de la Guimard at no. 9 rue de la Chaussée-d'Antin was a private theatre for 500 people at which, in the last years of the previous century, artists from the Comédie-Française, Comédie-Italienne and the Opéra had often appeared.[4]

It had been Louis XIV who decided that the old ramparts of Paris should go and be replaced by a tree-lined terrace starting near the Pont de l'Arsenal up to the Bastille and further on to the Porte du Temple (now the Place de la République) making one side of an upturned V and down the other to where the church of the Madeleine now stands. Completed in 1705 it was handsome and wide, lined on each side by two rows of trees with a carriageway down the centre. But there was little to encourage its use apart from looking over into the countryside from one's carriage, and at night it was totally deserted. By the middle of the eighteenth century, however, the Boulevard had begun to acquire its fashionable appeal as some of the rich and influential began to build fine mansions on the rural side, and particularly in the Chaussée-d'Antin area. By 1778 the Boulevard was paved and lit by oil lamps, assuring its place for many years to come as the centre of pleasure-loving Paris.

Nineteenth-century writers have given so many colourful accounts of boulevard life that it is easy to imagine what it was like in the middle of that century. The heart of the Boulevard stretched from the section called the boulevard du Temple to that of the boulevard des Capucines. (Most sections of the Boulevard were named after the major streets that joined it at various intersections, the boulevards des Italiens and Capucines being exceptions.) All day could be heard the clatter of hooves and iron rims of the four-wheeled fiacres, the two-wheeled cabriolets or the great 'omnibus-voitures', adding to the more subdued and measured percussion of the riders on horseback, and all mingling with the sounds of street cries and the noise of commerce. What the ear could not discern, the eye could pick up, as amongst the crowd of shoppers weaved the water-carriers, the messenger boys, the showmen and organ-grinders, and – everywhere – the flower sellers.

But it was in the evening that the Boulevard took on its most vivacious and colourful aspect, for along it were the cafés and theatres – those two fertile springs without which Parisian life seemingly would wither. These themselves provided a public 'stage' for those who wished to tread it, be they the true creative spirits or (more likely) the dilettantes and dandies. To be seen there gave the Boulevard at night its impetus, and as the middle class grew in wealth and power so the Boulevard thrived. It is not surprising that, so close to it, the Chaussée-d'Antin gained a character distinctly different from the faubourgs of Saint-Germain and Saint-Honoré and the Marais.

Music in the salons

Glimpses of private salon recitals can be caught through letters, diaries and – strangely enough – through the musical press which prided itself on being able to 'penetrate into the sanctuary and pierce the walls of private life', the *Revue et Gazette musicale* adding that indeed it may be said that 'walls have ears'.[5] Appendix A lists nearly a thousand private salon recitals offering performances of songs which were reported on in the pages of *Le Ménestrel*, the *Revue et Gazette musicale* and *Le Monde musical* during the period up to 1870.[6] It reflects only a fraction of what was on offer at that time in Paris, for, as these journals constantly reminded their readers, only a few salon recitals (both private and public) could be covered by their hard-pressed reporters. There are some that give a detailed account of what went on in the fashionable salons and in the homes of musicians themselves, but very often contented themselves with merely listing the performers and mentioning a fashionable romance (most usually the one published or distributed by the firm owning that particular journal). Despite their limitations, these reports amply confirm the integral part that the private salons played in the musical life of the capital and, as will be seen from Appendix A, they proliferated as the century wore on.

As mentioned earlier, many fashionable salons offered music as part of the afternoon or evening entertainment. One of the most celebrated literary salons of the day and which sometimes offered music to its guests was that of Emile and Delphine Girardin. Rising from humble – in fact, illegitimate – birth, Emile Girardin was to become one of the world's first 'press barons'. In 1831 he married Delphine Gay, daughter of Mme Sophie Gay, well known in her day as a gifted writer and lover of the arts, inheriting these qualities from her mother which were to blossom in the ambience of Mme Racamier's famous salon at the Abbaye-aux-Bois outside Paris. As beautiful as she was vivacious, she and her husband were friends with all the leading literary figures of that time, and to their salon first at 41 rue Lafitte and later in the Hôtel Marbeuf on the Champs-Elysées (both adjoining the Chaussée-d'Antin quarter) were drawn some of the liveliest minds of the day. It represented the quintessential Parisian soirée of the first half of the nineteenth century. An attaché at the Austrian Embassy in Paris, Count Rodolphe Apponyi, gives a description of a musical soirée at the Girardin's in March 1836.

> At Mme de Girardin's there were many literary figures. First, her mother Mme Sophie Gay; next Alfred de Musset, Lamartine, Balzac, Victor Hugo, Jules Janin, Emile Deschamps, Alexandre Dumas, Resseguier and others. Mme de Girardin recited some of her pretty poems to us with grace and, what is more, perfect simplicity. Lamartine spoke charmingly to us about these, which have not yet been published. These recitations alternated with romances, the words of which were composed by some of those present and put to music by Labarre who sang or accompanied them. Several of these romances have been composed by Mlle Lambert, a charming young person of great talent who sang them in inimitable fashion. Each time the performer was placed at the piano, Mme Gay named the author of the poem and explained what it was about.[7]

Le Monde musical 'penetrated the walls' of the Hôtel Marbeuf:

> M and Mme Emile Girardin recently gave a magnificent musical soirée. The audience comprised the elite of Parisian society. Among the politicians and literary men, were seen the prince de Ligne, MM Villemain, de Salvandy, Dupin snr, de Rambuteau, Reschid-Pacha, Victor Hugo, de Lamartine, de Balzac, L. Golzan etc. Mme de Girardin, with her usual grace, delightfully did the honours of her salon. M Balfe, the English composer, sang an air of his composition, which was pleasing. The two brothers, Alexandre and Laurent Batta, back from

their brilliant tour in Germany, played a duo on the motifs of *La Favorite*. The piece surpasses all that Batta had written and performed up to that day.

The romance *Pour tant d'amour*, which he inserted, profoundly moved the audience. Interpreted in that way by the artist, it will always enjoy an immense success. The romance from *Richard Coeur-de-lion, Une Fièvre brulante*, had been requested. It caused a real stir. We have been told wonderful things about a duo composed by Batta and Wolff, on motifs of *Lucrezia Borgia*. Let's hope we can hear it before long. Corelli, the new tenor of the Théâtre-Italien, sang with much taste the aria from *Roberto Devereux*, and with M Porto a duo from *Bélisario*. Mme Labarre closed the soirée with dignity by singing, with infinite taste and charm, two delightful romances by her husband.[8]

One of the centres of private musical soirées in Paris at this period was the Austrian Embassy, Rodolphe Apponyi's uncle the Ambassador being a devoted and knowledgeable music lover. Until 1838 the Embassy was in what was regarded as the most beautiful mansion in Paris, the Hôtel d'Eckmühl in rue Saint-Dominique in the faubourg Saint-Germain.[9] After its purchase by William Hope, a banker of English origin who was granted French nationality by Louis-Philippe, the Embassy moved to the Hôtel du Châtelet in rue de Grenelle-Saint-Honoré. At the time when it was in the faubourg Saint-Germain, on Sundays during the winter season it brought together amateur singers from that quarter for a matinée musicale, each aristocratic guest bringing his or her own music. We have already seen in the previous chapter that there were fine musicians amongst that exclusive circle – such as Prince Moskowa – and, given the Ambassador's musical discrimination and taste, there is no reason to doubt the talents of those who took part in these gatherings, especially those of the Countess de Sparre and Mme de Julvécourt who were recognized as possessing gifts of the first order. Ironically, it was the professional pianist Kalkbrenner who was the despair of the singers during the season of 1835 there, Apponyi complaining that he accompanied the singers as though he were playing a piano sonata and forgetting to keep in time with the soloist![10] Apponyi recalled a recital at the Embassy in 1832 at which Rossini accompanied the baritone Antonio Tamburini (in Paris for the first time to sing at the Théâtre-Italien), the tenor Giovanni Rubini (champion of Bellini's art), Giulia Grisi, who, like Tamburini, was making her Paris début in a Rossini season. (At that stage a number of fashionable salons prided themselves on offering only Italian music.) Also taking part in the same salon recital were Kalkbrenner, Liszt and Chopin.[11]

The scene of fine performers from the ranks of aristocratic or fashionable society was a feature of post-revolutionary Paris. Princess Czartoryska, Chopin's favourite pupil in Paris, became renowned as that composer's finest interpreter. Her salon in her home (the Hôtel Lambert on the Ile Saint-Louis) was a focus of the artistic community of Paris, as well as of expatriate Polish nobility. Accounts of musical life in the aristocratic salons are filled with the names of excellent performers who, but for their social position might have become professional musicians. In describing those who were excellent singers Apponyi pointed to the Marquises de Gabriac and Caraman, the Duchess de Vallombrosa, and Countess Potocka.

Amongst the finest was Countess Merlin who, from all accounts possessed a magnificent voice – she had studied with Manuel Garcia – and her salon was noted for its programmes presented by singers of the first rank. Born Maria de Las Mercedes de Jaruco in 1786, daughter of a Spanish nobleman who owned extensive properties in Cuba, her childhood was spent in Havana. Rejoining her mother in Madrid she met and married General Merlin who had served in Spain under King Joseph Bonaparte until the destruction of the Napoleonic army. They moved to Paris sharing a mansion with another Countess and General (Lariboisière) in rue de Bondy (now rue René-Boulanger). She became a driving force in Paris musical life, not only through her salon, but also in the many events in which she participated or organized, not least for charitable purposes. For example, in 1837, together with two other well-connected women and the musicians Meyerbeer, Habeneck and Halévy, she created a Philharmonic society to give concerts to raise funds for the poor both in the capital and in the provinces.[12] Until her death in 1852 her name is one of the most frequently encountered in the pages of the musical journals.

There were some well known opera singers who married into a title – or at least into wealth – and thus relinquished their professional careers: Countess de Sparre had been the opera singer Mlle Naldi; Countess Rossi was Henriette Sontag who had enjoyed a short but brilliant operatic career commencing in 1826, interrupted two years later following her marriage to Count Carlo Rossi, but taken up again to international acclaim in 1849 following the end of her husband's diplomatic career. Singers such as these appeared frequently in the programmes of private salons, so it is not surprising, therefore, that one music critic suggested in 1838 that concerts were multiplying so fast in aristocratic salons that in high society there would soon be more virtuosos than listeners![13] The aristocracy also boasted a number of composers praised by the musical press. As well as Prince Moskowa (see Chapter One), they included women such as Princess Scilla, Countess Beaumont, Mme de Maistre and, above all, Mme Vicountess de Grandval (1830–1907), whose output included seven operas, a mass, instrumental chamber music and a number of songs which were sung by amateurs and professionals alike from the 1860s onwards (see Appendix A).

Yet it was also in the homes of some of the wealthy middle class (which not only included financiers, but also doctors, lawyers and other professionals who were often passionately fond of music) and whose salons were noted for excellence of their music. One of the most frequently mentioned was that of the Orfilas.

Mme Orfila, wife of a well-known physician, was reputably a good musician herself as was her husband. His passion for singing was restricted to private occasions as the Faculty of Medicine regarded any public appearance as incompatible with his profession.[14] In their salon they offered their guests the finest performers in Paris, and not content with matinées and soirées in the winter season, they continued them during summer when they moved to their home at Passy, one critic exclaiming: 'With the Orfilas music is the flower of the four seasons – there is always singing there, Summer and Winter.'[15] In terms of the 'bourgeois' salons the only rival to the Orfilas' were those of the Crémieux, husband and wife, where one encountered the 'same love of fine music interpreted by the best artists.'[16] When Mme Orfila joined forces with Mme Mosneron de Saint-Preux, as she often did, their joint salon programmes would achieve 'an indescribable verve' as in February 1860 when their guests were offered not only two salon operas sung by leading singers, but also the rare appearance of one of the greatest dancers of her time Marie Taglioni who, though no longer young, revealed that she was still the personification of the art. Only Rossini and Mme Orfila, claimed Le Ménestrel, could have brought such an evening together.[17]

Not surprisingly, it was at the homes of the professional musicians that salons devoted solely to music were to be found, like those of Saint-Saëns who held his weekly gatherings on Mondays, or Pauline Viardot's who held hers on Thursdays; but these, like so many others, were not reported on by the musical press, unlike the soirées of Rossini, which, held on Saturday evenings at no. 2 rue de la Chaussée-d'Antin, were much sought after by music lovers and where programmes often included salon operas.[18] Those offered twice a month by the pianist and teacher Pierre Zimmerman (whose pupils included César Franck, Valentin Alkan, Antoine Marmontel and Louis Lacombe) were almost Parnassian in status, 'neither rank nor wealth alone sufficient to open Zimmerman's door'.[19] To have achieved success there, claimed the Revue et Gazette musicale, meant that an artist could tour Europe with head held high. On a more prosaic note – and one fully in accord with contemporary French sentiment – Le Ménestrel claimed that the Zimmerman salon was to music lovers what the Stock Exchange was to financiers.[20] Zimmerman and his wife lived in the beautiful Square d'Orléans off the rue Taitbout in the heart of the Chaussée-d'Antin quarter, its private courtyard flanked by nine buildings, the various floors of which were rented out. Nicknamed 'cité d'Orléans', it housed a virtual community of artists, its residents having included George Sand, Chopin, Pauline Viardot, pianists Marmontel and Loveday, the dancer Taglioni and the writer Louis Enault. The Zimmermans rented the first and second floors of no. 7. As an example of the kind of musician welcomed to his salon the music critic of the *Revue et Gazette musicale*, writing about a soirée in 1839 at which the young soprano Mlle de Rivière made her début, pointed out the composers Meyerbeer, Halévy, Donizetti, and Adam, the singers Duprez, Pauline Garcia and Géraldy, and the violinist Bériot amongst others, all of whom welcomed the young artist into their privileged circle. Some of them also performed at that recital.[21] One evening a few weeks later Clara Wieck appeared at the Zimmerman salon having made her Paris début only a few hours before at the Salle Erard.

The salon of the Lionnet brothers was another scene of purely musical events. Known affectionately as the 'Siamese twins of song',[22] they championed many a French composer, as reflected in the programme of a concert organized in their home in January 1860. Amongst the many who attended it were the composers Gounod, Delibes, and Victor Massé and the writer Alphonse Daudet. The length of the programme suggests a remarkable resilience on the part of the audience.

M Gounod sang some songs from his new opera *Philémon et Baucis*, which we shall be applauding soon at the Théâtre-Lyrique and which promises us a worthy companion to *Faust*. M Charles Delioux played two most remarkable pieces of his composition, *Le ruisseau* and his *Transcription sur Faust*. G. Nadaud performed for us some of his new songs, and notably *Le nid abandonné*, a touching mélodie full of sweetness. E. L'Epine sang with exquisite taste *Cousine Marie* and *Sous les tilleuls*, two of his prettiest mélodies. M Alphonse Daudet recited his delightful 'triolets', *Les prunes*. Then, at last, came the turn of the two hosts, who performed, with their usual style, several pieces from their album: *Le matin* (by Victor Massé), *Les cloches de Saint-Loup* (by Delsarte), *Fanchette* (by A. Hignard), *Les adieux à un ami* (by Nadaud), and *Les gardes françaises* (by Delioux). Each composer accompanied his work in turn. The Lionnet brothers received the most flattering congratulations from them all. But the greatest success of the evening was for M Delsarte, who made his audience shiver in *Les terreurs de Thoas* (from *Iphigénie en Tauride* [Gluck]). So he was given an ovation that he will long remember. People took their leave of each other at about three o'clock in the morning, their hearts still moved by the warm impressions of this delightful evening, impressions warmer than the coldness outside of two degrees below freezing.[23]

In the fashionable and aristocratic world of salon-giving host and hostess needed considerable wealth to maintain the tradition, for not only did artists have to be paid, but supper and often dancing concluded the evening. On the other hand, it is not clear whether Zimmerman, Rossini and others charged an entrance fee to those lucky enough to be invited to their salons, but it would not be at all surprising if they did, for some musicians depended upon their salon appearances for part (if not all) of their livelihood and many of the performers were amongst the most renowned, particularly the opera stars.

Adelina Patti, for example, appeared at the Rossinis in February 1864, a few days after she had sung for 'one of the princes of finance' M Emile Pereire, to whose home in the faubourg Saint-Honoré thronged more than a thousand people – ministers, men of state, bankers, literary people, and artists, and where she received a fee of 2500 francs – the price of performing at the Théâtre-Italien.[24] Bankers and politicians seem to have caught the general fever for giving lavish private concerts in the second half of the century, complementing the already growing number of intimate salons of the kind already described. Well might the music critic exclaim

> musical soirées are blossoming in most brilliant fashion in Paris during this winter of 1859. It has now become a genre in itself to serve one's guests a sumptuous programme of music. We take good care not to complain about it; it is a fashion that is desirably contagious. We offer it all our best wishes in the interest of art and artists.[25]

In 1837 the home of a Monsieur S … had been described as a centre for composers, painters, writers, and sculptors (always surrounded by young and pretty women),[26] and a few years later we read that Alexandre Dumas drew to his salon the leading lights of the artistic world,[27] but this mingling of the arts seems to have been more characteristic of the later part of our period. There were some in the 1860s, for example, that were described as musical/literary soirées, as at the home of Dr and Mme Mandl, in the rue Tronchet in the Chaussée-d'Antin quarter, where over thirty performers took part in a programme that began with music and concluded with theatre pieces, including a charade, for which there was a growing enthusiasm at this time in the salons. In this case, the word to be found was 'critique', the clue for the first syllable given in a performance of Weckerlin's *Cris de Paris*, the second syllable suggested through mimicking the gestures and mannerisms ('tics') of the leading Parisian actors. The entire word was then played out by a large group of musicians and actors.[28]

This was the time, too, when visual artists joined the fashion for giving musical soirées in their studios, the performers surrounded by canvasses and sculptures – as at the studio of Gustave Doré who welcomed musicians there every Sunday during the 1860s.[29] Nor were exponents of the new art of photography immune from the fashion, the celebrated Nadar turning his studio into a veritable Garden of Eden (as it was described), with flowers, greenery, fountains, lights, cascades and grottos amongst which was performed vocal and instrumental music of a high order.[30]

Yet, undoubtedly, the most striking assembly of the arts came about in the home of M Pitre-Chevalier in April 1863. It was inspired by a scene described by Giorgio Vasari in his monumental *Delle Vite de' più eccellenti pittori, scultori, ed architettori italiani* (1550), which had enjoyed two French translations early in the nineteenth century. The Parisian re-creation of this scene was described thus by a reporter:

> When Leonardo da Vinci painted the portrait of the Mona Lisa he surrounded it with the sweetest music. Last Sunday at the home of M Pitre-Chevalier while M and Mme Bettini-Trebelli sang the duet *Mira la bianca luna* by Morin, Six and Worms caught in crayon the pure profile of *La muette di Portici* – Mlle Marie Vernon, as on the previous Sunday they had caught that of the Olympian figure of [Joseph] Méry, under the eye of Giroux. While Mme Méric-Lalande sang the great arias of Rossini, M Jousse the romance from *Aladin*, Mme Garait (from the Opéra-Comique) with Berthelier the comic duet *Les tourtereaux*, Vizenti, winner of the grand prix in violin from Brussels drawing enchanting sounds from his instrument, Mlle Karoly, the tragedienne, together with Dubarry, declaiming a scene from Horace, M Boissière reciting one of his delightful fables, and Coquelin from the Comédie-Française with consummate artistry singing the chanson *Carcassone* by Nadaud. Finally, Mme Paër, Mlle Clara Lemonnier and M Dubois acted in costume, with props, lights and curtain *Le loup et l'Agneau* by Frédéric Barbier, words by MM Hipp. Tressant and Chol de Curcy, a jewel of the Théâtre-Déjazet, honoured by a soirée at Compiègne. Mme Causse, M d'Aubel and M Populus were acclaimed as accompanists that evening, as they had been the previous Sunday when they accompanied M and Mme Tagliafico, Mme Oscar Commettant, Levasseur etc.[31]

Thus, the scene offered by the private salons was a varied one. Some, of course, offered no music (particularly in purely literary salons), some offered it as only part of their entertainment – as a diversion or a break from conversation, the flow of which unfortunately was not always stoppable, to the great annoyance of music lovers and performers alike right throughout the century. At the Austrian Embassy, where chamber music was often played to an exclusive audience of about twenty, the wife of the English Ambassador irritated everyone by chattering throughout the performance.[32] Perhaps the Ambassador's wife was merely carrying on the tradition of her own country where, claimed *Le Ménestrel*, musical soirées were merely a pretext for social gatherings and conversation, noting also that although this happened frequently in Paris, there were still those where one encountered faithful followers of musical art.[33] Indeed, the *Revue et Gazette musicale* noted that in the salon of Countess Grabowska, music was listened to in 'religious silence by an audience both fashionable and knowledgeable'.[34] In 1863 *Le Ménestrel* compared those fashionable salons where 'ladies, diamonds, flowers and illuminations too often struggled against the music instead of assisting it', with one that its reporter attended where its invitees made their way as if on a holy pilgrimage to doors 'closed to noise and to luxury'.[35] (In this case, the salon – unnamed for reasons of privacy – featured Mme Camille Dubois who was said to have been a favourite pupil of Chopin.) On the other hand, as late as 1867, one critic, incensed by the conversation that accompanied a performance at

Princess Mathilde's salon asked why the most intelligent society in Paris listened so little and so badly to music,[36] although (as we shall see) at her purely musical gatherings the princess herself imposed silence upon her guests. We may safely say, however, that no chattering would have been permitted at salons in the homes of professional musicians or in those presided over by the many musically-gifted members of the aristocracy, or in those salons where politeness was the mark of the 'aristocratie bourgeoise'.[37] In any case, the overall seriousness towards music taken by Parisian audiences from the 1830s onwards was reflected by the way it was permeating all levels of society, a point that the musical journals never tired of reminding their readers.

*   *   *

The terminology of *matinée* (when gatherings took place in the afternoon, usually from 2.00 to 6.00 p.m.) and *soirée* (for evening events) was also adopted by the commercial salons, like the Salle Erard, Salle Pleyel and many others. Yet, as we have seen, no matter where or when they took place, recitals were invariably presented by a group of performers, which, except in the case of those gatherings devoted to instrumental chamber music, almost always included singers. Most of the songs did the rounds of both kinds of salons where very often the programmes and performers were the same.

Given the engagement of so many opera stars to sing in the private salons it is not surprising that the large majority of programmes featured excerpts from the operatic repertoire ranging from Mozart and Gluck to the latest Italian, French and German works including Wagner (*Rienzi*) and, very shortly after Berlioz's death, an excerpt from *Les Troyens*. Particularly popular was Flotow's *Martha*. Salon operas, notably those by Weckerlin, began to make an appearance in mid-century, and from this time also can be seen a growing appetite for lighter fare, such as operettas, *scènes bouffes* and charades, musical trifles relished by the aging Rossini himself.[38] At his salon a number of his unpublished works were performed, and on many an occasion elsewhere compositions by host or hostess saw their first (and perhaps last) performance to a captive audience – not least in the salon of the singer Duprez where performances were almost always devoted to his own works.

To conclude our brief glimpse of the private salons where music played a prominent part we shall turn to two of the most famous, one at the time of Louis-Philippe, the other during the Second Empire.

The Salon of Princess Cristina Belgiojoso (1808–1871)

Against the conformity of aristocratic French society under Louis-Philippe both the character and appearance of Princess Cristina Belgiojoso stood out in colourful contrast, or, in the opinion of many in high society, in colourful eccentricity. She was indisputably one of the most remarkable women of her age. Born into the immensely wealthy and privileged Trivulzio family of Milan, she inherited her mother's love of music and became an accomplished pianist. Liszt was to say of her that she had a rare gift for music, possessing what he described as an 'intuitive ear'.[39] Her father having died when she was four, she was brought up by her gifted mother (who counted Rossini and Bellini as amongst her closest friends) and, when her mother married again a year later, by a stepfather who encouraged and developed her love of the arts, science, history and philosophy. Yet it was a stressful childhood, not least because of the harsh Austrian rule that governed Milan after the collapse of Napoleon's empire, bringing with it a loss of freedom, many imprisonments and interrogations of Milanese leaders. At the age of 16 she married the young, tall and handsome Prince Emilio Belgiojoso, also from an ancient, but not wealthy, family. Amongst his attractions was a tenor voice so superb that Rossini tried, unsuccessfully, to tempt him into a professional career, for an aristocrat something not unknown in Italy although unthinkable in France. Unfortunately, he was also a flagrant womanizer, an urge which marriage to a young beauty did nothing to stifle. He once confessed that he had only married Cristina for her wealth.[40] Four years later the marriage broke up, and Cristina attempted to leave Italy against the orders of the Austrian authorities, but it was to be two years before she could reach Paris as a political exile where she worked tirelessly in the cause of Italian independence and in helping to alleviate the sufferings of Italian exiles in Paris. From what she could salvage from her fortune she set up her home at 23 rue d'Anjou-Saint-Honoré where her salon became an intellectual and musical centre of Paris. Here were to be found writers such as Heine, Musset, Janin and Balzac, musicians such as Bellini, Chopin and Liszt, as well as leading politicians of the day. Her pleasure in being surrounded by young writers and intellectuals who cared little for politeness shocked some, but Liszt was one who admired her deeply for being 'herself'[41] and his close friendship with her lasted many years. She became the model for some characters of fiction, such as in Balzac's *Le peau de chagrin*. Her physical appearance was startling and is best described by one of her contemporaries.

> she had quite a high slender waist, and an oval-shaped face like the Mona Lisa, but with an aquiline nose longer than that charming model. Very large black eyes illuminated her face, complemented harmoniously by her black hair. In looking at her, one's attention could have been riveted by these beautiful black eyes, by this lightly-arched nose, with its fine and dilated nostrils; but what held one's attention and provoked curiosity from a distance was the matt pallor of her complexion, which in the evening took on an absolutely fantastic hue in which

blue and green were mixed, thus giving the princess a strikingly ghostly appearance.⁴²

Although her spectral pallor gave rise to gossip that it was induced by the taking of drugs, few knew that the reason was to combat two unmentionable afflictions: epilepsy and syphilis, the latter transmitted to her by her philandering husband.

She enjoyed wearing bizarre and exotic dresses, often very low cut and transparent, robes and turbans that gave at least one observer the impression that she had a dagger secreted in their folds!⁴³ Her home was as unusual as the Princess herself.

> You entered through a little vestibule which communicated at the left with a dining-room, and at the right with the salon. The dining-room, in stucco, was decorated with paintings in fresco and mosaic style from Pompei. Long rather than wide, this room to where a piano was moved on reception days served thus as a room for dancing. The salon, quite large and square, was hung with brown, almost black, velvet, sprinkled with silver stars; the furniture was covered with the same material, and in the evening, when you entered, you could have believed yourself to have been in a silver chapel, the general aspect being lugubrious. ... From the funereal salon you passed into a bedroom, the walls hung entirely with white silk. The clock over the chimney piece, the flares, the candelabra, the entire decoration, in a word, was silver or silver pieces, providing a complete contrast with the salon.⁴⁴

It was in her salon that one of the most celebrated artistic events of the century took place: the musical 'duel' between the pianists Liszt and Thalberg on 31 March, 1837.

The idea came to Princess Belgiojoso as one of the ways to raise money for Italian political exiles – not that a charity concert was an innovation for Paris. From the Restoration onwards there had been concerts and balls in plenty to raise funds for victims of floods, wars and poverty – and this was to continue throughout the century. But the Princess's event was unique. Announced in *Le Journal des Débats*,⁴⁵ it began with three days of a 'sale of works' provided by leading artists like Delacroix, and sculptors like Mercier who offered two beautiful medallions he had made of Liszt and George Sand. A collector generously offered a Renaissance fresco from his private gallery, using a totally new technique to remove it from the plaster. Even members of the royal family gave tapestries that they themselves had woven. Meyerbeer offered an unpublished romance, and six of the leading pianist/composers – Liszt, Thalberg, Chopin, Pixis, Czerny and Herz – were asked to write variations on a duet from *I puritani*, the set called *Hexameron*. It was announced that a performance of this work (which also included additional movements by Liszt) was to be played by the six pianists, although recent research indicates that the work was not completed in time and therefore did not receive a performance then.[46] The climax came on the fourth day when Liszt and Thalberg performed as soloists on the same programme, the event hailed as a 'duel' between the two greatest pianists of the day; the general verdict of the 200 listeners who made up the fashionable audience being that Liszt was the champion.

Unfortunately, there are few reports about the private recitals given in Princess Belgiojoso's salon. Given her Italianate background and her love of the operas of Rossini and Bellini it can be surmised that this music took pride of place. Indeed there is a report of the Prince singing in the quartet from the second act of *Lucia di Lammermoor* in his wife's salon,[47] for, although they were legally separated, she generously gave him an apartment in her mansion in the rue d'Anjou-Saint-Honoré for his visits to Paris – until a scandal that rocked Paris, when Prince Emilio eloped at a ball with Countess Anne de Plaisance, the two of them making off to Italy to live. We hear of the princess herself accompanying other performers (in her 'usual musicianly style')[48] at a charity concert that she arranged in the salon of the Jardin-Mabille in the Champs-Elysées to assist a needy family, and it was in her salon on 25 March 1839 that Apponyi heard a performance of Mozart's Requiem.[49]

Here is not the place to describe the tangled web that was the life of Princess Belgiojoso. Suffice it to say that her political involvement with Italian independence led to a turbulent career following her departure from Paris (which, however, she continued to visit frequently) and she died in Milan in 1871, leaving behind not only memories of her musical prowess and influence, but also a stream of books and pamphlets that she published in France and Italy.

Princess Belgiojoso was nicknamed 'La muse romantique'. The second of our great hostesses, Princess Mathilde, was called 'Notre-Dame des arts'.

The Salon of Princess Mathilde (1820–1904)

A niece of Napoleon Bonaparte, Princess Mathilde's star rose when Louis-Philippe's fell and Napoleon III became Emperor of France. Before this, like all members of the Bonaparte family, she had lived outside France as an exile and while in Rome had met her cousin Louis-Napoleon. They fell in love and an engagement was announced but it went no further, for her 25-year-old fiancé, having initiated a hare-brained military scheme to win back the Bonaparte throne, was deported by Louis-Philippe to America and later that year went to England where he stayed until the revolutionary events of 1848. Then he saw that his hour had come. In the meantime, Mathilde had married

Prince Anatole Demidoff, an immensely rich Russian who owed his wealth to the iron ore found on the land of a peasant forebear who had turned his smithy into a munitions factory, and owed his title to the Czar's decision to grant this ancestor the hereditary title of Count Demidoff. The chance to gain social prestige through marriage to one of the best connected women in Europe (the Czar, for example, was her uncle) was undoubtedly his reason for marrying Mathilde, who, within a few months found that she had married a selfish, coarse and lecherous man whose violence towards her alarmingly betrayed his peasant antecedents. Nevertheless, the marriage gave Mathilde the first opportunity to visit the country to which she was so passionately attached but had never seen, for Louis-Philippe granted a temporary visa to the couple. When it was eventually made permanent they bought a house in the rue de Courcelles near the Chaussée-d'Antin. After six years Mathilde begged the Czar – who controlled all aspects of the lives of his subjects – to annul the marriage. The result was that Demidoff was banned from leaving Russia and was forced to pay a vast annual alimony to Mathilde. She never married again, but during the six years with Demidoff she met a man who was to dominate much of her life: Count Alfred-Emilien de Nieuwerkeke. Cultured and urbane, he was in every respect – except infidelity – the antithesis of Demidoff, and he helped Princess Mathilde, his mistress, establish one of the most brilliant salons in Europe.[50] Upon the accession of Napoleon III, first as President of the Republic, then Emperor, it became an extension of imperial power, and the annual salary he settled upon his cousin, together with her huge alimony, made her enormously wealthy. She relinquished the first home in the rue de Courcelles when Napoleon III presented her with a finer one in the same street at no. 23. It was here where appointments and honours were solicited and where many a ribbon of the Légion d'honneur was pinned on to a resplendent chest.

Warm-hearted, generous and, to those she admired, seemingly loyal to a fault – often impairing her political or artistic judgement – she befriended, encouraged and supported many artists. It was not for nothing that Saint-Beuve christened her Notre Dame des arts. Although she painted well, it would seem that she was neither truly intellectual nor innately musical, but she gained enormous pleasure in being surrounded by the most gifted people in Paris. On Sundays at the rue de Courcelles music reigned supreme.

In 1853, it was announced that the conductor Pasdeloup was to be placed in charge of forming an orchestra for her official receptions. Later she invited the violinist Eugène Sauzay from the Conservatoire to organize the music for her and in his memoirs he looks back to those days.

> Let us enter the beautiful hôtel de la rue de Courcelles. First of all, four large
> salons communicating through a huge conservatory. In the middle one the piano,

around which are grouped the singers, with the instrumental quartet at the left, and at the right a piano with pedal keyboard at which Saint-Saëns or Cohen used to improvise.

By the first chord each listener had taken his seat, the most musical near the piano exchanging compliments with the performers, the others dispersed around, some in the conservatory, some in the nearby salons where the poetry of flowers and perfume mingled with the charms of music.

... Come springtime, the Princess would have everything – piano, organ, music stands – taken into the great columned dining room where from then onwards the soirées would take place. This was the time of the year when the gatherings were the most frequented and the most brilliant. Then, whatever crowned head or whatever foreign prince was in Paris would not miss attending the Princess' home. ...

She had no trouble at all in obtaining silence and, according to her expression, to stop the chattering. She herself gave the example of discipline by moving away as soon as possible from those who surrounded her and coming to be near us to listen to the commencement of the work. ... Certainly the general aspect of the soirée was very different when it was exclusively musical.[51]

We catch another glimpse of music at the rue de Courcelles through the pages of *Le Ménestrel*. It was the end of the winter season of 1866, just before Princess Mathilde moved to her summer residence at St Gratien.

The salons of Princess Mathilde opened twice this week: Sunday as usual and last Wednesday in honour of Grand-Duchess Marie of Russia, invited to an intimate performance of *Le Cas de Conscience* by M Octave Feuillet, with Mme Arnold Plessy and Bressant as performers. Their majesties were present at this dramatic soirée. As for the preceding Sunday, the last Sunday for the winter held by Her Imperial Highness, it seems it was music that took up all the programme, and what a programme! Mme Carvalho sang some Mozart and Gounod so delightfully that the audience would have been happy to carry her aloft in triumph. Delle-Sedie (Monsieur) also sang some Gounod, in French, and with a rare perfection. The new member of the Academy [Gounod was elected to the French Academy the previous month on 19 May, 1866] was present at his double success. An amateur singer, who sings like a great artist, Mme Bouché, performed the new composition of Mme de Grandval: *Les lucioles* [Fireflies] with violin and organ accompaniment, without prejudice to the piano, played by the composer. The effect was delightful: these *Les lucioles,* thus accompanied, could go around the world. Mme Bouché also sang a charming duo by Campana with Mlle Rives, a young protégée of Rossini and Gounod, who, furthermore, had the honour of having her first singing lessons with the Countess de Sparre. With such a godmother and such godfathers, one must become a true artist, which Mlle Rives is already. It would be unjust to forget the instrumental section of the last programme of Princess Mathilde, all the more so since Franchomme, the official cellist of the salon played his transcriptions of Chopin with an exquisite feeling for this poetic music. A quartet by Haydn opened the soirée. MM Saint-Saëns and Sauzay shone in that, as in Gounod's *Ave Maria* and Mme de Grandval's *Les lucioles.*[52]

This, the decade of the 1860s, was the most brilliant period of Princess

Mathilde's salon, but as the decade came to a close her life was deeply troubled. In 1869 the ever-faithless Nieuwerkerke abandoned the very woman to whom he owed his honours, his appointments, his status and its effect on her was traumatic. These latter years of the decade also saw a rise of bitter resentment in France towards the Emperor, and, as his cousin, Mathilde was not immune from it. But the worst trauma of all was, of course, the catastrophe of the Franco-Prussian War. At its outbreak, which many blamed upon the Emperor (and more justifiably upon the Empress), the Princess was no longer safe in Paris, and she fled to Belgium where she was exiled yet again from the country she so deeply loved. Eventually granted permission to return – under certain conditions – by the founding President of the Third Republic, Thiers, the imperial pension and the mansion in the rue de Courcelles were taken from her. With the alimony from Demidoff she bought a smaller, though still spacious mansion in the rue de Berry where, as well as at her beloved St Gratien, she began to pick up the threads of her life once more. To her new salon came those artists, writers and musicians who had been the ornaments of the rue de Courcelles – Gautier, Flaubert, Goncourt, Balzac, Coppée, Saint-Saëns, Gounod, Bizet, and many others, and now the younger generation of genius – including Proust. When she died in 1904 the end of the most celebrated salon in Europe heralded the end of a three-hundred year tradition to which French civilization owed so much.[53]

*　*　*

In a famous article published in 1835 in the *Gazette musicale de Paris* Liszt condemned the way society treated its artists and contemptuously dismissed three-quarters of what music went on the Parisian salons at that time.[54] In the previous year the same journal had itself been critical of these gatherings, declaring they had little to do with musical art and the way it should be cultivated.[55] Yet six years later the *Revue et Gazette musicale* (which incorporated the earlier journal), was able to write: 'It is time for the grand musical soirées, but the finest of them are not those that you pay to go to. It appears that artists like to reserve the flower of their inspiration and the poetry of their talent for their intimate friends.'[56] In the next decade private salons were being widely recognized as rivals to public concerts.[57]

So too were the social barriers that had been encountered by Liszt and others in the 1830s being broken down as the century wore on. After returning from singing at a fashionable salon at that time Maria Malibran was known to have burst into tears, exclaiming 'I am merely the opera singer – nothing more – the slave whom they pay to minister to their pleasure.'[58] Yet even the most cursory glance at Appendix A reveals not only an extraordinary proliferation of private musical salons, but also the gradual association of fine aristocratic performers with those from the profession. It also becomes clear that music played an increasingly important part in official receptions and salons, some of whose eminent hosts were genuine music lovers. The President of the Senate M Troplong, whose official salons at the Petit-Luxembourg were a regular feature for a number of years, was himself known to be a good violinist and author of books and critical studies of Gluck and Mozart.[59] There can be no doubt that the best salons contributed much to musical life in Paris, not least because they provided opportunities for French music to be heard and encouraged. The works of Vaucorbeil, some of whose songs enhanced the early repertoire, were said to owe their initial success to being promoted in the salons of Mme Orfila and Marmontel.[60] Perhaps, above all, they provided a way whereby the ever-increasing number of professional musicians could earn their living. Aristocratic salons, like those of Countess Merlin, the princesses Czartoryska, Belgiojoso, Mathilde and others, offered 'rites of passage' to aspiring performers, both French and foreign, the support of these wealthy and influential patrons helping to launch successful careers. Musicians had every reason to be grateful to them.

Notes

1. For a detailed description of Parisian social life and the geographical location of the different coteries at this time see Anne Martin-Fugier, *La vie élégante ou la formation du Tout-Paris 1815–1848* (1990).
2. 'Le faubourg Saint-Germain s'est, depuis le premier Empire, toujours classé lui-même en petit et en grand faubourg Saint-Germain. Les nuances sont difficiles à saisir et la ligne de démarcation à indiquer, main, enfin, ces dénominations existent. S'agit-il de salons plus ou moins grands, d'hôtels plus ou moins somptueux, de moins plus ou moins retentissants? Évidement, le petit vaut le grand et le grand vaut le petit. C'est, et plus que toute autre chose, une affaire de coteries, de sociétés, d'individualités même; mais il est certain que les deux catégories ne fusionnent pas entre elles, et qu'il y a telles femmes, par exemple, reines dans le petit faubourg, ne pourront jamais parvenir jusqu'au grand. C'est un peu l'histoire de la noblesse de province et de la noblesse de cour.' E. F. Beaumont-Vassy, *Les salons de Paris et la société parisienne sous Louis-Philippe I* (Paris, 1866), 321.
3. Quoted in Jacques Hillairet, *Dictionnaire historique des rues de Paris* (1963), vol. I, 338.
4. Jacques Hillairet, *Dictionnaire historique des rues de Paris*, vol. I, 336.
5. 'Non seulement nous devons rendre compte dans notre feuille des concerts publics, mais nous pouvons aussi quelquefois pénétrer dans le sanctuaire et percer *les murs de la vie privée*. C'est ici le cas d'ailleurs, de dire que les murs ont des oreilles.' *RGM*, 11 April, 1839. How entry into the private salons came about in the early years is difficult to know. However, by the middle of the century some salon hostesses were sending details of their programmes to the

journals for reporting and reviewing in their columns. See *M*, 29 January, 1865.

6. While private salon recitals were never announced in advance in the columns of the music journals – only reported on after the event – it would seem that invitations, even to some of the most exclusive gatherings, regularly went out to reporters. See *M*, 26 January, 1868.

7. 'Chez MM de Girardin, il y avait beaucoup de gens de lettres, d'abord sa mère Mme Sophie Gay, puis Alfred de Musset et Lamartine, Balzac, Victor Hugo, Jules Janin, Emile Deschamps, Alexandre Dumas, Resseguier et autres. Mme Delphine de Girardin nous a récité de jolis vers de sa composition avec une grâce et, qui plus est, une simplicité parfaite. Lamartine nous en a dit de charmants et qui n'ont pas encore paru. Ces déclamations alternaient avec des romances, dont les paroles étaient composées par un des auteurs présents et mises en musique par Labarre qui les accompagnait ou les chantait. Plusieurs de ces romances ont été composées par Mlle Lambert, charmante jeune personne remplie de talent et qui chante d'une manière inimitable. Chaque fois qu'on se mettait au piano, Mme Sophie Gay nommait l'auteur du poème qui nous exposait le sujet.' Apponyi, vol. III, 209.

8. 'M et Mme. Émile Girardin ont donné dernièrement une magnifique soirée musicale. L'auditoire était composé de l'élite de la société parisienne. En hommes politiques et en littérateurs, on y remarquait MM le prince de Ligne, Villemain, de Salvandy, Dupin ainé, de Rambuteau, Reschid-Pacha, Victor Hugo, de Lamartine, de Balzac, L. Golzan etc. Mme de Girardin, avec sa grâce habituelle, a délicieusement fait les honneurs de son salon. M Balfe, le compositeur anglais, a chanté un air de sa composition, qui a fait plaisir. Les deux frères Alexandre et Laurent Batta, de retour de leur brillante tournée en Allemagne, ont joué un duo sur les motifs de *la Favorite*. Ce morceau surpasse tout ce que Batta avait écrit et exécuté jusqu'à ce jour. La romance *Pour tant d'amour*, qu'il a intercalée, a profondément ému l'auditoire. Ainsi comprise par l'artiste, elle obtiendra toujours un succès immense. La romance de *Richard Coeur-de-lion*, *Une Fièvre brulante*, avait été demandée. Elle a fait fureur. On nous a dit des merveilles d'un duo composé par Batta et Wolff, sur des motifs de *Lucrezia Borgia*. Espérons que nous pourrons l'entendre avant peu. Corelli, le nouveau ténor du Théâtre-Italien, a chanté avec beaucoup de goût l'air de *Roberto Devereux*, et avec M Porto un duo de *Bélisaire*. Mme Labarre a dignement clos la soirée en chantant, avec infiniment de goût et de charme, deux charmantes romances de son mari.' *MM*, 19 January, 1843.

9. Martin-Fugier, 143.

10. 'Nos matinées musicales, qui ont lieu tous les ans à cette époque, ont commencé de nouveau. Tous les dimanches, des amateurs de musique réunissent chez nous à trois heures, chacun apporte avec lui sa musique; on déchiffre des morceaux anciens et modernes. Kalkbrenner tient cette année-ci le piano au grand désespoir de tous les amateurs, car il ne les aide pas, il accompagne comme l'on jouerait une sonate, allant toujours en avant, sans s'inquiéter de savoir si on le suit on non.' Apponyi, vol. III, 140–41.

11. Apponyi, vol. I, 305.

12. *RGM*, 1 May, 1837.

13. 'Les concerts se multiplient dans nos salons aristocratiques et il y aura bientôt plus de virtuoses que d'auditeurs. Mmes la comtesse de Merlin, la baronne Delmar, de Pontalba, de Rigny, M William Hope ont fait assaut de merveilles

musicales; la première des dames que nous venons de citer, a soutenu, surtout avec éclat, la réputation traditionnelle et presque classique dont jouit son salon sous le rapport du chant; dernièrement, elle a exécuté d'une manière entraînante avec le concours du Prince de Belgiojoso, du comte Poniatowski et de Lablache, le quatuor qui termine le second acte de Lucia. On a dans la même soirée, entendu Mme la comtesse de Sparre (Mlle Naldi), dont la voix n'a rien perdu de la pureté comme de l'énergie passionnée qui la distinguaient jadis au théâtre.' *RGM*, 25 February, 1838.

14. Duchesse de Maillé, *Souvenirs des deux Restaurations* (1984), 121, quoted in Martin-Fugier, 317.

15. 'Chez Mme. Orfila la musique est la fleur des quatre saisons. On y chante toujours, été comme hiver.' *M*, 24 April, 1859.

16. 'Depuis nombre d'années les salons de M et Mme. Crémieux rivalisent avec ceux de Mme. Orfila, On y rencontre le même amour de la bonne musique et les meilleurs interprètes.' *M*, 17 April, 1859.

17. 'Mmes Orfila et Mosneron de Saint-Preux offraient à leurs habitués l'un de ces programmes qu'elles seules peuvent réaliser. Là, nos artistes se voient chez eux, au milieu d'amis jaloux et heureux de partager leurs plaisirs. Aussi les transformations les plus piquantes s'y produisent-elles spontanément et avec une verve impossible à décrire ... Il n'est que Rossini ou Mme Orfila qui puissent se donner le luxe de voir danser Mme Taglioni, l'idéal, en dépit du temps, de la grâce personnifiée.' *M*, 26 February, 1860.

18. It was not only music lovers who frequented the Rossini salon. *M* noted that its audience often included financiers such as Rothschild and Fould. *M*, 18 January, 1836.

19. 'Vous connaissez, au moins de réputation, le salon de Zimmerman; vous savez que deux fois par mois, le jeudi au soir, c'est un point de réunion pour les artistes célèbres et les amateurs, que le maître du salon daigne accueillir. N'entre pas qui veut chez Zimmerman; ni l'or ni le rang n'ouvrent sa porte à personne; mais de quelque coin du monde que l'on arrive, de quelque instrument que l'on joue; dans quelque la langue que l'on chante, pour peu que l'on possède une capacité musicale suffisamment justifiée, on y trouve un pupitre tout dressé, un auditoire tout préparé, des bravos empressés à récompenser le mérite fort, de même qu'à encourager le mérite qui grandit et l'élève. Avoir obtenu un grand succès chez Zimmerman, c'est avoir conquis ses lettres de noblesse, le droit de se présenter partout dans l'Europe tête levée.' *RGM*, 14 February, 1839.

20. 'Le salon de M Zimmerman est au monde musical ce que le temple de la Bourse est au monde financier.' *M*, 6 January, 1839.

21. *RGM*, 14 February, 1839.

22. The Lionnet Brothers were not the only family vocal groups. There were the Soeurs Marchisio and the Frères Guidon and Frères Castellani whose names also appear in accounts of salon recitals. (See Appendix A.)

23. 'M Gounod a chanté des airs de son nouvel opéra de *Philémon et Baucis*, qui nous applaudirons bientôt au Théâtre-Lyrique et qui nous promet un digne pendant à *Faust*. M Charles Delioux a joué deux morceaux fort remarquable de sa composition, *le Ruisseau* et sa *transcription sur Faust*. G. Nadaud nous a fait entendre quelques-unes de ses chansons nouvelles, et notamment *le Nid abandonné*, mélodie touchante et pleine de suavité. E. l'Epine a interprété avec un goût exquis, *Cousine Marie* et *Sous les tilleuls*, deux de ses plus jolies

mélodies. M Alphonse Daudet a récité ses délicieux triolets, *les Prunes*. Puis, enfin, est venue le tour des deux amphitryons, qui ont interprété avec leur style habituel, plusieurs morceaux de leur album: *le Matin* (de Victor Hugo), *les Cloches de Saint-Loups* (de Delsarte), *Fanchette* (d'A. Hignard), *les Adieux à un amie* (de Nadaud), et *les Gardes françaises* (de Delioux). Chaque auteur accompagnait son oeuvre tour à tour. Les frères Lionnet ont reçu les félicitations les plus flatteurs de chacun d'eux. Mais le grand succès de la soirée a été pour M Delsarte, qui a fait frissonner ses auditeurs dans *les Terreurs de Thoas* (*d'Iphigénie en Aulide*). Aussi lui a-t-on fait une ovation dont il gardera longtemps le souvenir. On s'est séparé vers trois heures du matin, le cœur tout ému encore des chaudes impressions de cette délicieuse soirée, impressions d'autant plus chaudes que l'atmosphère marquait 30 degrés Maryland.' *M*, 15 January, 1860.

24. *M*, 8 February, 1863.

25. 'Comme on le voit les soirées musicales prennent le plus brillant essor à Paris, cet hiver 1859. C'est maintenant un genre de servir à ses invités un sompteux programme de musique. Nous n'avons garde de nous en plaindre, c'est là une mode dont la contagion est à désirer. Nous l'appelons de tous nos veux dans l'intérêt de l'art et des artistes.' *M*, 6 February, 1859.

26. 'M S … rendez-vous des notabilités artistiques et littéraires, qui se trouvaient entourées par les plus jeunes et les plus jolies femmes. Compositeurs, peintres, littérateurs, sculpteurs, formaient l'aristocratie de ce salon.' *GM*, 24 December, 1837.

27. 'L'élégant salon de M Alexandre Dumas réunissait, mercredi soir, de sommités et de talents de tout genre. Peintres, sculpteurs, chanteurs, hommes de lettres, journalistes, jouissaient en commun de la plus aimable hospitalité. Les plus grands artistes du chant italien ont concouru à un concert qui, pour n'avoir pas été arrangé à l'avance, n'en a été que plus attrayant.' *MM*, 1 February, 1844.

28. *M*, 8 February, 1863.

29. *M*, 28 February, 1869.

30. 'Samedi soir, notre spirituel photographe Nadar avait transformé ses ateliers en salons champêtres et en jardins: lumières à profusion, verdures, fleurs, grottes et cascades, rien n'y manquait; c'était un spectacle féerique, y compris les jolies femmes. Dans cet Eden improvisé, Nadar donnait une belle et bonne soirée musicale.' *M*, 12 April, 1863.

31. 'Lorsque Léonard de Vinci peignait le portrait de la belle Joconde, il l'entourait des harmonies les plus suaves. C'est ainsi que, dimanche dernier, chez M Pitre-Chevalier, tandis que M & Mme Bettini-Trebelli chantaient le duo: *Mira la bianca luna*, Morin, Six et Worms saisissaient à la pointe du crayon le profil si pur de la Muette de Portici, Mlle Marie Vernon, comme le dimanche précédent, ils avaient saisi l'olympienne figure de Méry, sous la surveillance de Giroux. Pendant que Mme Méric-Lalande chantait les grands airs de Rossini, M Jousse la romance d'*Aladin*. Mme Garait, de l'Opéra-Comique, et Berthelier le duo bouffe des *Tourtereaux*, Vizentini, le violon grand prix de Bruxelles, tirait de son instrument des sons enchanteurs. Mlle Karoly, la tragique, disait avec Dubarry une scène d'Horace, M Boissière récitait une des ses charmantes fables, et Coquelin de la Comédie-Francaise, disait avec un art consommé, *Carcassone*, la nouvelle chanson de Nadaud. Enfin, Mme. Paër, Mlle Clara Lemonnier et M Dubois jouaient avec costumes, accessoires, lumières et rideau, le *Loup et*

l'Agneau, de Frédéric Barbier, paroles de MM Hipp. Tressant et Chold de Curcy, un bijou du Théâtre-Déjazet, honoré d'une soirée à Compiègne. Mme Causse, M d'Aubel et M Populus se sont signalés comme accompagnateurs, ce jour-là comme le dimanche précédent, où ils avaient accompagné M et Mme Tagliafico, Mme Oscar Commettant, Levassor [sic], etc.' *M*, 12 April, 1863.

32.   'On les reçoit en soupirant un peu, surtout l'ambassadrice qui nous désole avec son bavardage, tout spirituel qu'il soit. Dans ces occasions, c'est surtout moi qui suis à plaindre. L'ambassadrice, se voyant abandonnée par le maître et la maîtresse de maison, qui, dans leur passion pour la musique, ne lui répondent pas, ne me lâche plus; elle sait bien que je ne puis faire comme les autres; la seule liberté que je prends, c'est de l'inviter, de temps en temps, à parler un peu plus bas.' *Journal du comte Rudolphe Apponyi*, 239–40, entry for 27 March, 1830.

33.   'Les soirées musicales devancent la saison de Carême, et si beaucoup de ces soirées prennent la musique pour prétexte de réunion et de conversation – à la façon anglaise – il faut reconnaître encore dans Paris de ces salons hospitaliers où l'art musical retrouve ses vrais fidèles.' *M*, 13 January, 1861.

34.   'Les nouveaux salons de madame la comtesse de Grabowska se sont ouverts cette année sous auspices de talents remarquables: MM Ponchard, Sowinski, Robbrechts, mesdames Widemann, Loveday, etc., ont contribué à cette fête d'inauguration; mais ce que les artistes trouvent surtout de remarquable chez cette patronnesse des arts, c'est qu'ils sont constamment écoutés avec un religieuse silence par un auditoire à la fois fashionable et connaisseur.' *RGM*, 5 April, 1840.

35.   'Indépendamment de ces réunions où les femmes, les diamants, les fleurs et les lumières luttent trop souvent avec la musique au lieu de la servir, il est dans Paris de ces salons tranquilles, fermés au bruit et au luxe, vers lesquels un tout petit nombre de conviés s'acheminent silencieusement, tout comme pour un saint pèlerinage.' *M*, 1 February 1863.

36.   'Dans les salons de la princesse Mathilde, le programme n'était pas moins attrayant: on y a entendu Mmes de Grandval, Bouchet, Mlle Rives dans *la Serenata* de Braga; M.M. Saint-Saëns, Emile Durand et Sauzay. Mais pourquoi le public officiel de la rue de Coucelles écoute-t-il si peu et si mal la musique? Les salons de la princesse Mathilde reçoivent cependant la société la plus intelligente de Paris. Beaucoup d'artistes y sont invités: les musiciens, les peintres, les sculpteurs, les homme de lettres s'y pressent et sont les premiers, nous le constatons à regret, à se livrer aux conversations.' *M*, 24 February, 1867.

37.   For a fascinating study of Parisian listening habits from 1750 to 1850 see James H. Johnson, *Listening in Paris – a cultural history* (1995).

38.   'Rien n'égaye Rossini comme toutes ces scènes eccentriques.' *M*, 1 March, 1863.

39.   Quoted in Beth Archer Brombert, *Cristina: Portraits of a Princess* (1978), 384.

40.   Brombert, 20.

41.   *Correspondence de Liszt et de la comtesse d'Agoult 1833–1840*, ed. D. Ollivier, (1933), vol. I, 428.

42.   'D'une taille assez élevée et admirablement prise, la princesse Belgiojoso avait une figure ovale à la façon de *la Jaconde,* mais le nez plus aquilin que ce charmant modèle. De très grands yeux noirs illuminaient son visage, que des cheveux également noirs encadraient avec harmonie. En la contemplant, l'attention aurait pu être fixée par ces beaux grands yeux, par ce nez légèrement cambré, aux narines fines et dilatées. Mais ce qui s'absorbait le regard, et de loin

provoquait le curiosité, c'était le pâleur mate du teint, qui, le soir prenait une nuance absolument fantastique où le bleu et le vert se confondaient, donnant ainsi à la princesse une apparence de fantôme tout à fait saisissante. C'était l'usage, et peut-être l'abus, du poison médical nommé *datura stramonium*, qui chez-elle, disait-on, produisait cet effet si singulier.' Vicomte de Beaumont-Vassy, 123–124.

43. 'elle a des coiffures et des turbans d'une forme insolite, des robes excessivement décolletées et si singulièrement vaporeuses, des draperies si bizarres, qu'on croit découvrir sans cesse un poignard sous leurs plis.' Apponyi, vol. III, 264.

44. 'on passait dans une chambre à coucher tendue entièrement en étoffe de soie blanche. La pendule de la cheminée, les flambeaux, les candélabres, l'ornementation tout entière, en un mot, était en argent ou en matières argentées, ce qui formait avec la pièce précédente le contraste le plus absolu'. Beaumont-Vassy, 123.

45. *Le Journal des débats*, 21 March, 1837.

46. Brombert, 337–8. The absence of any comment about the work in *RGM* when it reported on the 'duel' (9 April, 1837) also lends support to Brombert's conclusion.

47. *RGM*, 25 February, 1838.

48. *RGM*, 20 June, 1847.

49. Apponyi, vol. III, 371.

50. Nieuwerkeke, who was appointed Directeur-général des Musées impérieux and Intendant des beaux-arts de la maison de l'Empereur, established his own weekly salon at the Louvre, the artistic direction usually under Pasdeloup.

51. 'Entrons donc dans le bel hôtel de la rue de Courcelles ... D'abord, quatre grands salons communiquant par une vaste serre. Dans celui du milieu, le piano autour duquel se groupaient les chanteurs, avec le quatuor instrumental à gauche, et à droite un piano-orgue sur lequel improvisaient Saint-Saëns ou Cohen. Au premier accord chacun des auditeurs avait choisi sa place, les plus musiciens près du piano échangeant des compliments avec les exécutants, les autres dispersés soit dans la serre, soit dans les salons voisins où la poésie des fleurs et de leur parfum se mêlait au charme de la musique. Le programme se composait des plus belles œuvres des grands maîtres, susceptible d'être jouées par un petit orchestre, et d'œuvres modernes chantées par les premiers chanteurs italiens ou français ... Le printemps venu, la Princesse faisait transporter tout le matériel – piano, orgue, pupitres dans la grande salle à manger à colonnes, où désormais avaient lieu les soirées. C'était l'époque de l'année où les réunions étaient les plus suivies et les plus brillantes. A ce moment arrivaient presque toujours à Paris quelque tête couronnée, quelques princes étrangers qui ne manquaient pas de paraître chez la Princesse ... Elle avait aussi bien du mal à obtenir le silence, et, selon son expression, à faire taire les bavards. Elle donnait elle-même l'exemple de la discipline en s'arrachant les plus possible à tous ceux qui l'entouraient pour venir écouter près de nous le morceau commencé. Bien entendu, l'aspect général de la soirée était très différent lorsque celle-ci était uniquement musicale.' Brigitte François-Sappey, 'La vie musicale à Paris à travers les Mémoires d'Eugène Sauzay', *Revue de musicologie*, LX/1–2, 1974. This extract is from pp. 204–10.

52. 'Les salons de la princesse Mathilde se sont ouverts deux fois cette semaine: le dimanche d'usage, et mercredi dernier en l'honneur de la grande duchesse Marie de Russie, conviée au régal d'une représentation intime du *Cas de conscience*, de M Octave Feuillet, avec Mme. Arnould-Plessy et Bressant pour interprètes, Leurs

Majestés assistaient à cette soirée dramatique. Quant au dimanche précédant, le dernier dimanche d'hiver de S. A. I. paraît-il, c'est la musique qui en a fait tous les honneurs, et quels honneurs! Mme. Carvalho a chanté du Mozart et du Gounod si merveilleusement, qu'on l'aurait volontiers portée en triomphe. Delle-Sadie a aussi chanté du Gounod, en français, et dans une rare perfection. Le nouveau membre de l'Institut assistait à son double succès. Une cantatrice amateur, qui chante comme une grande artiste, Mme. Bouché, a fait entendre la nouvelle composition de Mme. Grandval: *les Lucioles*, avec accompagnement de violon et d'orgue, sans préjudice du piano, tenu par l'auteur. L'effet a été délicieux; ces *Lucioles*, ainsi accompagnées, feraient le tour du monde. Mme Bouché a aussi chanté un charmant duo de Campana avec Mlle. Rives, une jeune protégée de Rossini et du Gounod. qui, de plus, a eu l'honneur de recevoir ses premières leçons de chant de Mme. la comtesse de Sparre, Avec une pareille marraine et de tels parrains, on doit devenir une véritable artiste, ce qu'est déjà Mlle. Rives. Il serait d'autant plus injuste d'oublier la partie instrumentale du dernier programme de la princesse Mathilde, que Franchomme, le violoncelliste en titre de la maison, a joué ses transcriptions de Chopin avec un sentiment exquis de cette poétique musique. Un quatuor d'Haydn ouvrait la soirée. MM Saint-Saëns et Sauzay y ont brillé, ainsi que dans *l'Ave Maria* de Gounod et *les Lucioles* de Mme. de Grandval.' *M*, 3 June, 1866.

53. For a study of Princess Mathilde see Joanna Richardson, *Princess Mathilde* (1969).
54. Franz Liszt, 'De la situation des artistes et de leur condition dans la société', *GM*, May–October, 1835.
55. 'Bien que le système des soirées musicales entre peu dans nos idées sur l'art et sur la manière de le cultiver, quelque peu d'importance que nous attachions par conséquent à rendre compte de ces réunions', *GM*, 28 December, 1834.
56. 'Voici le moment des grands soirées musicales, mais les plus belles ne sont pas celles où l'on peut aller pour son argent. Il semble que les artistes se plaisent à réserver pour leurs intimes la fleur de leurs inspirations et la poésie de leur talent.' *RGM*, 4 February, 1841.
57. As, for example, in *RGM*, 9 April, 1854.
58. Countess Merlin (Maria de las Mercedes de Jaruco), *Memoirs of Mme Malibran by the Countess Merlin and other intimate friends* (1840), 93.
59. *RGM*, 7 March, 1869.
60. 'C'est dams les salons de Mme Orfila & chez notre éminent professeur Marmontel, le digne successeur de Zimmerman, que le baptême du succès à été donné aux œuvres de M de Vaucorbeil, compositeur inconnu la veille, et fêté de son premier début par le monde musical et littéraire.' *RGM*, 22 March, 1857.

CHAPTER THREE

Singers in the Salons

As part of the 'industry' of musical Paris the salons offered frequent
employment – especially to singers – as reflected in those journals which
reported on the musical life of the capital and, sometimes, of the provinces.
Their pages are littered with the names of singers, many of them well known
in opera, who, when time permitted would appear in the salons – usually the
more exclusive ones, as well as other singers who made their living almost
entirely from doing the rounds of the salons. To judge from their reviews there
would be some fifty or more singing in one season. By the end of our period
there were considerably more.[1] The repertoire ranged from operatic arias
(sometimes exclusively Italian in some aristocratic salons) to French romances
and mélodies. From the 1850s onwards there was also a considerable vogue
for 'salon operas'.

With so many singers appearing in the salons a list of them would be
tedious. This chapter takes a handful of the most renowned, most of them
opera stars, all of whom, however, appeared regularly in the salons and who
sang from the repertoire that is the main subject of this book. To begin with,
however, we will briefly consider the changes that came over French singing
at the beginning of the nineteenth century, for it affected all who pursued the
profession of singing whether on stage or in the salon.

French and Italian Singing Styles

The influence on French music by that of Italy in the seventeenth and
eighteenth centuries is well known and well documented. Equally strong was
Italian influence on French singers in the nineteenth century.

French opera singers had prided themselves on their clarity of diction and
dramatic flair. But it was a style which, while requiring considerable lung
power, lacked line and cantabile, a view shared by so many writers of that time
that it cannot be dismissed out of hand.[2] French concern for diction, rather than
for vocal production, is confirmed also in the singing manuals in circulation

towards the end of the eighteenth century. For example, an instruction manual of 1770 published by a singing teacher at Lille, tells singers how they must know the 'rules' of short and long syllables in French prosody (a concept that stemmed from the latter years of the sixteenth century), but is remarkably unhelpful on technique.[3] Other manuals just prior to the changes occurring in French singing towards the turn of the century were equally conservative, usually just listing the ornaments that had been in vogue in the time of Couperin and Rameau. Antoine Bailleux, composer and publisher, described the 100 exercises in his singing manual as being 'in the new taste', but gives almost no advice on how to sing them.[4] We are forced to the conclusion that criticisms levelled at French singing may well have been close to the mark. Fétis describes it thus:

> French singing differed in certain ways to Italian singing. A pure and sonorous voice, clean and consistent diction and dramatic expression was about all one wanted for a long time in France from a singer. A rather unreasonable bias against roulades and ornaments has been held as unsuited to our language. Little by little, the Opéra-Comique has freed itself from these objections that have been put in its way; but the Opéra has resisted until now. They have just given way to what is up to date, and it's well done. ... One feels how much the world of French singing has expanded through the fusion of Italian styles and ours, and how much the art is becoming more difficult.[5]

The renowned tenor Adolphe Nourrit described how, until he studied with Donizetti he had always sacrificed sound for diction, the problem exacerbated by the profusion of nasal sounds in French.

One of the first to fuse French and Italian singing styles – and hailed as such by Fétis and many others – was Pierre Garat (1762–1823). He was born in Bordeaux with what seems to have been a naturally sweet voice of remarkable range. At his father's insistence, he came to Paris to study law (which he soon neglected), and it was there that he developed his vocal technique, largely by listening to Italian singers and studying with one of them. According to Fétis, Garat gained for the first time an idea of expressive singing in a pure and elegant style, beautifully in tune and with even tone and expressive diction. Although he was celebrated particularly for his performances of Gluck's music, he never became a professional opera singer, instead, cultivating the art of singing romances in the salons to which Fétis claimed he owed his reputation. Garat taught singing at the Conservatoire, amongst his students being Mme Branchu and the male singers Ponchard, Levasseur and the father of one of France's finest tenors, Adolphe Nourrit.

Another influence on the new generation of singers was Alexandre Choron who, it will be remembered, founded the Institution royale de musique religieuse de France in 1817. Like Garat, he was late in coming to music, having initially followed his father's wish to pursue studies at the Ecole Polytechnique, but his unquenchable love for music, further fired by his studies with the Italian singer Bonesi, led to his abandoning thought of anything else. He read widely and deeply and published a number of pedagogic works, some with a scientific bent. Like Garat, he admired the classical style of Mozart, Gluck and much earlier composers with their purity of line, a love which informed his vocal teaching. One of the finest singers of the day, Gilbert Duprez, was to emerge from Choron's school.

The major Italian influence on French singing, however, came about through Rossini's appointment as Musical Director of the Théâtre-Italien in Paris in 1824. Italian opera had found a champion in Napoleon Bonaparte who had united the forces of the Comédie-Française at the Odéon with the Italian Opera, the result being the Théâtre de l'Impératrice at which Spontini and, later, Paër, were conductors. At the Restoration the Théâtre de l'Impératrice became the Théâtre-Italien where Rossini's *Il barbiere di Siviglia* was given in 1819 to a rapturous reception, and when the composer arrived in Paris five years later he was offered the appointment as Musical Director there. It was the example of the first-rate Italian singers whom Rossini engaged, as well as his training of French opera singers, that was to have a decisive influence for the future, for he sought to fuse the best elements of both schools. He composed operas for both the Théâtre-Italien and the Opéra. For the latter he wrote *Le comte Ory* (1828) and *Guillaume Tell* (1829), the latter pointing the direction for Meyerbeer's French 'grand operas', the first of which was *Robert le Diable*, which, as we have already seen, ushered in a new era for the Paris Opéra under the directorship of Louis Véron.

In this chapter we shall look at a few of the leading singers whose names were household words in nineteenth-century Paris. Opera being the major musical form in the French capital they were nearly all opera singers, who, however, included French songs in their repertoire which they often sang in the salons. Any review of such singers must start with the Garcia family which boasted a father whose vocal methods produced two of the most celebrated singers of the century, and a son who refined and transmitted his father's method and whose pedagogical works and singing exercises are still well known to serious students today.

The Garcia Family

Manuel Garcia (1775–1832) was born in Spain where he made his name as a popular actor and a singer especially in Madrid. Leaving Spain to further his studies he came first to Paris in 1808 and then went on to Italy returning to

Paris in 1816 where he established his name as an opera singer, particularly in the operas of Rossini, and as a teacher. A man of violent temperament whose demands and denunciations would brook no opposition he must have been a remarkable teacher to have produced such magnificent singers as his daughters Maria and Pauline and to a lesser extent his son, also named Manuel.

Unlike his son, Garcia published no singing treatise, exercises or vocalises, but we gain a good idea of his teaching methods through Countess Merlin who had studied with him. Her description of Garcia's principles of voice production are worth quoting in full.

> The first objects to which the young singer should direct attention are: to equalize what may be termed the instrument of the voice, by correcting those imperfections from which even the finest organ is not exempt; to augment the number of tones by constant and careful practice [Here, in a footnote she quotes Garcia's own words: 'Those who wish to sing well should not practise without knowing how to practise. It is only by learning the secret of practising well that there is any possibility of learning to sing well'; to draw breath quietly and without hurry; to prepare the throat for emitting the tone with clearness and purity, swelling the note gradually but boldly, so as to develop the utmost power of the voice; and finally, to blend the notes in such a manner that each may be heard distinctly but not abruptly. But, on the other hand, it is requisite to guard against a false application of this principle, lest the student should fall into the defects of the old French method, by which one note was allowed to die away with a false expression of languid tenderness, and to fall, as it were, *en defaillance* [unsteadily] on the succeeding tone. To blend the tones of the voice according to the best Italian method, the note should first be emitted in a *straight line* (to employ a figurative expression) and then form a curve, the intermediate tones being given merely by sympathetic vibration, and the voice should again fall on the required note with decision and clearness.
>
> Whatever be the quality of the voice, the singer should take especial care of the upper notes, and avoid too much practice upon them, for that part of the voice being most delicate, its quality is most easily injured. On the contrary, by practising more particularly on the middle and lower notes, they acquire strength, and an important object is gained (which is in strict accordance with the one of the essential principles of acoustics) namely, that of making the grave [low] tones strike the ear with the same degree of force as the acute [high] tones. To the adoption of this rational rule is to be ascribed the great superiority of the Italian to the French school of singing. By softening the upper tones, and giving strength to the lower and middle tones, either by dint of the accent of the voice, or the accent proper to the words, the ear is never offended, and the music penetrates to the soul of the hearer without any of that harshness which shocks and irritates the nerves ...
>
> Exercises for strengthening the low and middle notes of the voice are more important for sopranos than for voices of any other class; first, because, in general, that part of the voice is most feeble; and next, because the transition from the *voce di petto* [chest register] to the *voce di testa* [head register] tends to deteriorate the purity of some tones, and to impart a feebler, or if I may so

express myself a *stifled* effect to others. It is, therefore, requisite to keep up a continual practice of the defective note with the pure note which follows or precedes it, in order to obtain a perfect uniformity in their quality ...

In proportion as the voice of the pupil improved it was Garcia's custom to prescribe exercises more and more difficult until every obstacle was surmounted; but he rarely noted down a set passage for his pupils. His method was to strike a chord on the piano, and to say to them, 'Now sing any passage you please'; and he would make them execute a passage in that way ten or twenty times in succession. The result was that the pupil sang precisely that which was suited to his voice, and suggested by his taste. Solfeggio exercises performed this way presented a character of individuality, being suggested by the feeling of the moment. Another advantage of the mode of practice was that the pupil gained a perfect mastery over his voice by dint of exercising his own inspirations, and that he was at liberty to follow the dictates of his taste without fear of hesitation.

Garcia never permitted his pupils, whilst they were in the course of tuition, to sing vocal compositions with the words; he confined them strictly to Solfeggi [vocalise]. But when he considered any one of them sufficiently advanced he would say, 'Now you are a singer; you may try anything you please – like a child out of leading-strings you can *run alone.*' It may be added that Garcia invariably applied his principles most rigorously to those pupils on whom he founded his highest hopes.[6]

At first, his highest hopes can hardly have been founded on Maria (1808–1836) whose voice was initially feeble and her intonation variable. Beginning her lessons with her father as a child, only someone with her character and resilience could have withstood the humiliating criticisms and exacting demands he made upon her during those tender years and beyond. Fortunately, she had a close and lifelong friend in Countess Merlin, nine years her senior and her first biographer. It was at Countess Merlin's salon that Maria sang before leaving with her father for London to make her début at the King's Theatre in June, 1825, and there, on her return to Paris two years later, where she sang to the directors of the Théâtre-Italien whom the Countess had assembled to hear her, and who were immediately won over by her performance. From then on her success was assured both in France and internationally.

But between her London début and her return to Paris she had contracted a disastrous marriage. It was during a tour to New York as part of an opera company directed by her father that she met an American businessman, Malibran, whose promise of happiness and wealth led instead, through his ineptitude, almost immediately to distress and bankruptcy, and with great difficulty she returned to Paris alone in 1827, her father having temporarily disowned her. Her success at the Théâtre-Italien, where she was known as Maria Malibran or as the phenomenon 'La Malibran', relieved her of her financial worries and she eventually obtained a divorce. Personal happiness came to her through the Belgian violinist Charles-Auguste de Bériot (1802–1870) whom she eventually married after bearing (in secret) his child, but her life was tragically short. She was in England to undertake various performances and was thrown violently from a horse when out riding in London. Although seriously injured, she typically refused to let this deter her from her engagements and during a performance at Manchester she became desperately ill, dying at the age of 28.

What was so special about Maria Malibran the singer? All who heard her spoke of the way she was able to bring together all the qualities desirable in an opera singer. As Countess Merlin described her, she had the good fortune to possess beauty, an admirable figure, a vibrant personality, and, as a born actress, she brought dramatic integrity, intensity and characterization to every role she played. Her voice had the quality of a contralto but with an extraordinary range that took her from E flat below middle C to C (or D) two octaves above middle C. She had a unique gift for embellishment appropriate to the dramatic and musical situation, which she improvised on each occasion, never repeating the same way she sang an aria. Embellishments added by the singer to their arias lost fashion after her death, but at that time it was a regular feature of operatic performance. Her memory was phenomenal, one that nowadays we would call 'photographic'. She could study a major role for the first time and sing it from memory that evening. She spoke fluent French, English, Italian and Spanish.

Maria also had a gift for composition – fluent rather than profound – and she especially liked writing romances. They are no better or worse than those then in vogue, but considering her very short and busy life, some thirty published songs is no small achievement. They were sung in the drawing rooms and salons of London, Paris and other places. It is no wonder that news of her untimely death was received with stunned grief – not least by those financially less fortunate who had every reason to be grateful for her warm-hearted and impulsive generosity, as on the day of her marriage to Bériot when she gave the Mayor 1000 francs to distribute to the poor in his district so that they could share some of her happiness.[7] It was considered that never again would there be such a singer. But following the début of her young sister Pauline she was seen to be 'reborn'. It was a sentiment felt most widely, and had already been given eloquent expression by Henri Blanchard after he had heard her at a matinée concert at the beginning of 1839, before her début as Desdemona in Rossini's *Otello* in October that year.

> And with the memory of Malibran, so sad, so painful, is mixed the certainty of seeing her reborn. Yes, we have in Pauline Garcia, her sister, those same musical faculties, so brilliant, so rich, so original: here we have the same vocal

equipment, the Shakespearean mixture of the tragic and the comic which does not grimace as in the Romantic school; here is the Spanish, French, Italian singer, inspiring by turns laughter and melancholy, noble and touching in the tones that are so gentle, in the reproaches that Euridice addresses to her spouse; lively and mad like an Andalousian in the pretty *séguidille* which she sang in such piquant fashion; melancholy and tender in *L'attente* ['Du bist die Ruh'] and *La poste* ['Die Post'], those songs of Schubert that are so lovely, the words of which have been so aptly translated by M Deschamps; original and comic in the *Tyrolienne* of Amédée de Beauplan. Pauline Garcia is called, by nature of the range of her talent to inherit the position of great artist that her illustrious sister seemed to have left vacant for ever.[8]

Unlike her older sister, Pauline (1821–1910) did not have the benefit of her father's training for long, for he died when she was only 11 years old. Manuel Garcia's principles, however, must have been well understood by her mother who took over the teaching of the young girl. Pauline's musical gifts took in more than singing. Under Reicha she became a versatile composer, and under Liszt an accomplished pianist who not only took part in chamber music recitals (there is a report of her participation in a performance of Beethoven's Piano Trio in C minor) but also achieved the probably unique distinction of accompanying herself in a performance of Schubert's *Erlkönig* at a concert in May 1862 given by Clara Schumann (by then a close friend) for the Société allemande.

It was as Pauline Garcia that the 18-year-old girl made her spectacular début in Rossini's *Otello*, first in London and then in Paris. The next year it was as Pauline Viardot that she sang, having married a distinguished writer Louis Viardot, twenty-one years her senior. The marriage stimulated her intellectual powers, and the Viardot's salon in the Chaussée-d'Antin became one of the intellectual and artistic centres in Paris. Many composers had reason to be grateful to her for championing their music – including Gounod, Massenet, Saint-Saëns and Fauré, to name the most important. In return, she became the dedicatee of many works from operas to romances. Berlioz made a new edition of Gluck's *Orfeo* for her to sing (this becoming the standard nineteenth-century edition of that work). For one of her London appearances he re-wrote and expanded his song *La captive*, a simple romance that he had written at the Villa Medici when he was a student there following his Prix de Rome, and to which he also added an orchestral accompaniment (see Chapter Five). Like her sister she had a gift for languages, and was the first to visit Russia and sing the music of Glinka and Dargomïzhsky in Russian. Following the Franco-Prussian War of 1870 she returned to Paris from Baden-Baden where she had gone with her family, and for the rest of her life devoted herself mainly to teaching and composition. Her compositions include 100 songs, works for piano and other instruments and four operettas. Of her publications, her vocal arrangements of some of the mazurkas by Chopin, with whom she worked (Pauline Viardot and George Sand being intimate friends) are amongst her best known. She sang them herself in London in 1848 at Chopin's last recital and obviously had the composer's blessing for them. Her best songs deserve a much wider recognition amongst today's singers, for they are very accomplished works. Her *Sechs Lieder*, for example, reveal both fine craftsmanship and imagination as do some of her settings of French poetry, such as *Sérénade* (to words by Bertrand).

As a singer, Pauline Viardot possessed the same extensive vocal compass as her sister's, but with less of a contralto than a mezzo-soprano quality. This was noted as early as 1838, the year before her operatic début, when she took part in a concert with her brother-in-law Bériot in Berlin. The well-known German critic of the time Rellstab declared it to stretch from F sharp below middle C to C two octaves above. (It was eventually to reach three notes above that.) He likened the lower notes not to those of a contralto, but to the sound of a cello, and the higher notes to the sound of a violin. Even though, like a number of writers who described her voice, he felt that it was not perfect in all its notes, Rellstab frankly confessed that not since the time of the 'miraculous voices' of Nanette Schechner (1806–1860) and Angelica Catalani (1780–1849) had he been so moved by a woman's voice as he was by this eighteen-year-old as she moved from one style to another – brilliant and virtuosic, simple and expressive, tragic and comic.[9]

Three other members of the Garcia family should be mentioned. Garcia's second wife, the singer Maria Joaquina (mother of Maria, Pauline and Manuel), outlived her husband by many years and, as we have seen in the case of Pauline, took over much of his teaching. Their son Manuel (1805–1906) studied singing under his father and harmony under Fétis. He sang with his father's company on the ill-fated tour to New York where his sister married Malibran, but gave up professional singing to devote himself to teaching, first at the Paris Conservatoire and then at the Royal Academy of Music in London. Apart from transmitting and developing his father's method, Manuel is also known for his invention of the laryngoscope. His most illustrious students were Jenny Lind and Mathilde Marchesi. His first wife Eugénie (1815–1880) also became a well-known teacher and her salon was celebrated for the fine singing that came from her students and from those in the professional world invited to sing there.

Adolphe Nourrit

Like Maria Malibran, Adolphe Nourrit (1802–1839) became a legend, not least because his exceptional career, like hers, was cut short by tragic circumstances, although in his case he lived nine years longer than did 'La Malibran'. Garat had trained Nourrit's father, a well-known singer at the Paris Opéra, but it was Garcia who trained the son. Adolphe possessed something of the range and quality of what was called *haute-contre* or high tenor, his voice described by the singer Duprez as having a 'white' tone and reaching very high in a mixed register.[10] Halévy described his style as clean and elegant, seducing the audience by the gracefulness of his singing.[11]

Following a triumphant début at the age of nineteen at the Paris Opéra in Gluck's *Iphigénie en Tauride*, he acquired a reputation over the next two years as the ideal interpreter of that composer's music, but the advent of Rossini was to mark a new stage in his career. On the Italian's advice he set about to develop greater vocal flexibility which even Garcia's training apparently had not achieved, and in 1826, following a period of study, he sang in the première of Rossini's *Le siège de Corinthe* to great acclaim.

It was not only Nourrit's operatic performances which made his name. He was also the first French singer to acquire a lifelong passion for Schubert lieder which he sang in the salons and, indeed, wherever he could. It was through Nourrit's performances and the enormous interest they stimulated that France became the first non-German-speaking country to cultivate the songs of Schubert, and in so doing unconsciously influence the course of song-writing there (see Chapter Six). In 1827 Nourrit was appointed to the Paris Conservatoire to teach singing. This appointment and the enormous prestige gained from his operatic performances promised a long and successful career.

In 1837 the Paris Opéra decided (with Nourrit's initial willingness) to appoint Gilbert Duprez as joint leading tenor. The quality of Duprez's voice was quite different from that of Nourrit's whose higher notes, for example, went into falsetto, while in Duprez's, rich quality was spread throughout his range, taking the high C in full voice, which when first heard caused a sensation. For Nourrit, Duprez was now not a colleague but a rival, and he resigned his post at the Opéra that year. The thought of retiring from the stage had, in fact, occurred to him the year before, for it was during that period in his life when, above all, he loved singing lieder, and he had broached the matter of devoting himself to it in a letter dated 26 October 1836 to his close friend the German composer and pianist Ferdinand Hiller who had lived in Paris for some years.[12] Probably a passing fancy at the time, it became a reality the following year, spurred on by Duprez's success and his own self-doubts.

In the event, it was to developing his technique and not to lieder that Nourrit spent the remaining years of his short life. Certainly his stylish performances of Schubert lieder (albeit always in French translations) reflected his serious nature – his contemporaries regarded him as unusually intelligent for an opera singer at that time – but his relentless self-criticism and hypersensitivity also led to a constant search for improvement. His retirement offered a unique chance.

After touring some provincial French cities and Brussels, Nourrit embarked upon a trip to Italy to study with Donizetti, reaching Naples in March 1838 where he began lessons with the celebrated Italian. Garcia's widow had already pointed out in Paris what she felt were weaknesses in his production, caused she said by problems when singing in French. In a letter to his wife from Naples after his first lessons with Donizetti Nourrit expressed the belief that he was partly overcoming the problem.[13]

Nevertheless, disillusionment about Italy, its music and its singers soon set in. It must have been particularly galling to Nourrit when, having gone to the trouble of visiting Italy, he was told by the castrato Velluti that singing was in decline in Italy and that nowadays the French sing better than the Italians – although this was probably just a pretty compliment to the visitor.[14] Moreover, after his discovery of Schubert's songs he found he was more and more drawn to German music.[15]

The example of Duprez's voice encouraged him to develop a richer and darker tone, but the result was to make it rough, and despite some success in singing opera in Italy he became more and more depressed. To a shocked and disbelieving Paris came the news that on the evening of 8 March 1839 he had flung himself to death from the top floor of his hotel in Naples. A subscription concert in Paris raised money to bring his body back for a funeral service at St Roch where the church was packed with leading artists and admirers of the celebrated singer. Extracts from Cherubini's Requiem were performed by Société des concerts and the cortege made a solemn progress through the hushed crowd in the street. The government announced that it would pay an annual indemnity of 1888 francs to Nourrit's seven children until the majority of the last child was reached.[16]

During his life the modest and retiring Nourrit assumed the status of a national hero. At his farewell recital at the Opéra the King and Queen, for example, had presented him with an inscribed gold ring, and his career at that time was crowned with tributes from all sides. Following his death, like the ill-fated Maria Malibran, Nourrit passed into nineteenth-century French musical legend.

Gilbert-Louis Duprez

Gilbert Duprez (1806–1896) was a product of Choron's school. While there as a child he studied, besides solfège and singing, French and Italian and the elements of Latin. This was followed by lessons in counterpoint, harmony and composition, his teachers there including an old Italian composer, Porta and Fétis. Choron seems to have divined the gifts of his young pupil, for according to one of Duprez's fellow students the master once said to the boy, who still possessed only his child's voice, that he would become the finest singer of his time.[17] After a brief visit to Italy he returned to Paris where in 1825 he made a début at the Théâtre-Italien with scant success. More serious study in Italy seemed necessary and he returned there to work under a teacher who helped turn his light voice into a darker and more powerful one. This was the voice that Paris heard when he made his début at the Paris Opéra in *Guillaume Tell* in 1837, his performance marking the beginning of his career and the end of Nourrit's. A review describes the new voice.

> A voice that is perfectly pure, even, sonorous, with excellent pronunciation, extraordinary declamation. Such are the qualities that strike one first of all in the new artist. Not one word lost, not one sentence neglected, not one phrase without charm and vigour. In his mouth the recitative acquires an importance that it had never had. It is no longer simply a transition from one piece to another; it is something that matches each piece both in terms of interest and meaning.[18]

Unfortunately for Duprez his voice was unable to withstand the demands he made upon it, and it deteriorated after only a few years. Thereafter, he devoted himself largely to teaching and composition. He had been appointed to the Paris Conservatoire in 1842, but in 1853 decided to open his own school of singing at his home in the rue Turgot. It became a celebrated studio, and the following year his influential book *L'Art du chant* appeared.

As a child Duprez had showed a passion for composition, something that never left him. His output was large but has not lasted. As he invariably sang his own songs in the salons rather than those by his contemporaries, none of the songs discussed in later chapters were championed by him. If his compositions have not survived, there can be little doubt, however, about his influence over nineteenth-century French singing.

François Wartel

Pierre-François Wartel (1806–1882) was Nourrit's most distinguished student. He studied with Nourrit during 1830/31 and gained from him not only a seriousness of purpose and constant desire for improvement, but also a love of the songs of Schubert. Wartel was admitted as a student at the Paris Conservatoire in 1825 but two months later changed to Choron's school. In 1828 he returned to the Conservatoire winning first prize in singing the following year. Nourrit had been appointed to the Conservatoire as a singing teacher the year before, and it was to him that Wartel turned for the last two years of his student days. He was appointed to the Paris Opéra, and in August 1836 master and former pupil appeared together in the first performance of Meyerbeer's *Les Huguenots*, the younger man making a very favourable impression upon the critics, one of whom spoke warmly of Wartel's progress, especially in the high notes of his tenor voice, these becoming more supple day by day, the delivery achieving greater ease and evenness.[19]

Yet some four years later Wartel resigned from the Opéra to devote himself to singing in the salons and concert rooms, particularly the songs of Schubert and those from the new generation of composers in France. He and his wife, a very accomplished pianist, made tours of Germany, Austria, Poland and Russia. At the height of his success he went to Italy as a student, working with the celebrated tenor Pasini who so reconstructed Wartel's voice by working on the lower notes that Wartel returned to Paris with a beautiful baritone voice. 'A high baritone, admittedly, but a voice that could still sing the role of William Tell without changing a note of Rossini's score', wrote one reviewer.[20]

The young generation of French songwriters had much to be grateful for to Wartel. It was he, for example, who in 1841 sang for the first time 'L'absence' and 'Villanelle' from Berlioz's then unpublished *Les nuits d'été*,[21] three years later taking these songs and 'Le spectre de la rose' on tour to Germany. On these tours he also sang works by Monpou, Morel and Proche, and thus helped disseminate abroad, as well as at home, this new romance style.

Jean-Antoine-Juste Géraldy (Géraldi)

Jean-Antoine-Juste Géraldy (1806–1869) was one of the few fine singers whose career was very largely made in the salons. He had been trained as a civil engineer and was working in Beauvais when the 1830 Revolution broke out in Paris. Going there on foot he was caught up in the fighting, and when peace was established three days later he decided to relinquish his previous career and follow his real passion – singing. Surprisingly, his father supported the idea, encouraging him to study with Garcia, to whom he paid 6000 francs to undertake his son's training, but it was less than two years that he had with him, for Garcia died in 1832 and his son Manuel took over. Géraldy also studied harmony at the Paris Conservatoire, and eventually continued his singing without a teacher.

It was in a private salon that Géraldy was heard for the first time, singing the Count's aria from *Le Nozze di Figaro*, but his first public appearance was on 16 March 1833 when he was a supporting artist in a concert given by his teacher Manuel Garcia (i.e. the son) and Franz Liszt. He was described as having a baritone voice, sweet and flexible in the middle register but lacking bite (*de mordant*) in the lower notes.[22] Nevertheless, his intelligent and stylish singing so impressed Meyerbeer that he entrusted the first performance of his dramatic song *Le moine* to the young man. From that time onwards, Géraldy's name was scarcely absent from reviews of public and private concerts.

Only once did he attempt to break into the world of opera – and that in Italy – but serious health problems thwarted this, and he wisely returned to Paris where he continued his successful career in the salons. During a concert tour to Brussels with the violinist Bériot, Fétis, now the Director of the Conservatoire there, invited him to become a visiting teacher for three-monthly, then six-monthly periods, the rest of the time spent in Paris singing and teaching. His students included Jenny Colon and Catinker Heinefetter. He also composed a number of songs which became popular, an unpublished opera and a set of thirty melodic studies for all voices.

His style of singing was described on a number of occasions. That of Fétis must suffice.

> despite a few weaknesses which sometimes marred his execution, he was a serious artist and a singer of the first order. He was distinguished through the training of his marvellous voice, excellent pronunciation – clean and clear – intelligent singing which, in its variety of tone, is difficult to find elsewhere to the same degree. Serious and masterly in the interpretation of great dramatic works, he excelled at the same time in comic ones.[23]

* * *

Space forbids more than a mention of a few of the many other singers who appeared in the salons and who included French songs in their performances. One of the most notable was Gustave-Hippolyte Roger who toured with Jenny Lind to England in 1848, but whose operatic ambitions were largely thwarted both by a relatively small tenor voice and a hunting accident in which his arm was pierced by a bullet necessitating amputation. His salon appearances in which, on at least one occasion he also sang Schubert, however, were highly regarded and his translation of the text of Haydn's *Die Jahreszeiten* was used for many years in France. A singer whose beautiful contralto voice was said to have created a sensation in the salons[24] was Lalo's future wife, Julie Bernier de Maligny who was to become the finest interpreter of his songs. Others who made their reputations in the salon rather than on the stage were composer/singers like Amadée de Beauplan, Loïsa Puget, Auguste Panseron, Romagnesi, Gustave Nadaud, the last-named appearing so often during the 1850s and 1860s that it seems that no salon concert was complete without him performing his latest chansons.

Opera singers whose names appear frequently in the salons included Mmes Battu, Bertrand, Frezzolini, Gaveaux-Sabatier, Iweins-Hennin, Stockhausen, Vandenheuvel (daughter of Duprez), Weckerlin-Damoreau (daughter of the celebrated Laure Cinti-Damoreau and married to the composer Wékerlin), and the male singers, brothers Lionnet and Guidon, Delle-Sedie, Gardoni, Lefort, Capoul, Zucchini, Ponchard, and, especially from the 1860s onwards, the celebrated French opera singer Jean-Baptiste Faure,[25] to whom many of the songs in the later repertoire were dedicated. And, of course, the brightest of all stars like Pauline Viardot, Adelina Patti and Marie Carvalho also made their welcome appearances in the salons.

* * *

Songwriting in France blossomed at the same time as French singing developed along the lines described in this chapter. It becomes clear from so many sources that the new style of singing was admired as much for its beauty of tone, derived from the Italian school, as for its clarity of diction, derived from French tradition. It was a perfect balance of the two, neither one at the expense of the other. Nothing could have been more advantageous to the development of an intimate art which at its best combines fine poetry with fine music. It is to that development that we now turn.

Notes

1. Isabelle Laspeyres, 'Les salons où l'on chante à la fin du Second Empire', *Revue internationale de musique française*, xvii, June, 1985.
2. For example, Merlin, Fétis, Scudo, to name a few. Fétis, for example writes 'Jusqu'à Garat *chanter* avait été synonyme de crier; il nous reste quelque chose de cela. Quant à nos agréments du chant ils étaient ce qu'on peut entendre de plus bizarre: les *ports de voix*, les *coulés*, les *flattés*, les *martellements* de Dumesnil, de Maupin, de Rochois, de Chassé, feraient aujourd'hui pousser de rire l'auditoire le plus sérieux.' *RM*, August, 1827, 73.
3. Raparlier, *Principes de musique, les agréments du chant et un essai sur la prononciation, l'articulation et la prosodie de la langue française* (Lille, 1772).
4. Antoine Bailleux, *Méthode pour apprendre facilement la musique vocale et instrumentale où tous les Principes sont développés avec beaucoup de clarté, et cent leçons dans le goût nouveaux ...* (Paris, 1770).
5. 'Les conditions du chant français diffèrent à certains égards de celles du chant italien. Une voix pure et sonore, une prononciation nette et régulière et de l'expression dramatique, est à peu près tout ce qu'on a désiré en France dans un chanteur pendant longtemps. Un préjugé peu raisonnable avait fait considérer les traits et les ornements comme peu convenable à notre langue. Peu à peu l'opéra comique s'est affranchi des entraves qu'on lui opposaient sous ce rapport, mais l'opéra résiste jusqu'ici; il vient de céder enfin l'empire de la mode, et il a bien

fait. … On sent combien le domaine du chanteur français s'agrandit par la fusion des formes italiennes avec les nôtres, et combien son art devient plus difficile. Nous avons eu un modèle de perfection de ces genres réunis: ce fut Garat.' *RM*, August 1827, 80.

6. Countess Merlin (Maria de las Mercedes de Jaruco), *Memoirs of Mme Malibran by the Countess Merlin* … (1840), vol 1, 41–2.

7. *RGM*, 3 April, 1836.

8. 'Et voilà, qu'à ce souvenir de Malibran, si triste, si douloureux, vient se mêler la douce certitude de la voir renaître. Oui, nous avons dans Pauline Garcia, sa sœur, ces mêmes facultés musicales, si brillantes, si riches, si originales: c'est la même organisation vocale, c'est ce mélange Shakespearien du tragique et du comique qui ne grimace point comme dans l'école romantique; c'est la cantatrice espagnole, française, italienne, excitant tour à tour le rire ou la mélancolie, *passant du grave au doux, du plaisant au sévère*, noble et touchante dans les sons si doux, dans les reproches qu'Euridice adresse à son époux; vive et folle comme une Andalouse dans la jolie *séguidille* qu'elle a chantée d'une façon si piquante; mélancolique et tendre dans *l'Attente* et *la Poste*, ces lieder si jolis de Schubert, dont les paroles ont été si heureusement traduites par M E. Deschamps; originale et comique dans la tyrolienne d'Amadée de Beauplan, Pauline Garcia est appelée par la nature de son talent varié à recueillir tout l'héritage de grande artiste que semblait avoir laissé pour jamais vacant son illustre sœur.' *RM*, 7 February, 1839.

9. … le journaliste [i.e. Rellstab] doit franchement avouer que, depuis les temps où retentissaient les voix miraculeuses des Schechner et des Catalani, il n'a jamais été remue par le son d'une voix féminine, aussi profondément que par celui de cette jeune cantatrice âgée de 18 ans. Ce n'est pas que ce son soit beau, absolument parlant; au contraire, l'organe a des parties défectueuses; mais on y sent une âme, un esprit, ou, si l'on veut, ce qu'on pourrait appeler la physionomie de la voix, et c'est cette expression individuelle qui émeut à ce point le soussigné. D'ailleurs cette voix est déjà fort remarquable à raison de son étendue des plus rares, car elle embrasse au moins deux grandes octaves et demie. Nous nous rappelons en effet avec certitude avoir entendu au grave *fa* dièse, et un *ut* à l'aigu. Il nous semble même que dans son premier air la cantatrice a vigoureusement attaqué des sons plus graves encore; mais comme nous n'avons pas pensé en ce moment à traduire ces sons en notes connues, nous ne pouvons rien assurer à cet égard, et pourtant cette voix n'a point au grave le caractère du contralto; nous la désignerions plutôt comme un mélange de soprano et de ténor, de sorte que la partie basse a de l'affinité avec le violoncelle, et la partie élevée avec le violon.' *RGM*, 6 June, 1838

10. Duprez, Gilbert-Louis, *Souvenirs d'un chanteur* (1880), 137.

11. F. Halévy, *Derniers portraits et souvenirs* (1863), 150.

12. Reproduced in Louis-Marie Quicherat, *Adolphe Nourrit, sa vie, son talent, son caractère, sa correspondence* (1867), 3 vols, Paris, 26.

13. 'C'est vraiment une leçon, et tout ce qu'il y a de plus leçon que je prends avec Donizetti. Malgré les progrès qu'il voit que je fais déjà, et ceux qui vont rapidement les suivre, il m'a repris hier presque à chaque mot, presque à chaque note, et t'assure que chacune de ses observations portait juste. Grâce à lui, je serai bientôt débarrassé d'un défaut qu'on m'a souvent reproché, et qu'entretenait chez moi la langue française: c'est de chanter parfois du nez. Notre langue est remplie de syllabes nasales; et plutôt que de sacrifier le mot, il m'est toujours arrivé de

sacrifier la qualité de la voix. En italien c'est tout autre chose; c'est même tout à fait le contraire: la voix est d'autant meilleure qu'on prononce mieux l'italien; et quand il m'arrive de donner un mauvais son, c'est que je le donne avec l'accent français; car dès que j'arrive à bien reproduire l'accent italien, ma voix est tout autre. Seulement cela me donne un peu de mal, et Madame Garcia avait raison quand elle parlait de trois ou quatre mois pour me corriger de ces défauts, auxquels m'a habitué notre harmonieuse langue ... le chant italien, qui en définitive est le premier chant du monde, vaut bien qu'on se donne un peu de mal pour l'apprendre, et la peine qui je prends aujourd'hui me sera comptée quand je posséderai à fond mon accent italien et celle façon si facile, si coulante d'émettre la voix sur des syllabes toutes propices à l'effet musical et sonore.' Quicherat, vol. 3, 168–9.

14. Quicherat, vol. 3, 112.
15. Letter to Hiller dated 6 July, 1838, reproduced in Quicherat, vol 3, 273.
16. *RGM*, 7 November, 1839.
17. Paul Scudo, *Critique et littérature musicales* (n.d. r. 1986), 378.
18. 'Une voix parfaitement pure, égale, sonore; une prononciation excellente, une déclamation extraordinaire, telles sont les qualités qui frappent tout d'abord dans l'artiste nouveau, Pas un mot perdu, pas une phrase négligée, pas une période sans charme ou sans vigueur. Dans sa bouche, le récitatif acquiert une importance qu'il n'avait jamais eue; ce n'est pas seulement l'intervalle d'un morceau à un autre, c'est quelque chose qui ne le cède en rien aux morceaux pour l'intérêt comme pour le sens.' *RGM*, 25 April, 1837.
19. 'Nous citerons également l'effet que produit dans *les Huguenots* la voix de Wartel. Ce jeune chanteur fait de véritables progrès, on voit qu'il travaille beaucoup les cordes hautes de sa voix, car elles s'assouplissent de jour en jour, et sa vocalisation en générale devient plus facile et plus égale.' *RGM*, 21 August, 1836.
20. 'Sans doute, Wartel, en sa qualité d'ex-ténor, est plutôt un baryton haut, mais il chante néanmoins le rôle de Guillaume Tell sans changer une note au texte de Rossini.' *MM*, 12 June, 1845.
21. Reviewed in *MM*, no. 9, 1841.
22. *RGM*, 16 March, 1833.
23. 'Géraldy était, on peut dire, en dépit de quelques inégalités de style qui parfois déparaient son exécution, un artiste d'école et un chanteur de premier ordre. Il se distinguait par une pose de voix merveilleuse, une excellente prononciation, une articulation nette et franche, une diction pleine d'intelligence, enfin, par une variété d'accent difficile à rencontrer à un pareil degré. Sévère et magistral dans l'interprétation des grandes œuvres du style dramatique, il excellait en même temps dans le genre bouffe.' F.-J. Fétis, *Biographie universelle des musiciens* (2nd ed. 1860–65, with supplement, ed. A. Pougin 1878–80).
24. *M*, July 30, 1865.
25. Not to be confused with the composer Gabriel Fauré. Jean-Baptiste Faure was also a composer, his *Les rameaux* being a popular work for performance at Easter (see Appendix A).

CHAPTER FOUR

The All-pervasive Romance

'That child of our soil' was how one Frenchman described the romance.[1] It was to France what the lied was to Germany and what the canzonetta was to Italy, and its most prized feature was its charming simplicity. While its champions were fond of tracing the romance's lineage to the troubadours of medieval times, its musical style as transmitted to music lovers in the nineteenth century came no earlier than from the classical period in the middle of the previous century.

Yet it also had an affinity with much earlier French music: the 'air tendre' often known as the 'brunette'. Composed for voice with lute (or theorbo or harpsichord) accompaniment, they were popular during the late seventeenth and early eighteenth centuries and derived their name from their texts, typical of which was

> Le beau berger Tircis,
>
> Près de sa chère Annette,
>
> Sur les bords du Loire assis,
>
> Chantait dessus sa musette:
>
> Ah! petite Brunette
>
> Ah! tu me fais mourir!

(The handsome shepherd Tircis, sitting next to his beloved Annette on the banks of the Loire, sang to the sound of his musette: Ah! little Brunette, How you are making me die!)

The seeming artlessness of such texts was, in reality, the juxtaposition of one stereotyped poetic image and phrase with another. So, too, was the style of romance poetry – at least in the first two decades of the century – dictated by polite poetic convention in both subject matter and language. Certainly, the Napoleonic Wars stirred some to write of heroism and battle, but the most characteristic texts dealt with the beauty of the beloved, or the pain of separation or unrequited love, and in a style that could offend neither the most prudish matron nor any self-respecting salon hostess. We are told that when Monpou's romance *L'Andalouse* (to a text by Théophile Gautier) was first sung in the salons in the early 1830s its text so scandalized some hostesses that its words were often discreetly modified or verses omitted.[2] One wonders if the demure daughter would have dared to catch her mother's disapproving eye if she had sung the sixth stanza of this song:

> Qu'elle est superbe en son désordre,
>
> Quand elle tombe, les seins nus,
>
> Qu'on la voit, béante, se tordre
>
> Dans un baiser de rage, et mordre
>
> En criant des mots inconnus!

(How superb she is in her disarray, when she falls, her breasts uncovered, how one sees her agape, twisting in a kiss of rage, and biting, crying out with unknown words.)

Even though this became one of the most famous romances of the day, neither its text nor its setting by Monpou is characteristic of the form, especially before 1830, that is, before the full force of nineteenth-century French romanticism was felt. Rather, the conventional romance sang of devoted, unstained love, spurned, betrayed or requited.

> Je le sais: vous m'avez trahi,
>
> Une autre a su mieux vous charmer;
>
> Pourtant quand votre cœur m'oublie,
>
> Moi, je veux toujours vous aimer.
>
> Oui, je conserverai sans cesse
>
> L'amour que je vous ai juré;
>
> Et si jamais on vous délaisse,
>
> Appelez-moi: je reviendrai.

(I know it: you have betrayed me; another woman's charms have been sweeter than mine; and yet, although your heart forgets me, mine would love you still. Yes, I shall never cease to nurture that love which I vowed to you; and if ever you are abandoned, summon me: I shall return.)

Romances were often classified according to their text and scenery. Those with their poetry evoking wild mountains were usually called tyroliennes. Rustic scenes were pastorales, water scenes were barcarolles. These poetic categories automatically set off stereotyped musical responses. Thus, barcarolles and pastorales inevitably flowed in compound metres, tyroliennes in triple time, redolent of yodelling tunes. French obsession at that time with the Middle East – its exotic culture of sultans, slaves, white captives, harems, caravans and the mysteries of the desert – found outlet in romance texts, these invariably called orientales. Unlike the other categories, orientales were free in their musical style, as were those romances which dealt with the general subject of love.

Clearly, there is a world of difference between texts of the nineteenth-century romance and the seventeenth-century brunette. Décor and vocabulary aside, however, they also have something in common: a simple and undramatic subject calling for no highly-charged musical response. In their simplicity both the brunette and the romance were regarded in their day as quintessentially French. Paradoxically, their slender content made them seem all the more difficult to compose and perform since such an art demanded, above all, what was seen as taste and sensitivity. The eighteenth-century composer Montéclair had believed that by learning how to sing brunettes one was able to cultivate both those qualities which would then stand a singer in good stead when he or she moved on to more complex music.[3] But whereas in the second and later verses of a brunette the singer was expected either to improvise highly embellished versions of the melody or to sing those which were often included in the publication, the romance called for only the lightest vocal embellishment – if any at all – to point up the expression. 'Good taste' in singing romances meant not drawing attention to one's vocal skills, or, as one writer put it, 'sacrificing' a large part of them.[4]

A good idea of the style of the romance can, in fact, be gained by advice given to the novice performer by Général Thiébault in 1813 and Romagnesi in 1846. (Despite being called Henri Romagnesi by Fétis in his *Biographie universelle*, his true name was Antoine-Joseph-Michel, although he was usually referred to by his surname alone.) That their descriptions of the form and their advice to singers still coincided, despite a difference of over thirty years, is in itself a sign of how the romance had become a national musical symbol, almost sacrosanct in style and form – at least, as far as the 'pure-blood' romance (the *'romance pur sang'* as it was sometimes called) was concerned, rather than its more expanded form that gradually became known as mélodie.

In the light of what was said about nineteenth-century singing in the previous chapter, it is not surprising that both Thiébault and Romagnesi stressed the need for clear diction and a thorough understanding of the sentiment of the text and the nuances of its poetry in this most French of all forms. Correct declamation should serve as much for its composition as its execution, declared Thiébault. While Thiébault also emphasized the need for well-connected, cantabile singing, Romagnesi had the advantage over him in making his professional career at a time when the older French style of singing was being transformed along the lines already described in Chapter Three. So it is that he also gives advice on breathing and posture and – up to a point – vocal production, stressing the need to join the notes evenly and cleanly rather than sliding from one to the other. Most useful of all, he takes a number of romances and in some detail describes how they should be sung. As far as good taste is concerned the singer of romances, he said, must seek only simple and natural means of expression, avoiding any exaggeration, and directing his voice only to expressing the delicate and nuanced sentiments of the song.[5]

The romance *'pur sang'* demanded no great range of notes from its interpreters – about a compass of a twelfth was the most, and usually it was much narrower than that. No 'passage-work' or grand melismas as in an aria, and nothing that required too much intensity of tone. The melody flowed in balanced phrases of two- or four-bar lengths and the music explored no keys beyond those closely related to the main one. So, too, was the accompaniment simple and stereotyped. The composers Auguste Panseron and Edouard Brugière introduced some obbligato instruments into their romances, meeting with some approval, but generally the accompaniment was for pianoforte alone. The great majority of romances were for solo voice, but there was also much call for romances composed for two equal voices, in which case they were invariably called nocturnes. Whether romance or nocturne, they were essentially a verse-repeating form, in most publications the first verse being printed out in full, with the voice part only provided for the remaining ones. These sometimes ran to as many as ten verses, but Thiébault recommended that only four should ever be sung. How was it possible to achieve anything of lasting value in a genre so confined?

This question would probably not have been asked. Even Thiébault, who laid down many strictures concerning its style and form, believed that the romance was a singer's rather than a composer's art. 'It is only after many efforts that one will convince oneself that singing a romance well is a difficult task in music, because perfection of method must stand in inverse ratio to the weakness of the genre.'[6] Depending so much upon beauty of performance romances were by nature ephemeral; fashionable for a season and then put aside like last year's hats. Perhaps too fashionable for the comfort of critics who had to endure the same songs sung so many times, a point made by one critic who used an extra exclamation mark each time he heard Mme Sabatier sing Pauline Thys's *La follette*; which by the end of the week had collected five of them.[7] (Perhaps she took the hint, for we hear no more of Mme Sabatier singing that romance.) The romance at this time was thus an annual bloom, which withered at the end of the season to be replaced by another of the species. No wonder that Fétis claimed that success for the composers of romances depended largely upon a prolific output. It was also to advantage, he added, if the composer were also a singer, for 'as each sings his own, the best would remain unknown if not presented by the composer'.[8]

The annual wave of newly composed romances flooding into the salons season by season, willingly performed by the composer/singer was, of course, a mixed blessing, especially for the hard-pressed critic – if not for the captive audience, as this wry comment makes clear:

> Then come the salon composers, that elegant, perfumed category, which is received everywhere with eagerness; for the composers of this genre are nearly all performers, and have no need of assistance to get their work appreciated. Should one of them appear at a salon, there is general rejoicing, everyone trying to outdo each other in welcoming him, celebrating him, begging him to present the delightful piece that he has just composed, for the last piece is always delightful. The composer smiles in what he considers to be a most modest way, does not require too much bidding – that's in poor taste – and delights, transports an audience always disposed to finding excellent music that is given to them over and above the punch, the brioche and the ice cream. A singer of romances takes over from the instrumentalist, and there are further transports of admiration. The same piece, transferred to the theatre, better executed perhaps by Mlle Jenny Colon or Déjazet, will pass unnoticed; but in the salon of Monsieur such and such, it is accepted that one always makes excellent music, and everything must be excellent. Sometimes, however, the enthusiasm is not feigned, if luck has it that you come across M Panseron or M A. de Beauplan, or perhaps one or two more celebrities of that kind; you will spend a very pleasant evening if M Plantade regales you with his delightful clowning.[9]

Panseron, Beauplan, Sophie Gail, Loïsa Puget, Romagnesi, Pauline Thys, Vimeux were amongst the composers regarded by nineteenth-century commentators as romance composers *par excellence*, their best works seen as the finest flowers of all. Yet few of their romances might appeal to modern tastes. If it is true that the singer was more important than the song it is highly unlikely that many would reach out from their faded pages when we turn over the thousands of such pieces accumulated in the first half of the century. Nevertheless, there is a sizeable number that deserve rescuing from oblivion. Such a romance is Romagnesi's *Belle rose, charmante fleur*, first published in 1806 and republished in a slightly revised version in the composer's complete romances, that came out in three volumes in 1838 (see Example 4.1). The words are by Mme Marie-Louise-Rose Levesque, also known as Pétigny de Saint-Romain, who published her *Idylles ou Contes champêtres* in 1786.

Catching something of the seventeenth-century style and imagery of the brunette these words inspired one of Romagnesi's loveliest melodies. We should see it, however, as nothing more than what it presumes to be: an elegant and gracefully moulded melody, moving within the exacting confines of the form – a perfect figurine in music.

Example 4.1   *Belle rose, charmante fleur* (Romagnesi)

(Lovely rose, charming flower, object of Flora's tender cares, go to the shepherdess whom I adore and carry my heart's vows; proud of your destiny, like me, live under her rule; perfume the air she breathes and do not leave her lovely breast.)

Romagnesi also deserves our attention for his useful description of the various romance-types in his *L'art de chanter les romances*. (See Appendix C for extracts from this work.) Although known in his day primarily as a composer his was not the ideal background for that career, for he came to it late. His leanings were first towards mathematics, which suggested a commercial career, while time in the army suggested a military one. Music finally exerted its appeal, and at the age of twenty-five he began studying with various teachers in Paris, discovering his natural talents as a singer and composer of romances. Both these talents led to a highly successful career in the salons. He also established himself as a singing teacher in Paris, and as well as his *L'art de chanter les romances* he also published *Psychologie du chant*, both of which appeared in 1846. In the later years of his career he widened his activities to include music publishing.

Romagnesi classified the romance into five different kinds: the sentimental, the heroic, the reflective and sombre, the dramatic and the light-hearted, which he called chansonnettes. Of these only the first two truly represented the traditional, 'pure-blood' romance. The dramatic kind were more in the nature of 'apprentice-pieces' for opera composers. In the light of the development of French song during the nineteenth century, the most interesting of the categories was the 'reflective and sombre' type which, Romagnesi said, recalled the style of German lieder, its accompaniment and its harmony being much stronger and highly-wrought than in the sentimental romance.[10] The voices best suited to this more powerful category, he declared, were contraltos, baritones and basses, although he felt they had a certain monotony which could be relieved by introducing a few ornaments in performance.

Songs composed for lower voices seemed, indeed, to be in short supply in France up until the 1840s. Romances were almost invariably composed for sopranos or tenors, although because of their limited range many could have been sung by mezzo-sopranos and baritones. Certainly, the convention of publishing the same song in different keys for different voice types became common only after 1840 when the romance was developing into the more sophisticated mélodie. When reviewing some songs composed for bass voice by Auguste Morel in 1841 the music critic of *Le Monde musical* welcomed what he saw as an important trend towards writing for lower voices.

> The French school can quite justifiably be severely reprimanded for the indifference that it has shown for so long towards deep voices. Indeed, while our composers were expending all the wealth of their imagination and of their genius on high voices, on the sopranos and tenors to whom the privilege of singing exclusively belonged, deep voices, used solely in the obscure labours of bass parts or of inner parts, were reduced, as it were, to a state of musical serfdom. When one had bass baritones singing solo – and this was done as rarely as possible and only when it was absolutely necessary – one only wrote for

them, virtually without exception, a sort of monotonous recitative whose heavy rhythm and slow, regular, diatonic pace were entirely devoid of any melodic feeling. As for contraltos, less than twenty years ago even the very name of this type of voice was unknown in France, and in spite of nature all women who dedicated themselves to the art of singing had to be or become sopranos.

Thanks to the salutary influence of the Italian school, whose superiority in all that has to do with the vocal genre is incontestable and uncontested, the French school has for some time fortunately been modified through this connection, and people are beginning to understand now that bass baritones and contraltos are capable of singing as well as sopranos and tenors. Our composers have set about writing for deep voices, and the resounding success enjoyed by composers of any merit who write for bass or contralto has shown how wrong it was to neglect them for so long.[11]

Two composers of romances became very well known from the 1830s onward: Pauline Duchambge and Albert Grisar.

Pauline Duchambge (1778–1858), born Antoinette-Pauline de Montet, was the daughter of a wealthy family in Martinique. Because of political upheavals there she lost what fortune she may have had when her parents died – she was then twenty years old – and she came to France having married an army officer Baron Duchambge d'Elbhecq whom she later divorced. She studied singing and piano (the latter with Dussek) and enjoyed a wide circle of musical friends, including Cherubini and Auber. Her warm and witty personality, as well as her beauty, gave her entrée into the salons, and when in 1814 she lost a modest pension she began composing romances. For this she had a decided gift and wrote some 400 pieces in this genre that enjoyed enormous popularity and gained for her much prestige as a composer of drawing-room romances, some of which still exert considerable charm. Such a romance is her waltz-like *Le bouquet du bal* which, although undated, probably appeared in the 1830s and was later re-arranged by her for flute and string quartet (see Example 4.2). The text for this charming melody was written by the well-known opera-librettist Eugène Scribe.

As the romance entered a new phase of development, to be described in the next chapter, so too did the sentimental romances of this most popular salon composer decline in popularity, and at her death those whom she had once charmed were reproached for allowing her to die impoverished. 'Remember the last song that your young daughter sang, the chaste romance which your eldest daughter sings today; it is almost sure to be a romance or chanson coming from the abundant and fluent genius of this elegant and delicate muse.'[12]

Amongst the poets whose verses she set were Emile Barateau, Jules de Rességuier, Casimir Delavigne, Pierre Jean de Béranger – to name just the better-known ones – and above all, Marceline Desbordes-Valmore, her exact contemporary with whom she enjoyed a close friendship.

Example 4.2   *Le bouquet du bal* (Duchambge)

(You are departing, lovely and adorned, for the ball to which I will not be going. When surrounded by vows and tributes, think of me, alas! Let this bouquet remind you of a faithful and absent lover. And though I am not there, there at least will be my bouquet.)

Marceline-Félicité-Joséphine Desbordes (1789–1859) was born in Douai under an unlucky star. Her father's trade – painting royal coats-of-arms – obviously had no future under the Revolution and the mixed marriage of her parents, Catholic and Protestant, led to separation. Mother and daughter left to live in Guadeloupe where they had relatives, but their arrival coincided with a revolution there causing the financial ruin of those they had planned to join. Worse was to come, for her mother caught yellow fever and died. Totally penniless, Marceline returned to France where she became an actress/singer, eventually marrying an untalented actor named Valmore whom she needed to support with her meagre income, travelling with him on his engagements to various provincial theatres such as at Rouen, Bordeaux and Lyon. It is not surprising that her poetry, which began appearing from the early 1830s, was sorrowful and elegiac and that she became known as 'the poet of tears'. Marceline Desbordes-Valmore and Pauline Duchambge were drawn together through their music, poetry, deep respect and love for each other and through the misery of their last years, made more pitiful by remembrance of the prestige they had once both enjoyed. They died in old age within a year of each other, and while little interest has ever been aroused in the works of the composer, those of the poet have attracted the attention of a number of modern scholars. Indeed, shortly after her death Verlaine and Baudelaire began to champion her poetry. The personal tragedies of both Pauline Duchambge and Marceline Desbordes-Valmore were partly the result of changing tastes in poetry and music through the impact of the full blast of romanticism. Theirs looked back to the taste of the First Empire and the early inroads of the romantic style.

Like that of Duchambge's *Le bouquet du bal*, the scene of the ball was also the background to the most celebrated romance of the early 1830s which had caught public imagination as much by its storybook-like first performance as by the flaunted sentimentality of its text. It was *La folle* (The Demented One) by Albert Grisar (see Example 4.3).

Albert Grisar (1808–1879) was born in Belgium, the son of a businessman who expected the young man to take up a commercial career, and to this end Grisar was sent to a firm in Liverpool in England in 1830. This was the year that revolution broke out not only in France, but also in Belgium which fought for independence from Holland. Learning of the outbreak, Grisar left England in secret, making his way first to Paris and then to Belgium where he joined the volunteers. After the war he had some composition lessons with Reicha in Paris and decided to make music his career, apparently with the support of his father. While at the family home at Antwerp in 1832 to celebrate his parents' 25th wedding anniversary, he was asked if he had any compositions that might be performed at the gathering, but he had brought nothing with him from Paris. Remembering that he had composed a song three years earlier, and which he had left at Antwerp with a neighbour, the copy was found and sung to the admiring family. It so happened that Adolphe Nourrit was in Brussels at that time, and Grisar decided to ask the singer's opinion of his youthful work.

Nourrit examined the manuscript and invited Grisar to come to the theatre that evening as his guest. To the astonishment of the young man Nourrit sang *La folle* during an entr'acte and we are told that the audience had 'never wept tears so sad, nor suffered such anguish'[13] as at that performance, which, of course, made Grisar's fame overnight. It was not only sung in all the salons; Maria Malibran took it into her repertoire and Chopin improvised upon it at a royal concert at St Cloud before the entire court.[14] Grisar went on to write mainly for the stage – 31 works in all, the most successful being *L'eau merveilleuse* (1839) and *Les porcherons* (1850).

Today it is hard to believe that such mawkishness could have been taken so seriously, but we shall never understand the popularity of the early romance without taking into account the sentimental tastes of the middle-class society that made up a large part of nineteenth-century Parisian audiences. While no great claims are being made here in its favour, it is easy to take a patronizing attitude to this repertoire as though the twentieth century were the guardian of good taste. Perhaps nowadays, however, we tend to draw a line between commercial and fine music, whereas the worst excesses of the (commercially-driven) sentimental romance were often confused with real art. The proliferation of salons at all levels of the social scale gave impetus to what became a veritable industry of uninspired romance composition by amateurs and musicians of no true creative talent, reflective of a society in which money and artistic discrimination did not often go hand in hand.

That the romance was fast becoming a commercial 'industry' was noted in 1845 by the writer J. A. Delaire, who described the romance after 1830 as a 'commodity' eagerly produced by publishers for a ready market, but who were unwilling to undertake publication of more substantial works like quartets and major pieces.[15] He estimated that, on average, 500 new romances were being published each year[16] and, with 250 000 copies sold in total at 2 francs a copy, the gross profit to the publisher was at least 500 000 francs. Payment to composers was usually 500 francs for a single romance, and up to 6000 francs for a collection of six by a fashionable composer, so that on a print run of 500, again estimated as average by Delaire, a publisher could expect at least a 50 per cent gross return on each title.[17]

As late as the 1860s the editor of *La Semaine musicale* complained of the mountain of second-rate romances which were continuing to pile up on his desk for review, and wondered why so many composers persisted in turning out such works when, according to his view, the public was becoming indifferent to them.[18] Clearly, the sentimental romance was all pervasive, and while its weakest examples are best forgotten, the spirit of the genre – with its emphasis upon tender lyricism, uncluttered harmonies and clarity of structure – informed much of the best vocal music of the French school. It flowered

Example 4.3 *La folle* (Grisar)

(Tra la la, now what is this melody? Ah! yes, I remember; the tuneful orchestra was beginning to play, with lively and joyous sounds ...)

through contact with French romantic poetry from Lamartine, Hugo, Gautier and many others, through the inspiration of Schubert's songs (which were to be championed in France more than in any other country outside the German-speaking ones for many years) and through the native genius of gifted composers from Berlioz to Fauré and Debussy. The simple romance was the starting point for them all.

Notes

1. 'La romance, ce petit poëme musical d'un tour si français, d'un caractère si élégant et si fin, cette enfant de notre sol.' Arthur Pougin, *Albert Grisar* (Paris, 1870), 37.
2. Théophile Gautier, *L'histoire du romantisme* (1874), 254.
3. Michel de Montéclair, Preface to *Brunètes anciens et modernes*, bk 1 (1703)
4. 'La manière de chanter les romances mérite une grande attention, tout le charme d'une romance étant nul si elle n'est parfaitement chantée. Son exécution n'admet pas en effet plus de médiocrité que son inspiration et sa composition; et il est si rare qu'elles soient bien chantées, que leur mérite n'est réellement apprécié que par peu de personnes. Pour être bien chantée, la romance demande non-seulement beaucoup de talent, mais même le sacrifice apparent d'une grande partie de ce même talent. Vouloir briller en chantant une romance est gâter sans profit la romance que l'on chante.' Général Thiébault, *Du chant, et particulièrement de la Romance* (1813), included in Gougelot, *La romance française* (Paris, 1943), 28–9.
5. 'Le bon goût l'avertit de ne chercher l'effet que par des moyens naturels et simples; d'éviter la manière et l'exagération; enfin, de conformer les inflexions de sa voix aux sentiments qu'il est appelé à exprimer.' Romagnesi, *L'Art de chanter les romances, les chansonnettes et les nocturnes* (1846), 16.
6. '... ce n'est même qu'à la suite de bien des efforts, que l'on se convaincra que bien chanter une romance est une tâche difficile en musique, parce que la perfection dans la manière, doit être en raison inverse de la foiblesse du genre.' Thiébault, 33–4.
7. *MM*, 9 March, 1843.
8. '... car c'est encore là une condition de la romance; les meilleures restent ignorées si elles ne sont produites par les auteurs eux-mêmes, car chacun chante les siennes.' Fétis, F.J., *RM*, 1829, 439.
9. 'Viennent ensuite les compositeurs de salon, classe élégante et musqué, accueillie partout avec empressement; car les compositeurs de ce genre sont presque tous exécutants, et n'ont besoin du secours d'aucun aide pour faire apprécier leurs ouvrages. Qu'un d'eux paraisse dans un salon, c'est une joie universelle, c'est à qui l'accueillera, le fêter, le suppliera de faire entendre le délicieux morceau qu'il vient de composer, car le dernier morceau est toujours délicieux. Le compositeur sourit d'en œil qu'il croit fort modeste, ne se fait pas trop prier, cela est de mauvais ton, et ravit, transporte un auditoire toujours disposé à trouver excellente musique qu'on lui donne par-dessus le marché entre le punch, la brioche, et les glaces. Un chanteur de romances succède à l'instrumentiste, et ce sont encore d'autres transports d'admiration. Le même morceau, transporté au théâtre, mieux exécuté peut-être par Mlle. Jenny Colon or Déjazet, passera inaperçu; mais chez monsieur tel ou tel il est reconnu que l'on fait toujours d'excellente musique, et tout doit être excellent. Quelquefois cependant l'enthousiasme n'est pas factice si

le bonheur veut vous rencontriez M Panseron ou M A. de Beauplan, ou peut-être encore une ou deux célébrités du genre; vous pourrez passer une soirée fort agréable, si M Plantade vous régale de ses délicieuses bouffonneries.' Adolphe Adam, *Souvenirs d'un musicien* (1857), 58–9.

10. 'Les mélodies rêveuses et graves, dont le style rappelle celui des *lieders* allemandes, veulent, ainsi qu'eux, un accompagnement d'une harmonie plus forte et plus travaillée que les autres espèces du genre romance ... Cette espèce de romances, à cause de la monotonie des voix graves et de celle des sujets sérieux, peut être ornée de notes d'agrément, mais dans le genre soutenu qui convient surtout à cette spécialité.' A. Romagnesi, *L'art de chanter les romances, les chansonnettes et les nocturnes* (1846), 17–18.

11. 'L'école français peut à bon droit être sévèrement blâmée de l'indifférence qu'elle a, pendant si long-temps, témoignée pour les voix graves, En effet, pendant que nos compositeurs dépensaient toutes les richesses de leur imagination et de leur génie pour les voix hautes, pour les sopranos et les ténors auxquels appartenait sans partage le privilège du chant, les voix graves, uniquement employées aux obscurs travaux des parties basses ou des accompagnements intermédiaires, étaient pour ainsi dire réduites à un état d'ilotisme musical. Quand on faisait chanter les basse-tailles seules, et on ne le faisait que le plus rarement possible, lorsqu'il y avait nécessité indispensable, on n'écrivait pour elles, à peu d'exceptions près, que des sortes de mélopées dont le rythme lourd et la marche diatonique lente et régulière étaient entièrement dépourvus de tout sentiment mélodique. Quant aux contraltos, il n'y a pas encore vingt ans que l'on ignorait en France jusqu'au nom même de ce genre de voix, et il fallait, en dépit de la nature, que toutes les femmes qui s'adonnaient à l'art du chant fussent on devinssent des sopranos. Grâce à la salutaire influence de l'école italienne, dont la supériorité pour tout ce qui tient au genre vocale est chose incontestable et incontestée, l'école française s'est depuis quelques temps heureusement modifiée sous ce rapport, et l'on commence à comprendre maintenant que les basses-tailles et les contraltos sont aptes à chanter aussi bien que les sopranos et les ténors. Nos compositeurs se sont mis à l'envie à écrire pour les voix graves, et le succès éclatant obtenu par les compositions pour basses-tailles ou contraltos qui offraient quelque mérite a montré combien on avait en tort de les négliger si long-temps.' *MM*, no. 20, 1841.

12. 'Rappelez-vous la dernière chanson que chantait votre jeune fille, la chaste romance que chante aujourd'hui votre fille aînée; il est presque sûr que romance et chanson sortent du génie abondant et facile de cette muse élégante.' *RGM*, 30 May, 1858.

13. *L'Avant-scène*, Marseille, 28 May 1837, 305–6.

14. *RGM*, 13 October, 1839.

15. 'Sous le rapport commercial, la romance est une denrée qui a du débit lorsqu'elle est lancée dans les salons sous le patronage d'un chanteur à la mode ...' J. A. Delaire, *Histoire de la romance considérée comme oeuvre littéraire et musicale*, Paris 1845, 21.

16. *M* (16 January 1853) estimated that in 1852 1367 pieces of vocal music were published in Paris. Thus, in the middle of the century romances would account for nearly half of these publications.

17. J. A. Delaire, 21 and footnote.

18. *SM*, 2 March, 1865.

CHAPTER FIVE

The Romance and Romanticism

If the word 'romanticism' still challenges neat definition today it was even more puzzling to those living in the early nineteenth century. '*Romantisme*' hesitatingly entered French usage towards the beginning of that century, but even by 1830, Victor Hugo its chief voice in France, was only prepared to define it as 'liberalism in literature'.[1] As far as music was concerned a similar view was taken in an article that came out in the same year as Hugo's celebrated play *Hernani*, in which Edouard Fétis spoke of romanticism's spirit of 'independent thought'.[2] Edouard's more famous father was to speak of the 'spirit of renovation' that was preoccupying artists at that time,[3] a description echoed a century and a half later by Jacques Barzun who characterized romanticism as embodying 'the same spirit of renovation that ... was at work in the streets of Paris, the desire to replace the old, crumbling structures with new and more spacious ones.'[4]

As in other countries, the first artistic manifestation of this 'liberalizing' spirit in France was in literature, music needing, it would seem, a little more time to adjust its techniques to the expressive demands of the new style – as much in the act of performance as in composition. Not that there was much need for singers to develop different techniques when the romance was touched by the new spirit stirring in France; but for some composers the old-fashioned romance – the 'romance *pur sang*' – must have seemed at odds with romanticism. Stemming from the style of the late classical period the romance moved in symmetrical periods of two- and four-bar phrases (as in Romagnesi's *Belle rose, charmante fleur*), a regularity not always appropriate for a sweep of melody attempting to convey the intensity of a romantic text. Because the romantic urge in song, both in Germany and France, was quickened by the example of lyric poetry, the latter must be the starting point for any consideration of either lieder or romance.

The romantic spirit in literature had already been at work in Germany (and in England) well before the turbulent première in 1830 of Hugo's *Hernani*, which has gone down in history as one of the most decisive literary events in France. Yet, while that play may have been the loudest and most powerful early shot in the cause of romanticism in that country, it was certainly not the first. Ten years before, Lamartine, reacting against the loftiness and impersonal nature of the classical style, rejoiced that he had brought poetry 'down from Parnassus, and in place of a seven-stringed lyre had given to the so-called muse the very cords of man's heart, touched and set in motion by the countless tremblings of the soul and of nature.'[5] His *Méditations poétiques* are filled with images of the romantic artist as passionate, solitary, disenchanted, ill at ease with all but nature, and forever on the brink of tears – a state of lonely melancholy later called 'le mal du siècle', as in *L'isolement* (later set to music by Niedermeyer)

> Si je pouvais laisser ma dépouille à la terre
> Ce que j'ai tant rêvé paraîtrait à mes yeux;
> Là je m'enivrerais à la source où j'aspire,
> Là je retrouverais et l'espoir et l'amour
> Et ce bien idéal que toute âme désire,
> Et qui n'a pas de nom au terrestre séjour.
> Que ne puis-je porté sur le char de l'aurore,
> Vague objet de mes vœux, m'élancer jusqu'à toi!
> Sur la terre d'exil pourquoi reste-je encore,
> Il n'est rien de commun entre la terre et moi.
> Quand la feuille des bois tombe dans la prairie
> Le vent du soir se lève et l'arrache au vallon:
> Et moi je suis semblable à la feuille flétrie;
> Emportez moi comme elle, orageux aquilon.

(If I could leave my mortal remains on earth, then that of which I dream so much could appear before my eyes; there I would drink to the full from the spring which I long for; there I would find again Hope and Love and this ideal Goodness which every soul longs for and which has no name on earth. Would that I, carried on dawn's chariot, could soar towards you, shadowy object of my desires. On exile-earth why do I yet remain? We have nought in common, the earth and I. When the woodland leaf falls in the meadow, the evening's wind rises up and snatches it from the valley. And I, I am like the withered leaf; carry me away like it, thou stormy north wind.)

Yet, emotional and deeply personal as this outpouring may be, the structure of that poem was, in fact, very traditional – cast in a mould of the classical alexandrine.[6] Lamartine's 'freedom' – his romanticism – came through the subjective nature of his themes rather than through a loosening of form. It was to be Victor Hugo, Alfred de Musset and their contemporaries who were to explore new forms to convey their romantic vision, and the first composer to try and match them in his romances was Hippolyte Monpou.

Today, the name of Hippolyte Monpou (1804–1841) is scarcely likely to raise a questioning nod of recognition. Rather, a smile, for even in his own day one of his most affectionate admirers admitted that he was as ugly as his name.[7] But he was a much-loved personality, as well as an admired composer whose romances seemed to point in a new direction, winning – rare achievement – the whole-hearted approval of the writers whose poetry he set. He was, in fact, a frequent figure at gatherings of the early romantic poets, often held in an artist's studio where, after quickly smoking half a cigarette, he would sit at the piano and sing his romances. Gautier remembers that when Monpou felt he had been understood after having sung a romance, he would say: 'And that one, how do you find it?', and the poet recalls how he would continue in that way, to everyone's great pleasure, until the candles came to their end, making the candle-rings explode. 'Never has a composer had for his art a more wild and enthusiastic love; nobody limited himself less', claimed Gautier who put Monpou and Berlioz together as the first two romantic composers in France.[8]

As a boy Monpou had been trained in music as a chorister at Saint-Germain-L'Auxerrois, and as a youth in Choron's famous school, where amongst his fellow students was Gilbert Duprez. Originally intending to follow a career in church music, he decided that his future lay in writing operas, and like so many with this ambition began composing romances to gain initial reputation. He achieved a modest success as an opera composer, but opera was, indeed, to be his undoing. He was working on one to a libretto by Scribe with a guaranteed performance at the Opéra-Comique on condition that if it were not finished by a prescribed date he would have to pay a penalty of 30 000 francs. The effort of trying to finish the work brought on an illness of such severity that he died after having completed only two acts. A pyramidal monument of black marble erected at Père Lachaise has been a more lasting reminder of this 39-year-old composer than has his music.

Of his 86 songs the best loved – and certainly the finest – was his setting of Musset's *L'Andalouse*.[9] It was also his first, and there is a charming story recounted in the journal *L'Echo musical* about the events of its publication in 1830. Written some twelve years after the event, and undoubtedly embroidered, it tells of the composer's last-ditch attempt to interest a publisher in what was to become a best-selling romance. Antoine Lemoine gave him fifty francs which he and his three fellow students, who included the singers Wartel and Duprez, spent in a riotous gastronomic and musical spree (maybe holding only a grain of truth, it nevertheless gives a delightful glimpse into Monpou's personality. (See Appendix D for a transcript and translation.)

Example 5.1 reproduces the first verse of this romance (in this romance each musical verse comprises two of Musset's verses).

Example 5.1   *L'Andalouse* (Monpou)

* staccatos added in this measure

Avez-vous vu, dans Barcelone,
Une Andalouse au sein bruni ?
Pâle comme un beau soir d'automne !
C'est ma maîtresse, ma lionne !
La Marquesa d'Amaëgui !

J'ai bien fait des chansons pour elle,
Je me suis battu bien souvent,
Bien souvent j'ai fait sentinelle,
Pour voir le coin de sa prunelle,
Quand son rideau tremblait au vent.

(Have you seen in Barcelona an Andalusian woman, with breasts pale brown,
pale as a beautiful autumn evening. She is my mistress, my lionness, my
Marquise of Amaëgui.

I have written many songs for her; often have I fought, often have I kept
watch so to catch a glimpse of her eyes when her curtain trembled in the
wind.)

On the surface the poem suggests a classical form, but there are no
regularly placed caesuras and, above all, there is a rich interplay of rhythms
amongst the words themselves. In eighteenth-century poetry the euphony of
the words contributed to a line which flowed smoothly to its end, pointing up
the rhyme, whereas in this poem we are more aware of the rhythm of
individual words and phrases with their natural 'breaks' and the startling use
of words with strong musical sounds and evocative power not frequently used
in French poetry before this time ('sein bruni', 'ma lionne', 'beau soir
d'automne' etc.).[10]

Monpou's setting catches much of this although, obviously, a verse-
repeating form such as the romance must inevitably be a compromise, the
melody clearly suiting some verses better than others. Just as Musset's poem
uses a form in which its regularity of syllables and rhymes is overridden, as it
were, by the counterpoint of the words themselves, so too does Monpou
overcome the regularity of his two- and four-bar phrases by employing various
musical devices. There are some metre changes, for example, that ruffle the
symmetry, as do the cross-accents in the fourth line of the piano part. The first
three vocal phrases are fused to give a sweep of six bars, followed by one of
four bars, thus upsetting the symmetry of the spans. And how well Monpou
catches the lover's flickering hopes of seeing the Andalusian girl when her
curtain flutters in the breeze – by the simple means of dislocating the verbal
phrase through rests inserted in unusual places – even in the middle of a word:
'quand ... son rideau trem ... blait au vent'). These impatient moments are also
underlined by sharp dissonances in the piano part punctuating the relentless
bolero rhythm. Never had there been a romance quite like this. It was almost
inevitable that Monpou should be accused of lacking taste as well as technical

ineptitude, but this no doubt drew him closer to those poets who had been accused of precisely the same shortcomings.

Monpou's range of expression was, however, limited by a very narrow harmonic vocabulary. It is not noticeable in those romances which have great rhythmic verve and ebullience, such as *L'Andalouse* and *Gastibelza, le fou de Tolède* (to words by Victor Hugo), but in the more dreamy and slow-moving ones the dependence upon tonic and dominant chords and few key-changes hampers a fuller reflection of the text. Nothing could illustrate this better than a comparison between Monpou's and Berlioz's settings of Victor Hugo's *La captive*. (See Examples 5.2 and 5.3.) Some of the earliest works by Hector Berlioz were, in fact, romances, including his superb setting of this evocative poem from the poet's collection *Les Orientales* (1829).

The element of the exotic runs like an idée fixe through much romantic French poetry, writers – like painters – finding endless fascination in the terrain and culture of the Middle East. A number of them, unable to resist its beckoning call visited Egypt and other Arabian lands, importing into their writings and paintings visions of the sensuality, cruelty and mystery of this world apart. It was not a uniquely nineteenth-century phenomenon, however. French fascination with the exotic can be traced back at least to the early years of the previous century when Galland translated the *Thousand and One Nights* into French, and as the century neared its end it was brought closer to France through scholarly studies of eastern languages and religions. Some scholars saw Eastern cultures and religions as catalysts for a new 'renaissance' through their impact on Western thought, just as the classical culture of ancient Greece had transformed medieval Europe four hundred years before.[11] Thus, at the beginning of the nineteenth century the mystic east was deeply embedded in French consciousness, perhaps to a greater extent than found elsewhere, not least through the publication in 1811 of Chateaubriand's three-volume account of his pilgrimage to Jerusalem. Although the primary purpose of *L'itinéraire de Paris à Jérusalem* was to demonstrate the superiority of Christianity over Islam, it stimulated enormous interest in eastern culture, inspiring literary works from those who journeyed to the great deserts in person or in imagination.

Though closer to France, Spain was another country that caught the imagination of the early French romantics, as we have seen in Musset's *L'Andalouse*, which, like Hugo's *Les Orientales* (1829), was written before the poet had actually visited the place of his inspiration, Musset's fascination with Spain having been aroused by literary works such as Byron's *Childe Harold*. In the words of Lloyd Bishop 'Spain was for Musset a country of sensual luminosity and bright colours, picturesque architecture and picaresque mores. It was also the homeland of intense, excessive emotions: burning passions, ferocious jealousy and revenge ...'[12]

While the 'orient' also inspired writers outside France – such as the Irish writer Thomas Moore (*Lalla Rookh*) and Goethe (*Westöstlicher Divan*) – yet English and especially German romantics seemed to be more drawn to medieval Europe, drinking in the mythology of gothic times with more gusto than did French romantics who, in their search for the exotic and unusual, reached out rather to 'orientalism', which at that time could mean anything from China, Turkey, Spain, 'Arabia', or what one wished.

The literary and artistic interest in 'oriental' cultures was, however, a pale reflection of the scholarly passion for them evident from the later years of the eighteenth century, not only in France, but in England, Germany and elsewhere where the results of intensive investigations by scientists and travellers were read to learned societies and their books published in ever increasing numbers. Arabian culture, in particular, held a special fascination for the French, not least because Egypt had become part of its history when Napoleon and his Grande Armée invaded it in 1798. For this campaign, in addition to 55 000 soldiers, Napoleon had brought together a large group of scientists, technicians and artists (Méhul was invited but declined) to study and record Egyptian civilization, resulting in a ten-volume *Description de l'Egypte*, published from 1809 to 1828, in which Guillaume-André Villoteau recorded his early researches into Arabian music. From 1836 Parisians were permanently reminded of the presence of Egypt when the Luxor Obelisk was erected in the Place de la Concorde.

Musicians and music lovers could catch glimpses of exotic music through the pages of the *Revue et Gazette musicale*, which, before the middle of the century was reached, had published articles about music in China, Turkey, Egypt and Algeria, Spain and Mexico; transmitted the latest findings about the ancient 'statue vocale' of Memnon; and reproduced diagrams and descriptions of instruments ranging from the Indian *Vina* to those played in ancient Greece and Rome. Nor were readers spared the mathematical complexities of Arabian scale structures, or the metallurgical processes for making authentic Chinese gongs.

Oriental music itself was regarded as a curiosity rather than a work of art to be taken seriously by music lovers and only one example of such a melody found its way into the *Revue et Gazette musicale* when, in its issue of 28 October 1838, one from Turkey was offered to its readers. However, at the end of 1844 Félicien David incorporated an Arabian melody into his symphonic ode *Le désert*, which, following a rave review by Berlioz, catapulted the composer into fame. As we shall see later, David was one of the few composers who had experienced Arabian music at first hand, and *Le désert* may fairly lay claim to being the first example of musical exoticism in European orchestral music.

In their settings of *La captive* – a poem depicting the scene of a European girl captured for the Sultan's harem – neither Monpou nor Berlioz strike the exotic musical note. This remained exclusively in the realm of the text which begins

> Si je n'étais captive,
> J'aimerais ce pays,
> Et cette mer plaintive,
> Et ces champs de maïs,
> Et ces astres sans nombre,
> Si le long du mur sombre
> N'étincelait dans l'ombre
> Le sabre des spahis.

(If I weren't a captive, I would love this country, and this plaintive sea, and these cornfields, and these stars without number, if along the dark wall were not gleaming in the darkness the Spahis' sabre.)

Although it finishes rather limply, Monpou's setting is a pleasant enough melody, but in no way matches Berlioz's youthful romance, which faithfully captures the young girl's yearning in long musical phrases that lift and open out into superb lyrical arches, the opening ones gaining intensity through constant modulation and the ever-upward movement until reaching F#. As the long phrases fall to the final cadence they briefly recapture the rising hopes of the opening. It is a melody that combines beauty of form and touching eloquence.

Berlioz wrote this song when he was a student in Rome, having gained the Paris Conservatoire's coveted Prix de Rome that included an obligatory period at the French Institute in the Villa Medici. Perhaps Berlioz felt a bond between Hugo's captive and himself – an 'exile' from Paris, as he claimed to be. Whatever the reason, his romance expresses the loneliness and yearning for home with wonderful feeling. In his memoirs he describes the genesis of the song.

The song called La captive [is] a piece whose popularity I never foresaw when I wrote it. I am wrong, however, to say it was composed at Rome; it dates from one of my visits to Subiaco [early February 1832]. I remember the occasion. It was in the inn where we used to stay; I was watching my friend Lefebvre, the architect, drawing at a table, when a sudden movement of his elbow knocked a book onto the floor. I picked it up. It was a copy of Hugo's *Orientales*; it had fallen open at that enchanting poem La captive. I read the poem, then turning to Lefebvre [a Prix de Rome prize-winner in the field of art] said, 'If only I had some manuscript paper, I would set this to music – I can *hear* it.' 'Don't let that deter you – I'll make you some', and taking a pen and a ruler he rapidly drew a few staves, on which I jotted down the tune and the bass. I put it away among

Example 5.2   *La captive* (Monpou)

my papers and thought no more of it. A fortnight later in Rome, during some music at the Director's, I remembered La captive. 'I must show you a song that I thought up in Subiaco', I said to Mlle Vernet; 'I am curious to know whether it is any good, I haven't the faintest idea.' I scribbled a piano accompaniment and we performed it there and then; and so well did it catch on that a month later the desperate Vernet [the Director] admonished me, 'Look here, Berlioz, next time you go up to the Mountains, for God's sake don't bring back any more songs. That Captive of yours is making my life in the Villa a misery. It's everywhere – in the palace, the gardens, the wood, the terrace, in all the passages. One can't move a yard without hearing someone bawling or mumbling "Le long du mur sombre ... le sabre de Spahis ... je ne suis pas Tartare ... l'eunuque noir", and the rest of it. It's driving me mad. Tomorrow I'm

Example 5.3   *La captive* (Berlioz)

getting rid of one of my servants, and I shall engage another on the strict understanding that he does not sing La captive.' I later developed and orchestrated the song. To my mind it is one of the most colourful I have written.[13] (Translation from David Cairns, *The Memoirs of Berlioz* (1970), 224–5.)

It appeared in a number of versions. The first, in 1832, was for voice and piano to which in the same year he added an ad libitum cello part. Two years later the accompaniment was orchestrated, and in 1848 he re-cast the song into a much longer work that Pauline Viardot sang at Hanover Square in London with Berlioz conducting. In this longer version he sets some of the verses differently from the simple melody of the romance, but whether or not this is an improvement is a matter of personal opinion.

La Captive was not, however, Berlioz's first published song, two years earlier he had published, at his own expense, settings of nine texts from Thomas Moore's *Irish Melodies*. Thomas Moore (1779–1852), an extraordinarily versatile and gifted Irishman whose engaging personality helped popularize his works at home, started putting together in 1808 a collection of Irish tunes (mainly from an existing collection by Edward Bunting), supplying words for them and working in collaboration with John Stevenson who provided the piano accompaniments. They were published serially until 1834 and became enormously popular, not only in Ireland and England, but also on the continent where they helped slake the romantic thirst for things foreign. Berlioz's settings were to translations by his friend Thomas Gounet and by Louise Belloc who translated only the final song of the collection, which in Berlioz's original edition was called *Neuf mélodies* (later changed to *Irlande*). Some settings are for solo voice, others for duet or chorus, each with piano accompaniment, and although the collection as a whole is of variable quality it contains a song that is truly remarkable – *Elégie en prose*. This is a setting of Louise Belloc's translation of the Irish song 'When he who adores thee', and unlike the other translations it made no attempt to be in verse – hence its title. That this song stood out from the simple romance-type settings of the other songs in the collection was recognized by the composer himself: 'I have rarely found a melody of such truth and poignancy, steeped in such a surge of sombre harmony. The piece is extremely difficult both to sing and to accompany … To hear it done poorly would be inexpressibly painful to me.'[14]

In its greater complexity in both vocal and piano parts and the range of its expression *Elégie en prose* looks forward to Berlioz's vocal masterpiece *Les nuits d'été* composed some ten years later, and hence to those developments in songwriting that will be the concern of Chapter Seven. Its original version was for solo voice with piano, but in 1856 it was published with orchestral accompaniment, the version that is most frequently heard nowadays. Settings of six poems by Théophile Gautier, *Les nuits d'été* is a collection rather than a song-cycle, and is, in fact, not always comfortable in range for one voice. Like so many romantic French songs of this later period, those in *Les nuits d'été* owe much to the simple romance, not least to its verse-repeating form. The strophic nature of *Villanelle*, for example, is very clear. In *L'isle inconnue*, however, this is most skilfully disguised as are others in the collection where Berlioz's mastery of varied repetition hides the bare strophic form, giving instead the impression of a spacious, 'through-composed' form. By the time Berlioz had come to compose *Les nuits d'été* the forces that were to develop the simple romance into a more sophisticated form were already at work. One of them was the songwriting of a foreign composer who was to make his home in Paris: Louis Niedermeyer (1802–1861).

Born at Nyon in Switzerland, Niedermeyer had music lessons with his father before going on to Vienna to study piano under Ignaz Moscheles and composition under the ageing Emmanuel Förster. At the age of seventeen he went to Italy where he studied and became close friends with Rossini. Moderate success came with a performance in 1820 of his first opera *Il reo per amore* at Naples, and when Rossini was appointed Director of the Théatre-Italien in Paris in 1824 it was performed there, although, like his later operas, it failed to impress Parisian audiences. Their 'nose' for detecting a born operatic composer was, in this case, correct, for Niedermeyer's real gifts as a composer lay in sacred music and songwriting, as well as in conducting and teaching. Recognizing the huge gap that the closure of Choron's school had left he founded his Ecole de musique religieuse in 1853 (also known as the Ecole Niedermeyer) for the training of church musicians and the study of choral masterpieces. Supported by a government subsidy it flourished to become one of the most influential schools of music in the second half of the nineteenth century, attracting teachers of the calibre of Saint-Saëns, and producing students of the calibre of Fauré. He followed this up three years later by founding a journal to spread a taste for fine religious music, *La maîtrise*. Together with Prince Moskowa, Niedermeyer was made a member of the Academy of Saint-Cecilia in Rome in 1843, while in Paris a mark of his reputation lay in his being one of three musicians short-listed for a seat in the French Academy the year that Berlioz was chosen (1865). The other two were Félicien David and Charles Gounod.

It was after leaving Naples that Niedermeyer came across Lamartine's poem *Le lac*, and story has it that he set it to music while sitting on the banks of Lake Geneva. That was in 1821, only a year after the poem itself had appeared, but it was to be several more years before the song was published. Niedermeyer arrived in Paris in 1823 and soon afterwards approached the publisher Pacini with his song, but Pacini was in a quandry, for he had already

Example 5.4 Opening of *Le lac* (Niedermeyer)

agreed to publish a setting of the same poem by an Italian singer Balocchi and the plates were already engraved. While recognizing the quality of Niedermeyer's song, he was reluctant to issue two settings of the same text and we are told by the composer's son that Pacini solved the problem by waiting until Balocchi left Paris and then destroyed his plates.[15] It was the most fortuitous act of Pacini's commercial career, for Niedermeyer's *Le lac* became one of the most justifiably celebrated songs of the century, immediately establishing the composer's reputation in France and beyond, and during the century was published in various arrangements from mandolin to military band. Although Niedermeyer wrote *Le lac* before coming to France, and

Example 5.5   Romance from *Le lac* (Niedermeyer)

therefore it can hardly be claimed as being written by a French composer, it marks one of the turning points in French songwriting. Saint-Saëns went so far as to say that the resounding success of *Le lac* marked out the path for Gounod and all those who followed.[16]

Of the sixteen stanzas of Lamartine's *Le lac* Niedermeyer set six of them in music that magnificently conveys the elegiac mood of the poem, creating an expansiveness new to French song. In bringing together the declamatory and lyrical elements the hand of an operatic composer was clearly at work, the first three stanzas being set in the style of a measured recitative, while the last three are set in the style of an 'aria', in reality a romance with three verses. (Niedermeyer actually places the word 'romance' at the head of each of those stanzas.)

The blending of declamatory and lyrical elements, so successfully accomplished in *Le lac*, was an approach taken in a number of other early songs by Niedermeyer, such as in his settings of Lamartine's *Isolement*, *L'automne* and *La voix humaine*, all of which are fine large-scale works. If others in a more ballad-like style, with supernatural décor – as in *La noce de Léonor* – strike us as having too strong a whiff of sulphur called forth by a surfeit of diminished-seventh chords (chords that might with justification be called the musical 'mal du siècle' of that century), others are less pretentious. Indeed, some of Niedermeyer's most felicitous songs are close to the simple romance tradition, but imbued with warm and expressive harmonies and subtle expression.

Thus, around 1830 Monpou, Berlioz and Niedermeyer were writing songs that were lifting the romance, on the wings of romanticism, to a new level of artistry. Of these composers Niedermeyer was undoubtedly the most influential, Monpou and Berlioz offering songs that were perhaps a little too idiosyncratic to establish models for others to follow. At the same time the most potent influence of all was to come from outside France. The discovery by music lovers in France of the songs of Franz Schubert, was to conquer their hearts and reveal new possibilities for French composers in the art of songwriting.

Notes

1. 'Le romantisme, tant de fois mal défini, n'est, à tout prendre, et c'est là sa définition réelle, si l'on ne l'envisage que sous son côté militant, que le *libéralisme* en littérature.' Victor Hugo, *Hernani* (Paris, 1830), Préface.
2. 'En musique, comme en littérature, que l'indépendance de la pensée soit le principe de toutes choses.' Edouard Fétis, *RM*, 1830, 236.
3. *RM*, 15 April, 1833.

4. Jacques Barzun, 'Paris in 1830', *Music in Paris in the Eighteen-Thirties* ed. P. Bloom (c. 1987), 4.

5. 'Je suis le premier qui ai fait descendre la poésie du Parnasse, et qui ai donné à ce qu'on nommait la muse, au lieux d'une lyre à sept cordes de convention, les fibres mêmes du cœur de l'homme, touchées et émues par les innombrable frissons de l'âme et de la nature.' Alphonse de Lamartine, *Méditations poétiques* (1820), Préface.

6. The alexandrine consists of lines of twelve syllables subdivided into two groups of six each, the subdivisions being marked by a tiny break (caesura), each of these equal subdivisions presenting a phrase that is both grammatically correct and complete in sense. An alternation between 'feminine' rhymes (unaccented endings) and 'masculine' rhymes (accented endings), as well as a relatively limited vocabulary of words that were acceptably 'poetic', were further limitations. Such rigidity was once likened by the early twentieth-century writer Paul Valéry to the toughness of marble, which, under the hands of a Michelangelo, could be shaped in a way that represented a triumph of mind over material. (Paul Valéry, *Variétés*, Paris, 1924, 62–3.)

7. 'Monpou est une physionomie, non pas au point de vue, bien entendu, car le pauvre garçon était au moins aussi laid que son nom.' Léon Escudier, *Mes souvenirs*, 1886, 315.

8. 'Jamais compositeur n'eut pour son art un amour plus furibond et plus enthousiaste; nul ne se ménageait moins. Quand il était au piano et qu'il se sentait compris après avoir chanté une romance, il disait: "Et celle-là, comment la trouvez-vous?" et il continuait ainsi, à notre grand plaisir, jusqu'à ce que les bougies arrivées à leur fin éclater les bobèches.' Théophile Gautier, *Histoire du romantisme*, (1874), 223.

9. Musset's text was also set by Amédée de Beauplan who called his song *La marquise d'Amaëgui, bolero.*

10. For a detailed analysis of musicality and euphony in Musset's lyric poetry see Lloyd Bishop, *The Poetry of Alfred de Musset* (New York, 1987), 113–44.

11. See Raymond Schwab, *La renaissance orientale* (1950).

12. Lloyd Bishop, 2.

13. '… cette mélodie qui a nom *La Captive*, et dont j'étais fort loin, en l'écrivant, de prévoir la fortune. Encore, me trompé-je, en disant qu'elle fut composée à Rome, car c'est de Subiaco qu'elle est datée. Il me souvient, en effet, qu'un jour, en regardant travailler mon ami Lefebvre, l'architecte, dans l'auberge de Subiaco où nous logions, un mouvement de son coude ayant fait tomber un livre placé sur la table où il dessinait, je le relevai; c'était le volume des *Orientales* de V. Hugo; il se trouva ouvert à la page de *La Captive*. Je lus cette délicieuse poésie, et me retournant vers Lefebvre: Si j'avais là du papier réglé, lui dis-je, j'écrirais la musique de ce morceau, car *je l'entends*. – Qu'à cela ne tienne, je vais vous en donner. Et Lefebvre, prenant une règle et un tire-ligne, eut bientôt tracé quelques portées, sur lesquelles je jetai le chant et la basse de ce petit air; puis, je mis le manuscrit dans mon portefeuille et n'y songeai plus. Quinze jours après, de retour à Rome, on chantait chez notre directeur, quand *La Captive* me revint en tête, "Il faut, dis-je à mademoiselle Vernet, que je vous montre un air improvisé à Subiaco, pour savoir un peu ce qu'il signifie; je n'en ai plus la moindre idée." L'accompagnement de piano, griffonné à la hâte, nous permit de l'exécuter convenablement; et cela prit si bien, qu'au bout d'un mois, M Vernet, poursuivi,

obsédé par cette mélodie, m'interpella ainsi: "Ah çà! quand vous retournerez dans les montagnes, j'espère bien que vous n'en rapporterez pas d'autres chansons, car votre *Captive* commence à me rendre le séjour de la villa fort désagréable; on ne peut faire un pas dans le palais, dans le jardin, dans le bois, sur la terrasse, dans les corridors, sans entendre chanter, ou ronfler, ou grogner: *Le long du mur sombre ... le sabre du Spahis ... je ne suis pas Tartare ... l'eunuque noir*, etc. C'est à en devenir fou. Je renvoie demain un de mes domestiques; je n'en prendrai un nouveau qu'à la condition express pour lui de ne as chanter *La Captive*." J'ai plus tard développé et instrumenté pour l'orchestra cette mélodie qui est, je crois, l'une des plus colorées que j'aie produites.' Hector Berlioz, *Mémoires*, ed. Pierre Citron (1969), vol. 1, 249–50.

14. 'Mais je crois que j'ai rarement atteindre à une aussi poignante vérité d'accents mélodiques, plongés dans un tel orage de sinistres harmonies. Ce morceau est immensément difficile à chanter et à accompagner; ... L'entendre médiocrement interpréter serait pour moi une douleur inexprimable.' Berlioz, *Mémoires*, 126; Cairns, *Berlioz*, 110.

15. A. Niedermeyer, *Vie d'un compositeur moderne* (1853), 20.

16. *A. Niedermeyer*, Preface by Saint-Saëns.

CHAPTER SIX

Paris Discovers the Songs of Schubert

It seems that Parisian music lovers first heard the songs of Schubert when Adolphe Nourrit began singing them in the early 1830s. It was apparently Liszt who introduced Nourrit to them through his piano arrangement of *Erlkönig* which he was playing in a salon when the singer entered the room. Nourrit was so overcome by the music that he asked Liszt to play it once more, to which the pianist replied that it would be far better for Nourrit to sing it.[1] This encounter through Liszt was probably about 1833 or 1834, for in an article published in 1837 the writer Legouvé claimed that it was 'our dear and admirable Nourrit' who initiated the public into Schubert's songs some three years before, although only in recent months, he says, had they been heard outside the circle of those who loved his music.[2] A press report tells of a public concert in the Salle Petzold as early as the end of 1834 when Nourrit sang *Ave Maria*,[3] and a few weeks later he sang *La religieuse* ('Die junge Nonne') for the Conservatoire's Société des Concerts, prompting one critic to exclaim that it would be difficult to imagine anything 'more poetic, more original and more dramatic' than this wonderful song.[4] Two years later Nourrit and Liszt were to perform Schubert lieder together when they came across each other at Lyon while touring. Rehearsing every day during their sojourn there they performed in a fashionable salon in that city, their own enthusiasm for the songs communicating itself to those who heard them.[5]

Despite his growing reputation as an interpreter of Schubert's songs Nourrit was keenly aware of his lack of German and his dependence upon French translations. He revealed it in a letter to a Monsieur Ed. P. ... at Le Havre, which, although undated, is believed to have been written in January or February 1835.

> I have acquired some new songs by Schubert which are magnificent. The translations which you have left for me have served me very well and I have succeeded in arranging their rhymes for the music and they could pass for fine verse. How lucky you are knowing German! For if you could sing you could unite the poetry of Goethe with the inspirations of Schubert. Teach me German, and I will teach you singing. It's a deal ...'[6]

During the six or so years left to him before his tragic death in 1839 Nourrit depended either upon published translations or upon the help of friends to render the German texts into French. As might be inferred from the above, he may also have liked to have had a literal translation which he could then transform into his own poetic singing version. In his dependence upon friends for translations it would not be surprising if he had sought the help of two German emigrés who were to make Paris their home, one temporarily, the other permanently: the composer/pianist Ferdinand Hiller and the poet Heinrich Heine.

Of these two, only Hiller was to become a very close friend of Nourrit. Yet it is probable that Heine and Nourrit would also have struck up an amicable relationship as early as June 1831 at a soirée they both attended shortly after Heine's arrival in Paris.[7] Whether or not Hiller or Heine ever came to Nourrit's assistance in the matter of translations we do not know; what is not in doubt, however, was their influence in forming his taste for German music, especially during the period 1831–1832 when the three of them (together with Liszt) attended meetings of the Saint-Simonians (see Chapter Seven) the musical bias of which was at that time towards German music.[8]

Nourrit's admiration for German music (so unusual at that time for a French opera singer) is touchingly revealed in a letter written to Hiller in 1836 in which Nourrit confides in him his desire to retire and sing all the German songs he loves.[9] Two years later in Naples he wrote again to Hiller and his words suggest that his love of German music was further strengthened through a growing disenchantment with Italian music.

> Nothing can make us forget our old divinities, our Glucks, our Mozarts, our Beethovens, our Schuberts, and without being ungrateful to Italy, to which we come to ask for that which other countries cannot give us, we must carry our respects beyond the Alps, and believe that there are some things better to do than that which is done today under the beautiful sky of Ausonie. [6 July 1838][10]

The best account we have of a Schubert performance by Nourrit comes from Gustave Bénédit (1802–1870). Trained as an opera singer at the Conservatoire, Bénédit seems to have recognized his own shortcomings as a performer and returned to Marseilles (his birthplace) where he took up the position of *Professeur de chant et de déclamation* at the Conservatoire there and also that of music critic. If Bénédit's knowledge of instrumental music was very limited, his judgement about vocal matters was, apparently, to be trusted.[11] This lends weight to his somewhat passionate account of Nourrit's performance of Schubert songs at Marseilles in 1837, and published in *La Revue musicale* shortly after the news of Nourrit's death two years later. It gives us an idea of the effect Nourrit's singing had on his listeners.

And *Les Astres* ['Die Gestirne'] – what noble magnificence Nourrit gave to this immortal song, in which the composer, to lend his thought more poetic flight, freed himself from cadence and [regular] rhythm. The translator, M Legouvé, followed Schubert's example. The words of *Les Astres* are in prose, such that there reigns in this space without horizon an indefinable quality ... This was what Nourrit was able to communicate in Marseilles. He sang the first part of *Les Astres* with a calm and solemn majesty, then, as if struck by a sudden flash during the last verse, he signalled to the accompanist to speed up the tempo and, yielding to the secret voice of his soul which was drawing him towards a torrent of poetry, he abandoned himself to it with a frenzy of inspiration that nothing could describe. What fine enthusiasm! His voice and his face were resonant with celestial brilliance as he delivered these last words: 'Qui joint la terre avec les cieux. ...' Oh! if in such a moment those who have accused Nourrit of lacking religious philosophy could have seen and heard him, perhaps they would have prostrated themselves before him, like that listener whose emotion I questioned, and who replied with a voice full of tears, 'Ah, monsieur, there is no praise great enough for such marvels; it makes one believe in God'.[12]

Soon after Nourrit's death in 1839 the torch for Schubert's songs was carried by one of his pupils, François Wartel, an intelligent musician of wide taste who often championed the cause of French composers. Nourrit's love of Schubert's songs must have inspired his most gifted student, for so closely was Wartel to become identified with the German master that one critic teasingly referred to him as Frantz [sic] Wartel,[13] another as Wartel-Schubert.[14] As early as 1841 one writer said of him: 'He has conquered Schubert, Schubert belongs to him, Schubert is his possession, his thing, his idol, his manitou.'[15] Having established a fine reputation in Paris as a lieder singer (albeit in French translations) Wartel set off in October the next year for Vienna where he gave four concerts which were extensively reviewed in the *Allgemeine Wiener Musik-Zeitung*. The appearance of a French singer presenting their beloved Schubert in French guise was at first something of a curiosity to the Viennese, but his first concert allayed any fears they may have had:

Herr Wartel has made a significant name for himself in Paris as a Beethoven and Schubert singer; this has not stopped us here in Vienna of being somewhat mistrustful of a French performance of such truly German songs. Having heard this performance by a foreign artist, however, I have no hesitation in declaring that there are few German singers who can surpass or even match him in inwardness of feeling and unvarnished conception. Without falsification he gives us the composer's idea, and with a finesse and nuance which can only come about through a deep understanding of the master's intentions.[16]

By the end of his three month sojourn in Vienna, despite some criticism of the second concert, Wartel's performances had become a sensation. As far as the music critic Lewinsky was concerned, Wartel demolished the widely-held belief that the French had no depth of spirit and feeling. An artist such as he transcended narrow national boundaries, Lewinsky declared; his citizenship was not of a country, but of the spirit, his concerts providing a true demonstration that 'The Fatherland of Art is the World'.[17]

Although Wartel's tenor voice was not regarded in Vienna as outstanding (as we have seen in an earlier chapter he was to develop into a baritone later in his career) his gift for interpretation rose above all such considerations. In his performance of *Erlkönig*, for example, the only weakness that Lewinsky pointed to lay in the translation. It was a pity, he said, that Wartel had to sing lines such as 'Voyez le cavalier hattant le pas' for 'Wer reitet so spät durch Nacht und Wind', and 'Viens vite, si non reconnais ma puissance' for 'und bist du nicht willig, so brauch'ich Gewalt'.[18] Nevertheless the enthusiastic public demanded a repeat of *Erlkönig*, something that the singer was unable to do from the exhaustion of having already repeated in that concert every song but one. It was no wonder that Wartel's success during this tour and a later one in 1844 was reported with utmost pride by the French musical press.

Another singer who did much to spread a love for Schubert's songs in Paris was the baritone Jean-Antoine-Juste Géraldy who, as we saw in Chapter Three made his début as a supporting artist for Liszt. Great singers such as Pauline Viardot also included Schubert's songs in their repertoire, in her case sometimes singing them in German. Yet Schubert in translation remained normal for many years – many of them dedicated to Nourrit, Wartel and Géraldy. Thus, some of the credit of popularizing Schubert's songs in Paris – and France – must also go to the translators, and in particular to Bélanger.

Almost nothing is known about Bélanger (including his first name), despite the existence of two collections of verse inspired by Walter Scott's *Kenilworth* and *Ivanhoe* (set to music in 1845 by Giuseppe Concone – the Italian singing teacher and composer then resident in Paris), as well as a volume of dramas, comedies and essays published in 1855, translations of Mendelssohn's *St Paul*, Goethe's entr'actes in *Egmont*, six sacred songs of Beethoven and hundreds of songs by Schubert. Even the correspondence between him and a Joachim Dupont published in 1824 gives little clue to his life. Yet, for lovers of Schubert's songs circulating in France at this time, his name must have been almost as familiar as the composer's.

Bélanger's translations are usually regarded as poor specimens, but the pressure upon him to provide a seemingly endless supply must have been intense. While it is easy to laugh at his romantic sensibilities that seemed so to baulk at the prosaic subject of *Die Forelle* that he transformed a trout into a mischievous sprite, he also provided some very felicitous translations as, for example, *Sois toujours mes seules amours* ('Sei mir gegrüsst'), made so popular by Nourrit. And although it was Bélanger's translation of *Erlkönig* which was found so tame when Wartel sang it in Vienna, it certainly has more punch than that of another by Emile Deschamps who rendered the famous line 'und bist du nicht willig, so brauch'ich Gewalt' into 'Viens donc? un refus pourrait être fatal'. But perhaps there are few words in French (or English) that can match the abrasiveness of the German at this dramatic point.

As well as Bélanger and Emile Deschamps (who was also well known for his translations of Shakespeare, Goethe and Schiller) others who helped in the spread of Schubert's songs in France by their translations were Ernest Legouvé (especially the eight religious songs: *Pax vobiscum, Vom Mitleiden Maria, Dem Unendlichen, Himmelsfunken, Das Marienbild, Die Gestirne, Gebet während der Schlach* and *Litanei* – translations all dedicated to Nourrit) and, somewhat later, the librettist Jules Barbier. Schubert in translation remained a feature of French performances throughout most of the century, those in the original language most usually being given by visiting German singers at the Association de bienfaisance allemande in Paris, active from the 1850s onwards.

Finally, amongst those directly responsible for the widespread cultivation of Schubert's songs in France were, of course, the Parisian publishers and in particular, Charles-Simon Richault.

Publications of Schubert's songs in Paris

When Franz Schubert died in 1828 only 185 of his total song output of 631 songs were published. Most of these had been issued, with opus numbers, by Diabelli, but there were also a dozen or so that had appeared as supplements to various musical periodicals. A large number of songs were thus still in manuscript at the composer's death, and in 1830 these were sold by Schubert's brother to Diabelli who began the daunting task of putting them into some order before gradually publishing them from 1830–1850. This collection Diabelli called *Nachgelassene musikalisches Dichtungen* (usually shortened to *Nachlass*). As well as this collection of songs there were over 50 others that were also published posthumously from 1829–1843. Yet even by mid-century 270 songs had still not been published.[19]

Schubert's songs being in the 'public domain' as far as France was concerned (no international copyright laws then to prevent this) Diabelli signed a contract with Richault, enabling the latter to publish them in Paris, a situation which some German composers found offensive. Stephen Heller, for example, called Richault an 'unbridled counterfeiter').[20] The result, however, was that through these publications, as well as performances by Nourrit and others, France became the first country outside the German-speaking ones to cultivate the songs of Schubert and develop a deep love for them there. If, when Richault died at the age of 86, his publications were his memorial, a brief appreciation in *Le Ménestrel* could be its inscription:

> He was one of the first to make known in France all the German vocal and instrumental works that have become classics here, as they are beyond the Rhine. It was he who revealed to us the songs of Schubert, first of all with the assistance of Adolphe Nourrit, then with that of Wartel. Our composers of chamber music and of instrumental works found a welcome in the catalogue of M Richault, who, in this connection, rendered a true service to serious art in France.[21]

Charles-Simon Richault (1780–1866) began his career in publishing as an apprentice in the firm of De Momigny (a publishing house that later went bankrupt), but by 1816 had established his career as an independent publisher.[22] It is estimated that on average he published between 300 and 400 musical works a year. By 1840 he had issued some 270 separately published Schubert songs, all translated into French, each in folio size with an appropriately engraved picture on the front page, usually enclosed in a blue, red or green border. The musical notation, carefully engraved, is very clear, and these handsome copies sold from 2 francs to 7.50 francs according to the number of pages. They were sold separately as well as put together in shorter collections and the full series was called *Oeuvres complètes de Schubert; paroles Françaises de Bélanger.*[23] The first songs of the series were announced in June 1834 as *Six mélodies célèbres: Marguerite* ('Gretchen am Spinnrade'), *La poste* ('Die Post'), *Sérénade* ('Ständchen'), *Au bord de la mer* ('Am Meer'), *La jeune fille à la mort* ('Der Tod und das Mädchen'), and *La fille du pêcheur* ('Das Fischermädchen'). Four years later Richault was ready to offer a collection of sixty songs, and the next year he published a collection of twenty (to translations by Deschamps). As well as the solo songs, the collection contains eleven choral settings as well as *Le berger sur la montagne* ('Der Hirt auf dem Felsen') for clarinet, voice and piano. Publication of this large collection of songs, all of which were available separately, ceased in 1840.

It is clear from the *cotage* assigned to each work (and placed at the foot of each page) that Richault did not publish the songs in any special order. By comparing these serial numbers with a list of them established by Lesure and Devriès from Richault's catalogues, it is possible to gain some idea of the years when the songs were published.[24] A glance at the songs published in 1835 gives an idea of the 'disorder':

French Title	German Title	Opus No.	Cotage
Le secret	Geheimes	14/2	3317
Vision	Der Doppelgänger	(Schwanengesang)	3320
La verrai-je encore	Dass sie hier gewesen	59/2	3321
Nuit et songes	Nacht und Träume	43/2	3322
Le voyageur	Der Wanderer	4/1	3323
Le printemps	Frühlingsglaube	20/2	3324
La truite	Die Forelle	32	3325
La chanson de nuit de voyageur	Wandrers Nachtlied (Uber allen Gipfeln ...)	96/3	3327
Marie	Alinde	81/1	3330
La cloche des agonisants	Das Zügenglöcklein	80/2	3331
Le berger sur la montagne	Der Hirt auf dem Felsen	op. posth. 129	3332

Included in the 1835 publications (but not shown in the above list) was a song translated as *Adieu*, which became one of the most popular in the collection and described by Legouvé as 'the most marvellous "last sigh" from any artist'.[25] Deutsch, however, has shown it to have been composed, not by Schubert, but by August Heinrich von Weyrauch with the title *Nach Osten!* to a text by Karl Friedrich Gottlob Wetzel beginning 'Nach Osten geht, nach Osten der Erde Flug'.[26] There are also some errors in opus numbers, and in the collection the same song occasionally appears twice in different translations.

Perhaps it was in recognition of this disorder and duplication, as well as the fact that Diabelli had now published many of the *Nachlass,* that Richault took the step to abandon the folio edition and embark upon an octavo size edition which he called *Seule collection complète des mélodies de François Schubert avec acc^t de piano.* This necessitated re-engraving all the songs published so far, as well as engraving the remainder. With the exception of six translations by Legouvé (of the so-called 'religious' songs), all other translations were by Bélanger and it required new plates for 336 songs. These he arranged in fifteen volumes, each containing some twenty-five pieces, each volume selling for the very reasonable price of 8 francs. The new edition, which was published in 1845, kept the order of the opus and *Nachlass* numbers as issued by Diabelli, and most of the errors of numbering found in Richault's earlier publications were corrected. Nevertheless, a few anomalies remained. *Amour et mystère* is a vocal arrangement of the second of the Waltzes for piano, opus 9, transposed down a semitone to G, while the final song in the collection, entitled *Dernière pensée de Schubert* and described by Richault as 'hitherto unpublished', had, in fact, been published eight years earlier in Germany although not by Diabelli. It was *Die liebende Schreibt* (op. posth. 165 no. 1), published on 26 June, 1832, as a supplement to the *Wiener Zeitschrift für Kunst, Literatur,*

Theater und Mode.[27] (See Appendix B for a list of the songs published in this edition, with German titles added.)

Richault also published another collection of twelve songs by Schubert to translations by Emile Deschamps, whose texts, however, were more usually used by other publishers, such as Mme Launer who produced a luxury edition of forty songs by Schubert in 1845. Schlesinger, publisher of the *Revue et Gazette musicale*, was also active in publishing some. Clearly, France was in the forefront of the publication of Schubert's songs outside Germany and it was to be many years, for example, before an English complete edition appeared.

The impact of Schubert's songs in Paris

Within a few years of Nourrit's public performances of Schubert's songs in Paris, and because of their wide circulation when French editions began to open up the repertoire in France, the name of Schubert was on everyone's lips. Music lovers in France were even able to catch a glimpse of Schubert's 'human side' through the eyes and memory of a musician who had recently come to live and work in Paris after a successful career as a violinist and singer in Germany. The claims by the Silesian-born Henri Panofka (who had studied violin and composition in Vienna in 1827) to have known Schubert during that year added special interest to his long article in October 1838 published in the *Revue et Gazette musicale* about the composer's songs.

> I had the good fortune to know Schubert personally; I met him in Vienna, in 1825, and we saw each other often, for, in Vienna, artists get together much more often than they do in Paris; intimate circles are established, and it is usually in a beer-hall that the most poetic and the most dreamy ideas are exchanged: one should not find that ridiculous; beer is an expensive and precious drink for the Viennese person; surrounded by vines, he finds no charm in wine; and even the majority of correct people, in Vienna, only drink, so to speak, water. But beer, which combines so nicely with the pipe, becomes a more real, a more delicate enjoyment, and nourishes conversations better; for don't go thinking that it is drunk in great gulps; it is enjoyed slowly, and one thus gains time. It was, then, in such gatherings that I became connected with Schubert; in our midst were Fratnz [sic] Lachner, today master of the chapel of the king of Bavaria, the poets Schober and Hofzinser, and the violinist Slawik. The one of all of us who was most full of cheer was Schubert; he always knew a good number of anecdotes, and witticisms sprang from his lips, which were continually animated by a smile and benevolence; and then it was his moments of rest, of relaxing that he came to spend with us; for Schubert started work at 7 o'clock in the morning, and until two o'clock his door remained irrevocably closed; but barely had the clock struck two and he headed either for the country, or to see his friends, and the rest

of the day was devoted to business, to going for a walk, to those charming meetings that I have just been speaking of.[28]

Yet Panofka's long article (of which only a small part has been reproduced above) was far more than a mere pen-sketch of the composer. It included penetrating comments on his style, amplifying and illustrating his main point that 'the great merit of the works of Schubert lies in a profoundly poetic conception of the words, the originality of the melodies, the novelty and the beauty of the harmonies, and above all in the intimate union between voice and accompaniment.'

It was inevitable that the 'discovery'of Schubert's songs in Paris would have an impact upon the art of songwriting in France. In 1837 Ernest Legouvé had already prophesied doom for the French romance.

The introduction into France of Schubert's melodies will kill the romance ...

We have had and still have some *romanciers* (excuse the word, I know no other) who lack neither grace nor charm, and Mme Duchambge above all has very remarkable qualities of melody and a poetic sadness; but all the compositions of these musicians sin in terms of form; their accompaniment is a series of non-arpeggiated chords, of little flat and insignificant drummings which do not combine at all with the melody; and their works are old after two or three years, because they have no artistry.[29]

How could French composers fail to be affected by Schubert's example and by the respect and enthusiasm his songs seem to have been engendering in France in the late 1830s and early 1840s? The possibility of an alliance between German lied and French romance, was amusingly suggested in the leading article in the *Revue et Gazette musicale* when, at the end of 1840 it looked ahead to what might happen to music in 1841: An 'encounter' between 'Romance', pictured as a damsel in distress ('I am so very French, please protect me') and 'Lied', an unsmiling German, is witnessed by the patron saint of the New Year St Sylvestre, who suggests that, despite the German's execrable French, 'Lied' might care to become a 'naturalized' Frenchman. 'I don't vant to be naturalized; I vant to stay Cherman. But I vant to leef in Paris, to seeng in Paris ...', rebutting St Sylvestre's suggestion that he should marry 'Romance', 'She ees to ohld', he complains. 'Go to the devil', exclaims the exasperated saint, 'or sing me something. I'd rather hear you sing than hear you talk'.[30]

For those to whom the romance was almost a sacred national trust the idea that there might be a union beween the two was, of course, anathema; but there was no holding back the inevitable – this had already started. By 1840 the reviewer Blanchard felt moved to complain that

The simple and naïve romance, this national and true song, is no longer considered adequate by our salon composers to express a tender, gentle or sad sentiment. Just like Victor Hugo, who was made the leader of a school in poetry, and who had so many grotesque imitators, Schubert is the focal point of the young musical school who now only dream of *Lieder* with pretentious, tortuous melodies and harmonies and ambitiously ridiculous modulations.[31]

On the other hand, in the eyes of some, no greater compliment could be paid to a composer than the description 'French Schubert', an accolade given to at least three songwriters: Félicien David, Henri Reber, and Auguste Vaucorbeil. Legouvé's prophecy that Schubert's songs would kill the romance was only partly fulfilled. Certainly the romance as envisaged by Thiébaut and Romagnesi had little time left. But the qualities of lyrical charm, unpretentiousness and immediate appeal, which were its essence, were so deeply embedded in the tradition of French songwriting that even its transformation into what was eventually called mélodie could not banish them.

Notes

1. 'C'était chez un banquier hongrois, M Dessauer, un ami de Liszt. L'artiste était au piano, et jouait *le Roi des Aunes*, lorsque Nourrit entra. Double raison pour continuer. Nourrit était tout oreilles. A mesure que cette musique si dramatique le pénétrait, il manifestait une vive émotion; son visage s'illuminait. Le morceau terminé, il redemanda. Liszt lui dit qu'il ferait bien mieux de la chanter. Nourrit s'excusait sur ce qu'il ne savait pas l'allemand. Liszt expliqua le sujet, et Nourrit consentit à vocaliser simplement le chant; ce qu'il fit avec l'expression d'un interprète inspiré. *longumque bibebat amorem.* Il s'éprit dès lors d'une grand passion pour ces mélodies; à sa demande, on en traduisit un certain nombre* et il fit l'infatigable propagateur. (*fn. Il y a une traduction de M. Bélanger, une autre de M. Emile Deschamps; il les modifiait sans cesse, surtout au point de vue de la musique.) L.-M., Quicherat, *Adolphe Nourrit, sa vie, son talent, son caractère, sa correspondance*, 3 vols. (1867), vol 2, 32.
2. *RGM*, 15 January, 1837.
3. *Le Moniteur*, 22 December, 1834.
4. *RGM*, 25 January, 1835.
5. Letter from Liszt written from Chambéry in September 1837 and published in *GM*, 11 February, 1838.
6. 'Je me suis procuré de nouvelles mélodies de Schubert, qui sont magnifiques. Les traductions que tu m'as laissés m'ont beaucoup servi, et j'ai réussi à les arranger en rimes sous la musique, qui est assez belle pour se passer de beaux vers. Es-tu heureux de savoir l'allemand! Car si tu savais chanter, tu pourrais unir les poésies de Goethe aux inspirations de Schubert. Apprends-moi l'allemand, je t'apprendrai à chanter. C'est dit ...' Quicherat, vol 3, 7.
7. Fritz Mende, *Heinrich Heine Chronik seines Lebens und Werkes* (1986), 91.
8. Ralph P. Locke, *Music, Musicians, and the Saint-Simonians* (1986), 58–9.
9. Quicherat, vol 3, 26.

10. '... rien ne peut nous faire oublier nos vieilles divinités, nos Gluck, nos Mozart, nos Beethoven, notre Schubert, et, sans être ingrats envers l'Italie, à qui nous venons demander ce que les autres pays ne peuvent nous donner, nous devons porter nos regards au delà des Alpes, et croire qu'il y a quelque chose de mieux à faire que ce qui se fait aujourd'hui sous le beau ciel de l'Ausonie.' Quicherat, vol. 3, 273.

11. Fétis, *Biographie universelle des musiciens*, Supplement, vol. 1. (1878), entry on Bénédit supplied by Edouard de Hartog.

12. 'Les *Astres*, avec quelle noble magnificence Nourrit posa ce chant immortel, où l'auteur, pour donner à sa pensée un essor plus poétique, s'est affranchi de la cadence et du rythme; le traducteur M Legouvé a suivi l'exemple de Schubert. Les paroles des *Astres* sont en prose, de sorte qu'il règne dans cette période sans horizon, je ne sais quel caractère de grandeur et d'indépendance qui touche presque à l'infini ... Voilà ce que Nourrit sut faire comprendre à Marseille. Il dit la première partie des *Astres* avec une majesté calme et solennelle, puis comme d'un éclair soudain, en présence de la dernière strophe, il fit signe à l'accompagnateur de presser la mesure, et cédant à la voix secrète de son âme qui l'entraînait vers un torrent de poésie; il s'y abandonna tout entier avec une frénésie d'inspiration que rien ne saurait décrire. Quel bel enthousiasme! son visage et sa voix résonnaient d'un éclat tout céleste, quand il fit entendre ces dernières paroles: *Qui joint la terre avec les cieux. ...* Oh! si dans un pareil moment ceux ont accusé Nourrit de manquer de philosophie religieuse avaient pu le voir et l'entendre, peut-être se seraient-ils prosternés devant lui comme cet auditeur dont j'interrogeais l'émotion, et qui me répondit avec une voix pleine de larmes: Ah! Monsieur, il n'y pas d'éloges assez grands pour de telles merveilles, *cela fait croire en Dieu.*' *RM*, 25 April, 1839.

13. H. Blanchard, *RGM*, 28 February, 1847.

14. *M*, 2 February, 1862.

15. 'Il a conquis Schubert, Schubert lui appartient, Schubert est son bien, sa chose, son idole, son manitou.' *RGM*, 4 April, 1841.

16. 'Herr Wartel hat sich in Paris als Beethoven-und Schubert-Sänger einen bedeutenden Namen gemacht; dieß hinderte aber nicht, hier in Wien gegen einen französischen Vortrag so echtdeutscher Gesänge etwas mißtrauisch zu seyn. Jetzt aber, da wir diese ausländische Darstellung selbst gehört haben, nehme ich wenigstens keinen Anstand zu erklären, daß es wenige deutsche Sänger gibt, die an Innigkeit des Gefühls und ungeschminkter Auffassung, Herrn Wartel gleichstehen oder gar ihn übertreffen; er gibt aber die unverfälschte Idee des Komponisten, und zwar mit einer Feinheit der Nuancirung, wie sie nur ein tiefes Eindringen in die Intentionen des Meisters erzeugen kann.' *Allgemeine Wiener Musik-Zeitung*, 15 November, 1842, 550. This concert was held on 8 November in the Musikvereinssaal, at which Wartel's pianist-wife Thérèse also appeared, as she did on the other three occasions. During this tour she did not accompany the songs, but always performed as a soloist.

17. 'Die Vaterland der Kunst ist die Welt', *Allgemeine Wiener Musik-Zeitung*, 9 March, 1843.

18. 'Wir bedauern ihn nur, das er so prosaische Verse wie folgende singen mußte: "*Voyez le cavalier hattant le pas*" für das Deutsche "Wer so spät durch Nacht und Wind." dann: "*vois-tu les noirs enfants,*" statt: "Sieht du nicht hort Erlkönigs Töchter am düstern Ort" und endlich: "*Viens vite, si non reconnais ma*

puissance," für: "und bist du nicht willig, so brauch'ich Gewalt." Ibid.

19. John Reed, *The Schubert Song Companion* (1985), 484. The statistics in this paragraph come from this study.

20. 'effréné contrefacteur', Devriès and Lesure, *Dictionnaire des éditeurs de musique française*, vol. 2, 1820–1914, (1988), 91.

21. 'L'un des premiers il fait connaître en France toutes les œuvres vocales et instrumentales allemandes, devenues classiques parmi nous comme au delà du Rhin. C'est lui qui nous révéla les mélodies de Schubert, d'abord avec le concours d'Adolphe Nourrit, puis avec celui de Wartel. Nos compositeurs de musique de chambre et d'œuvres instrumentales trouvaient leur place hospitalière dans le catalogue de M Richault, qui, sous ce rapport, a rendu de véritables services à l'art sérieux en France.' *M*, 25 February, 1866.

22. See Anki Devriès and François Lesure, *Dictionnaire des éditeurs de musique française*, vol. 2, 1820–1914, (1988), 362–4, for corrections to errors which have appeared in all accounts of Richault's life.

23. Only the British Library seems to have a large (perhaps complete) collection of the songs in this folio edition, collected in 6 volumes (H2146). They appear to have been bound in no special order.

24. Anki Devriès and François Lesure, *Dictionnaire*, 369. While Lesure and Devriès warn that the *cotages* must be treated with caution (Richault sometimes used early numbers again in later years, and also set aside some *cotages* for particular composers) from the evidence of advertisements and reviews, it would seem that the *cotages* are, for this particular time, fairly reliable for establishing dates for his publications of Schubert's songs.

25. 'L'Adieu est le plus admirable dernier soupir qu'ait jamais trouvé aucun artiste.' *RGM*, 15 January, 1837.

26. Otto Deutsch, *Franz Schubert Thematisches Verseichnis seiner Werke in chronologischer Folge* (1978), 657.

27. Deutsch, 391.

28. J'ai eu le bonheur de connaître Schubert particulièrement; je le rencontrai à Vienne, en 1825, et nous nous vîmes souvent, car, à Vienne, les artistes se réunissent beaucoup plus entre eux qu'à Paris; des cercles intimes s'y organisent, et c'est ordinairement dans un estaminet (*bierhaus*) que se fait l'échange des idées les plus poétiques, les plus rêveuses: qu'on ne trouve pas cela ridicule; la bière est une boisson chère et précieuse pour le Viennois; entourée de vignes, il ne trouve point de charmes dans le vin; et même la plupart des personnes comme il faut, à Vienne, ne boivent pour ainsi dire que de l'eau. Mais la bière, qui se lie si heureusement à la pipe, devient une jouissance plus réelle, plus délicate, et alimente mieux les conversations. Car n'allez pas croire qu'on la boive à grands coups; on en jouit avec lenteur, et on gagne du temps. Ce fut donc dans de semblables réunions que je me liai [*sic*] avec Schubert; parmi nous se trouvaient Fratnz [*sic*] Lachner, aujourd'hui maître de chapelle du roi de Bavière, les poètes *Schober* et *Hofzinser*, et le violoniste *Slawik*. Celui de nous tous qui avaient le plus de gaieté, c'était Schubert; il savait toujours bon nombre d'anecdotes, et les mots spirituels jaillissaient de ses lèvres. qu'animait continuellement le sourire de la bienveillance; et puis c'étaient ses moments de repos, de laisser-allez qu'il venait passer avec nous; car Schubert se mettait au travail dès sept heures du matin, et jusqu'à deux heures sa porte restait irrévocablement fermée; mais à peine deux heures étaient-elles sonnées qu'il se dirigeait soit vers la campagne,

soit chez ses amis, et le reste de la journée était consacrée aux affaires, à la promenade à ces charmants réunions dont je vins de parler.' *RGM*, 14 October, 1838.

29. 'L'introduction en France des mélodies de Shubert [sic] tuera inévitablement la romance ... Nous avons eu et nous avons encore quelques *romanciers* (qu'on me pardonne ce mot, je n'en connais pas d'autres) qui ne manquent ni de grâce ni de charme, et Mme Duchambge surtout a des qualités de mélodies et une tristesse poétique très-remarquable; mais toutes les compositions de ces musiciens pèchent par la forme; *ils ne savent pas*; leurs accompagnements sont une suite d'accords plaqués, de petites batteries plates et insignifiantes, qui ne se lient en rien avec la mélodie; et les oeuvres sont vieilles au bout de deux ou trois ans, parce qu'il n'y a pas d'art chez eux.' *RGM*, 15 January, 1837.

30. '*La Romance:* Je suis éminemment française, et je viens vous prier de me protéger, de prendre ma parti.' *1841 [Saint Sylvestre]*: Contre qui? *Le Lied*: Parplé! contre moi qui fiens prendre sa blace. Ché suis faporeux comme elle et plis qu'elle; ché plis te naïfeté qu'elle. Ché été le Binchamin té Schubert et ché lé suis à présent té Proch et Dessauer. *1841*: C'est bien, c'est bien. Malgré votre accent, nous vous accordons droit de bourgeoisie chez nous, en attendant que vous vous fassiez naturaliser. *Le Lied*: Ché feux pas me naturalisser; ché feux rester Allemand. *1841*: Eh bien, restez Allemand. *Le Lied*: Mais ché feux habiter Paris, chanter tans Paris et enchanter Paris. *1841*: Eh bien! habitez Paris, chantez dans Paris et enchantez Paris. *Le Lied*: Mais ché feux pas qué la romance mé disse qu'elle m'a tonné le chour, que ché fiens t'elle. *1841*: Oh! quelle tête carrée! Arrangez-vous ensemble, Marriez-vous; il ne peut résulter de votre union que quelque chose de joli. *Le Lied*: Elle est trop fieille. *1848*: Allez au diable! ... ou chantez-moi quelque chose, car j'aime mieux cous écouter que discuter avec vous.' *RGM*, 27 December, 1840.

31. 'La simple et naïve romance, ce chant national et vrai, ne suffit plus à nos compositeurs de salon pour exprimer un sentiment tendre, doux ou triste. De même que M Victor Hugo qu'on a fait chef d'école en poésie, et qui a eu tant de grotesques imitateurs, Schubert est le point de mire de la jeune école musicale qui ne rêve plus que plus que *Lieder* d'une mélodie et d'une harmonie prétentieuse, contournées, et à modulations ambitieusement ridicules.' *RGM*, 6 December, 1840.

CHAPTER SEVEN

Romance into Mélodie

It may have been Berlioz's *Neuf mélodies* (1830) – his settings of texts from Moore's *Irish Melodies* – that gave rise to the use of the word 'mélodie' when describing songs more musically sophisticated than the simple romance. Yet, as is often the case when new musical terminology appears, its usage was haphazard.

Richault and other publishers usually described their editions of Schubert's songs as 'mélodies', while reviewers were inclined to call his songs 'German romances'. On the other hand, in 1839 the publisher Maurice Schlesinger issued five new songs by Niedermeyer, all to words by Emile Deschamps, describing them as *Cinq Lieder Nouveaux*. Three of these were in the ballad style, but, as the reviewer Blanchard correctly pointed out, the remaining two were in the style of the simple romance. Even in the second half of the century some French songs were still being described as 'lieder'. In 1859 the musical periodical *Le Ménestrel*, which, like many others, often included songs or piano works in its issues, declared that, in the interests of good music of average difficulty and accessible to the greatest number, it would in future no longer publish romances but instead the 'more developed mélodies' (mélodie plus développée). The very fluidity of the two terms 'romance' and 'mélodie' reflects how the style of the earlier form permeates the later one.

The romance style is, in fact, never far away from even the most imaginative 'mélodies' which, if they slip into a simpler expression, irresistibly recall the earlier form and the world of the salons which nurtured them. In contrast, the simpler songs of Schubert seem to evoke not the world of the salon, but that of the countryside and its folk songs. As we have seen in the previous chapter, Schubert's songs were 'in the air' in the 1830s, so it is appropriate to start with one of the earliest of our composers to be dubbed the 'French Schubert'. This was Henri Reber.

Regarded in his old age as an arch-conservative, in his youth Henri Reber (1807–1880) had been in the vanguard of new developments in French music – in particular, his affection for the German repertoire, not least the songs of Schubert. He had, in fact, grown up not far from Germany – at Mulhouse on the Upper Rhine, and athough his parents had hoped for a commercial career for their son the young man's love of music overcame this, and in 1828 he moved to Paris, entering the Conservatoire where his teachers were to include two well-known musicians: Reicha and Le Sueur. By the mid-1830s Reber's music was beginning to attract discerning attention. Three songs, including a setting of Victor Hugo's *La captive*, were published during 1837/38 and the following year the first of his four symphonies was performed at the Conservatoire in the same week as a concert given by Berlioz. In a review of Reber's concert published in the *Revue et Gazette musicale* a comparison was drawn between the two men, both of whom were seen as gifted young composers treading totally different paths: Berlioz, like Victor Hugo, breaking new ground in form and language, and, with the exception of Gluck and Beethoven, turning his back on the classical masters; Reber, drawn to the German tradition and finding inspiration from it, which, at that time in both politics and music, it was suggested, required the greatest courage of all in daring to display good sense, calm and moderation – not always evident in the 'modern school', a point of view from which the Editor of the *Revue et Gazette musicale* and his editorial committee (which included Berlioz who had recently joined it) were quick to distance themselves.[1] Reber's alliance with Young France was that of a 'reformer' rather than an 'innovator',[2] being deeply influenced not only by Haydn, Mozart and Beethoven, but also by Bach, and feeling most at home in writing chamber music and songs. Nevertherless the seeds of his musical conservatism were sown early, and some of his contemporaries were puzzled by what they saw as 'severe ascetism' in one so young and so biased towards bringing back the 'dated and outmoded forms of the past.'[3]

Although, like most French composers, he had sought success in opera, his first, *La nuit de noël* (1848), while highly praised by Berlioz, who particularly admired its orchestration – achieved only a *succès d'estime*. This was also the fate with later ones. Saint-Saëns was to say of him that 'he belonged to that rare species of those who speak briefly, fearing long discourse and writing nothing useless', so it is no wonder that the smaller canvass of song seemed to suit him better than did the larger one of opera. Of his songs, in particular, Saint-Saëns wrote

> [they] are notable for their charm and their melodic simplicity, and for the respect for the prosody and for that strange peculiarity whereby vocal ornaments, often considered incompatible with a pure style, are not banished, Reber forbade in his songs neither trills nor scales nor arpeggios; gracious arabesques frequently accompany the lines of his architecture, arabesques of a very pure style, it goes without saying, and having nothing to do with those gargoyles of the old Italian school.[4]

He wrote fifty-six songs for voice and piano. Of them *Au bord du ruisseau* (to a poem by the seventeenth-century dramatist Philippe Quinault) most clearly shows the composer's debt to Schubert in the style of its flowing accompaniment – evoking a scene by the banks of the stream – its vocal line supported by harmonies and modulations that beautifully convey the gentle melancholy of the words.

It is not surprising that Reber's setting of a translation of Goethe's *Mignon* also brought a Schubertian response from him, and a sure sign that Reber was regarded as following the German master was that his attractive setting of a seventeenth-century poem by Charles Malherbe – *Stances* – was described as being in a 'severe' style.[5] Yet the majority of his songs are not haunted by Schubert's ghost, except insofar as they show how, under the influence of German lieder, Reber was one of the first of that generation of French composers to regard solo song as an art form to be taken seriously.

Honours came to him in the form of election to the French Academy in 1853, the award of the Legion of Honour the next year and in 1862 the appointment as teacher of composition at the Conservatoire where he had already been teaching harmony for some years. Well before this, in 1830, a young man, provincial and poor, came to him seeking lessons in harmony. It was Félicien David.

Félicien David (1810–1876) had come to Paris from Provence where he had tried to eke out an existence for two years following the closure in 1828 of a Jesuit College in Aix where he had been studying. Not that the rigorous training by the Jesuits was what he had wanted. But for a young man with no prospects and who, as a child with a good soprano voice from a poor village family near Vaucluse had been taken into the choir school of Saint-Sauveur in Aix, enrolment in the college seemed a natural step to take. The decision to remain having been taken out of his hands by the closure of the college he arrived in Paris in 1830 and presented himself to the Conservatoire where he studied with Fétis for composition and Benoist for organ. His lessons in harmony with Reber were as a private student. However, other strong influences were at work on him, and after only a year he quit his studies at the Conservatoire and took the decisive step to join the Saint-Simonians.

This was a movement, a fraternity, inspired by the writings and teaching of the social philosopher and reformer Henri Saint-Simon (1760–1825). His vision of a society in which talent, labour and productivity were more important than class distinction or the accident of birth, was resonant with those ideals which had fermented the French Revolution and with the spirit of regeneration that was still at work after it. Following Saint-Simon's death, leadership passed to Barthélemy-Prosper Enfantin (1796–1864) who, while

Example 7.1 *Au bord du ruisseau* (Reber)

(Stream, which with water so pure, bathe these brilliant flowers. In vain does your delightful murmur humour the torment I endure; nothing can soothe my fatal woes.)

not losing sight of the founder's ideals, transformed what had been a reforming movement into a cult, calling himself 'The Father' and his followers, now wearing special tunics, 'Disciples'. A search for a 'female Messiah' worthy to sit next to The Father was started, and women's rights began to play an important part in this phase of the Saint-Simonians. Even conventional morality was questioned, Christian belief in 'original sin' and the denigration of sexual pleasure being rejected. The Saint-Simonians were now more controversial than ever, and some of those who had embraced the movement in its earlier days found that associating with it could be an impediment to a career, and so turned their back on it or played down their earlier connections. There is a possibility, for example, that Henri Reber may have had some kind of association with the Saint-Simonians – perhaps because of Félicien David – for he composed a choral and instrumental piece for them called *A l'Orient!*, but nowhere in the biographical material is there any mention of his connection with the organization.

Despite Enfantin's innovations that changed the outward appearance of its members and widened its beliefs, the basic ideals of Saint-Simon remained intact, and its meetings at which Enfantin and others gave public lectures regularly drew enormous crowds. Liszt, Berlioz, Halévy, Mendelssohn, Hiller and Nourrit were amongst musicians attracted to them – at least for a time. Music, indeed, played a central role in the activities of the Saint-Simonians. German music, in particular, was highly regarded for its uplifting and spiritual power, and for its capacity to communicate the Saint-Simonian message to outsiders. But music was also brought into the daily routine of the Disciples: those who joined it as members of the fraternity living together on what was then the outskirts of Paris at Ménilmontant. Here there was music to be sung at thanksgiving before and after meals and at its public ceremonies. A composer of real gifts was needed – and found. Félicien David had arrived in Paris at the right time.[6]

It may have been that David was attracted to the movement as much for the shelter and fraternity that it offered a young man – until then lacking security and friendship – as for its ideals and the opportunity to propagate them through music. Thus, most of his compositions at this early stage were male voice choruses. But the collapse of the movement was already in sight. There were internal dissensions amongst the Disciples themselves and in 1833 the movement was outlawed by government decree leading to Enfantin's imprisonment and the closure of the Retreat at Ménilmontant. A number of the Disciples obeyed Enfantin's decree that the missionary work of the movement should be continued both in France and overseas. So it was that Félicien David travelled with some of the others to Egypt, Algeria and other Middle East countries where the seeds of his artistic maturity were sown. There he transcribed some Arabian melodies and absorbed something of the musical culture of those countries.

When he returned to Paris in 1835 the Saint-Simonian movement had totally collapsed and he spent the next few years in solitariness in the village of Igny near Palaiseau, making a thorough study of Beethoven's scores, and composing or polishing his early works. These included songs inspired by his sojourn in the desert, such as *Le chibouk* and *L'Egyptienne* to texts by fellow Saint-Simonians who had been with him in the Middle East: Jacques Cognat and Auguste Colin, the latter providing him with the text for his most famous work *Le désert*. Other friends from his days with the movement supplied a number of texts which he set over a period of time, some of these authors achieving distinction in later years, such as Charles Poncy, a stone mason in his Saint-Simonian days and whose writings were encouraged by George Sand and Béranger. Another friend from those days, Tyrstée Tastet, was not only to write stage works but also a history of the French Academy, while other writers of lesser achievement associated with the movement were Sylvain Saint-Etienne, and Emma Tournier, wife of a Saint-Simonian. All provided David with song texts, while another, Charles Chaubet, wrote the words for his symphonic ode *Christophe Colombe*. Not all his poets, however, were from the brotherhood. Théophile Gautier, himself a traveller to Egypt and whose writings are sometimes touched by exoticism, wrote the poem of one of David's loveliest songs: *La tristesse d'odalisque*, while other poets included Musset and Barateau.

His earliest publication was a collection of piano pieces entitled *Mélodies orientales* (1836), but despite their alluring title they aroused little interest. However in 1840, by which time he had moved to Paris to live with his brother, his name was beginning to appear in reviews of concerts and salon recitals. His Nonetto (for 2 cornets, 4 horns, 2 trombones and ophiclide) made a very good impression at a concert that year given by the conductor Valentino[7] (well known for performing the German classics), and in that same year one of his songs gained great popularity – but for political rather than artistic reasons.

A political furore had erupted in 1840 between France on the one side and England, Germany, Russia and Austria on the other. Its roots stretched a long way back to events following the defeat of Napoleon Bonaparte in 1815 when the victorious allies had signed a treaty in which the left bank of the Rhine was taken from the French. When in 1840 Egypt waged war on Turkey, France sympathized with the Pasha, the other four countries with the Sultan. Old antagonisms were awakened, including the question of the Rhine, and a German poet Nicolas Bekker wrote an inflammatory poem entitled *Der deutsche Rhein* this in turn prompting Musset to retort in like-kind with *Le*

Rhin allemand. It reminded the Germans (and fellow Frenchmen) that during the French Revolution Prince Louis-Joseph de Condé had formed a great army (known as Condé's Army) on the banks of the Rhine. The poem commences

> Nous l'avons eu votre Rhin allemand,
> Il a tenu dans notre verre.
> Un couplet qu'on s'en va chantant
> Efface t'il la trace altière
> Du pied de nos chevaux marqué dans votre sang?
>
> Nous l'avons eu votre Rhin allemand.
> Son sein porte une plaie ouverte,
> Du jour ou Condé triomphant
> A déchiré sa robe verte.
> Où le père à passé, passera bien l'enfant,

(It has been ours, your German Rhine! It has remained in our glass. Does a verse that one goes off singing erase the proud trace of our horses' hooves marked in your blood?

It has been ours, your German Rhine. Its breast bears an open wound from the day when Condé, triumphant, tore up its green robe. Where the father has passed, there will the child pass ...)

David's was only one of many settings of this poem, but it was one of the most popular selling 150000 copies,[8] and, as we shall see in the Postscript to this study, it received a new lease of life during the Franco-Prussian War.

1843 found Félicien David 'the delight of all the salons'[9] and a review of two of David's songs for bass voice suggested that if the composer were to persevere on the road he had chosen there would be no doubting his eventual success.[10] One of those songs – *Le jour des morts* to a poem by Lamartine – has been described by the late Frits Noske as 'one of the remarkable French songs of the Romantic era'.[11] It is one of his few 'grand' songs, for most of them are in the unpretentious style of the romance.

David's eventual success was not long in coming. On 8 December the following year his symphonic ode *Le désert* was performed, drawing from Berlioz a rave review which turned the composer overnight into a celebrity. Scored for choir, narrator and orchestra, *Le désert* deserves to be far better known today than it is, for it is a remarkably beautiful and evocative work.[12] An Arabian melody, transcribed by the composer, which in *Le désert* becomes 'Hymne à la nuit', was so keenly appreciated that David brought it out as a solo song in its own right, although as such its 'oriental' nature is certainly dampened by the greyness of the piano accompaniment in comparison with the radiant colours of the orchestral one. As a song for voice and piano it was published in three different versions and under three different titles: *Le soir*, *Le batalier du Nil*, and *Rêverie orientale*, the last named also bearing a different text, as the somewhat sensual nature of the original was deemed to be unsuitable for 'young people'. The opening of the original text is, however, reproduced in our extract from the song.

The immense success achieved by David with *Le désert* prompted Parisian music lovers to look forward to more of the same. He obliged with two more symphonic odes: *Moise au Sinaï* (1846) and *Christoph Colombe* (1847), but neither of these seemed to meet all their expectations. His most successful dramatic work was his opéra-comique *Lalla-Roukh* (1862), based upon

Example 7.2   *Le soir* (David)

(My lovely night, oh! tarry longer! Yes, you make me love and live; oh night, whilst my voice sings, my beloved is drunk with love.)

Thomas Moore's tales of the same name. We have already seen how translation of Moore's *Irish Melodies* stimulated some of Berlioz's earliest songs and choral works, and it was only natural that Moore's 'oriental romance' (comprising four Indian-inspired narrative poems with a connecting tale in prose) should have attracted David.

Song writing occupied David throughout his career. Those depicting oriental scenes are perhaps a little too 'europeanized' to seem very striking today, and many of the other songs tread predictable paths of harmony and melodic turns of phrase. There is undoubted truth in the reproach made in his own day for his 'sitting indifferently in the shade of the green palm trees of the Nile, of the pagodas of India or of the banana plantations of South America, and yet always singing the same tone.'[13] Nevertheless, his songs are undeniably attractive and deserve to be better known than they are today. In his day the composer enjoyed the prestige of success, and was elected to the French Academy in 1869, filling the chair of the man to whom he owed so much – Hector Berlioz.

Contemporary with Reber and David (as well as with Berlioz and Monpou) was Auguste Morel (1809–1881). Born in Marseille where he lived until he was 25 his father having envisaged (like so many other fathers of budding composers discussed in this study) a commercial career for his son. During those years in Marseille he set about studying the scores of chamber music by Haydn, Mozart and Beethoven, and then the pedagogic works of the composer/teacher Reicha. In 1836, with his eye on the Paris Conservatoire he left Marseille not realizing that at 25 he was just beyond the age of admission. Nevertheless, he was encouraged to continue his career.

Like Berlioz, Morel turned to the writing of musical criticism to gain an income, his fellow writers on *Le Monde musical* seeing to it that their young colleague also gained good press as a composer. Thus from 1841 we begin to hear of Morel's success in the salons with his first songs, including *Il est dans les étoiles*, which, because of its serious nature was inevitably compared with Schubert's songs.[14] By 1845 his songs seem to have become permanent fixtures in the salons, *Le fils de Corse* regarded as one of the greatest successes of that year's season (together with songs by Quidant, Boieldieu and Massé). They were taken up by some of the leading singers of the day, particularly by Wartel, who on various European tours included songs by Morel, Berlioz and Monpou. The tenor Alexis Dupont was another fine singer who made Morel's name known in Germany. In addition to his songs his output included chamber music, symphonic and religious works and an opera.

Invited in 1850 to become the Director of the Conservatoire in his hometown of Marseille Morel sought to build this up along the lines of the Paris Conservatoire. Unfortunately, in 1873 the municipal council decided to downgrade the institution where he had laboured for some 20 years, and he returned to Paris. During his lifetime his achievements were recognized by the award of the Legion of Honour in 1860, while the Académie des Beaux-Arts twice awarded him the Chartier Prize for composition. In 1863 the Music Section of the Union des arts in Marseille opened a subscription to cover the costs of publishing his chamber music. His songs are unknown today, so we reproduce the opening of *L'invocation* to words by Lamartine, which both Wartel and Dupont included on their tours outside France. Its sentimental nature, simplicity, sweet lyricism and harmonic warmth places *L'invocation* on the borders between romance and mélodie.

Reber, Morel and David all helped to take the romance to a serious level, but they are hardly household names today. Their younger contemporary Charles Gounod (1818–1893), however, so dominated French music throughout the nineteenth century that it is hard to believe that he was also one of the first generation of composers to help develop the romance into mélodie. His first songs were composed when he was at the Villa Medici following the award of the Prix de Rome which he won in 1839. He recalled his time there:

> My favourite distraction was reading *Faust* by Goethe, admittedly in French, for I knew not a word of German; I read, on the other hand, and with great pleasure, the poems of Lamartine. Before worrying about sending my first consignment of compositions from Rome, for which I had much time ahead of me, I was busy writing several songs amongst which were *Le vallon* as well as *Le soir*, the music of which would be adapted for the crowd scene in the first act of my opera *Sapho*, to the beautiful words of my friend and celebrated collaborator Emile Augier ... I wrote both within several days of each other and almost at the time of my arrival at the Villa Medici.[15]

Two other songs come from this early period, *La chanson du pêcheur* and *Venise*, but exposure to the music of Palestrina while at Rome seemed, amongst other influences, to have drawn him away from romantic literature and music. His new absorption in sacred music and religious contemplation sits oddly with the picture of him left by Fanny Mendelssohn who, after visiting him at the Villa Medici, described the young Gounod as 'passionate and romantic to excess'.[16]

On his return to Paris he took up studies in theology and became organist and director of music at the Eglise des Missions étrangères in rue Vaneau, where, to the amazement of his friends and those who had predicted a brilliant musical future for him, he remained for five years. His return to the 'world' (without taking holy orders) coincided with the 1848 Revolution and Pauline Viardot's début at the Paris Opéra in Meyerbeer's *Le prophète*. She had known Gounod in his days in Rome when she had visited him at the Villa Medici with Fanny Mendelssohn, and no doubt had looked forward like

Example 7.3 *L'invocation* (Morel)

(O you who appeared before me in this desert of the world, Heaven-dweller, staying but a short while in these places, a ray of love in my eyes.)

everyone else to his spectacular career on his return to France. Her own now opening up, she invited him to write an opera for her. The result was not only *Sapho*, but a release of creative energy that led to twelve operas including two of the most deservedly popular operas of the century: *Faust* and *Roméo et Juliette*.

Gounod wrote nearly 200 songs, some of which were to English texts, and some he transcribed for piano solo. He himself was something of a singer – although he later lamented that forcing his voice in adolescence had spoilt its potential – and this is evident in all his vocal writing in its gratefulness to the voice. It is true that amongst his songs are those in which his extraordinary facility too often tempted the trivial and his religiosity the sentimental. But there are other wonderful songs so embedded in romantic repertoire that it would be difficult to imagine the nineteenth century without them. With Gounod arrives a repertoire of romantic French song that celebrated singers began to include in their programmes alongside the lieder of Schubert and Schumann; no longer the encore piece or the light-weight song for the salon as the romance had been, the mélodies of Gounod gave new-found status to French solo song.

Another towering figure in French music who also contributed to the early repertoire of mélodie was Giacomo Meyerbeer (1791–1864) who was, of course, far senior in years to almost all other composers featured in this book. His French songs began appearing during the 1830s and 1840s. Meyerbeer had come to Paris in 1825, conquering it with his *Robert le diable* in 1831 – by which time he was almost forty.

It is sometimes forgotten that Meyerbeer commenced his career as a concert pianist, a background often reflected in the brilliant accompaniments to some of his 52 songs. His subsequent operatic career is equally reflected in vocal lines of these songs, which make far more demands on the singer that any other French songs of this period. Inevitably, some have the feel of opera about them – especially *Le moine* and *Rachel à Nephtali*, but many are more intimate in style, sensitive to their texts, and fitting happily into the category of solo song rather than aria. His *Le poète mourant* – analysed and highly admired by Berlioz[17] – was dedicated to Nourrit who performed it with Liszt at the piano when they gave a concert in aid of impoverished, unemployed workers at Lyon in 1837,[18] where, it will be recalled, they also sang a programme of songs by Schubert. Amongst his most deservedly popular songs was *Chanson de mai* which, sung many times by Wartel and other singers in the salons and elsewhere, is indeed a deliciously witty example of his gifts as a songwriter.

Lightheartedness and wit were not dominant features of romanticism and French songwriting of the period was no exception. One composer, however,

Example 7.4 *La cuisine du château* (Nadaud)

(From before dawn everywhere they're bustling and scurrying, moving around lightly; the door opens and closes to take in eggs from the farm and herbs from the garden. In the iron pot the stew or soup bubbles away all day.)

whose songs delighted the salons by their essentially good humour was Gustave Nadaud (1820–1893) who, significantly, called his songs chansons and, as a result, was sometimes affectionately known as the 'Paris chansonnier', not least because he was both singer and composer and welcomed everywhere on both counts. His chansons, which so often concluded a salon recital, included some of a sentimental nature, although the majority, like *La cuisine du château*, are light hearted (Example 7.4).

A composer whom we might associate with a later generation is Louis Lacombe (1818–1884) whose songs did not start appearing until the second half of the century. When they did they had all the hallmarks of romantic French song in its mature stage; yet he was born in the same year as Gounod. As a child prodigy who had won the Conservatoire's 1st Prize in piano at the age of eight, Louis Lacombe matured into a musician of stature in France as pianist, composer and writer. In February 1869 he took the unusual step of offering three recitals at the Salle Erard devoted to his own music: mainly his songs, but also some chamber music performed by the Armingaud String Quartet. By the time his songs were published the term 'mélodie' had largely supplanted 'lied' for songs in a more 'serious' style, but not so in Lacombe's songs, and they were welcomed by those who looked for greater originality and sophistication than was offered by the songs in the traditional romance style. Although the music of Schumann was not widely performed in Paris at that time, some reviewers detected the influence of that composer in some of Lacombe's 'lieder'. They were certainly regarded as being out of the usual run, one critic writing. 'An austere thinker and musician, Louis Lacombe allows no compromise with the audience; he gives it his impressions such as he felt them, in all their honesty and integrity, without futile ornaments, scornful of rendering them more pleasant by clothing them in a weft of gold or silk; and it is on this account that we consider him a serious composer to be reckoned with.'[19] They range in expression from gentle, lyrical songs such as *Nuits de juin* and *L'attente*, to powerful utterances such as his setting of Hugo's bitter and violent poem *La ville prise* in which the cruel destruction of an ancient city by soldiers is graphically described. As in Example 7.5, the accompaniments betoken the pianist-composer (in this case including directions for pedalling) supporting a vocal line set out with details of expression and rhythmic nuance. Most striking is the harmonic intensity, powerfully revealed in the concluding bars of the song (shown here) where the E♭ major tonality is abruptly and passionately dislocated by the minor version at the words 'Que mon sort est amer', which run like an idée fixe throughout the song. Even more striking are the two occasions when the tonalities of E♭ major and E♭ minor (the latter being the prevailing tonality) collide with the simultaneous use of G natural and G♭.

Example 7.5   *Lamento – La chanson du pêcheur* (Lacombe): (a) closing bars; (b) bars 7–8

Example 7.5   concluded

(My lovely friend is dead: I will weep forever; into her tomb she has carried
away my soul and my love.)

Both Wagner and Liszt composed songs to French words, mostly to texts
by the early French romantics, including Hugo, Dumas and Béranger.
Comprising only a handful (thirteen by Liszt, six by Wagner) they were
published during the 1840s, but not in France where they seem to have either
been unknown or ignored by French singers, who, in any case may have been
discouraged by their difficulty, lacking as they often do, that suave lyrical flow
which is a hallmark of romantic French song, a quality that French composers
up to and including Debussy were to preserve.

Notes

1. 'En musique comme en politique, le plus grand courage aujourd'hui, c'est d'oser
    avoir du bon sens, du calme, de la modération, de la logique.', *RGM*, 29
    December, 1839. An editorial note reads: 'Les idées qui sont exposées dans cet
    article concernant l'école moderne sont peu conformes à celles du directeur et
    principaux rédacteurs de la *Gazette musicale*; mais nous craindrions de dévier de
    la ligne d'impartialité dans laquelle nous marchons, si nous refusions d'admettre
    les opinions consciencieuses comme celle de notre collaborateur M Guéroult.'
2. Dieudonné Denne-Baron also expresses this point in an article about the
    composer in *M*, 14 September, 1862.
3. '... il nous semble qu'il s'y trouve toujours quelque chose de raide et empesé, un
    certain sentiment de sévère ascétique, qui la déparent un peu.' *MM*, 28 May,
    1846.
4. Les mélodies de Reber pour chant avec accompagnement de piano sont d'une
    grande distinction. Remarquables par le charme et la simplicité mélodiques, elles
    le sont encore par le respect de la prosodie et par cette particularité curieuse que
    les ornements du chant, souvent considérés comme incompatibles avec un style
    châtié n'en sont point bannis. Reber ne proscrivait de ses chants ni les trilles, ni

les gammes, ni les arpèges, et ces gracieuses arabesques accompagnent volontiers les lignes de son architecture; arabesques d'un goût très pur, cela va sans dire, et n'ayant rien de commun avec les gargouillades de l'ancienne école italienne.' Camille Saint-Saëns, *Harmonie et mélodie* (1885), 289.

5.   *RGM*, 6 June, 1847.
6.   For a study of Félicien David's association with the organisation see Ralph P. Locke, *Music, Musicians and the Saint-Simonians* (1986).
7.   *RGM*, 29 March, 1840.
8.   *RGM*, 23 January, 1842.
9.   *MM*, 28 December, 1843.
10. *RGM*, 19 March, 1843.
11. Fritz Noske, *French Song from Berlioz to Duparc*, trans. Rita Benson, 2nd edition (1970), 149.
12. For an interesting background to David's career and especially his period in the Middle East see P. Gradenwitz: 'Félicien David (1810–1876) and French Romantic Orientalism', *Musical Quarterly*, lxii (1976), 471–506.
13. Quoted (and rebutted) in the tribute to Félicien David read to the French Academy by Ernest Reyer on the composer's death.
14. *MM*, 1841, issue 18 (no month given).
15. 'Ma distraction favorite était la lecture de *Faust* de Goethe, en français, bien entendu, car je ne savais pas un mot d'allemand; je lisais, en outre, et avec grand plaisir, les poésies de Lamartine; avant de songer à mon premier envoi de Rome, pour lequel j'avais de temps devant moi, je m'étais occupé à écrire plusieurs mélodies au nombre desquelles se trouvaient *le Vallon* ainsi que *le Soir*, dont la musique devait être, dix ans plus tard, adaptée à la scène de concours du premier acte de mon opéra, *Sapho*, sur les beaux vers de mon ami et illustre collaborateur Émile Augier … Je les écrivis toutes deux à peu de jours de distance et presque dès mon arrivée à la Villa Médicis.' Charles Gounod, *Mémoires d'un artiste* (1896), 84–5.
16. 'Gounod passionné et romantique à l'excès', quoted in Hugues Imbert, *Nouveaux profils de musiciens* (1892), 118.
17. *RGM*, 4 February, 1838.
18. *RGM*, 6 August, 1837.
19. 'Penseur et musicien austère, Louis Lacombe n'admet pas de transactions avec le public; il lui livre ses impressions telles qu'il les a ressenties, dans toute leur loyauté et leur intégrité, sans futiles ornements, dédaignant pour les rendre plus aimables de les revêtir d'une trame d'or ou de soie; et c'est à ce titre même que nous le considérons comme un compositeur sérieux avec lequel on doit compter.' *M*, 13 March, 1870.

CHAPTER EIGHT

Reaching out to Full Bloom

Of the composers mentioned so far in the history of romance and mélodie probably only Berlioz, Meyerbeer and Gounod are well-known names. Most of those discussed in the present chapter – all born in the third decade of the nineteenth century or later – will be more familiar to singers and music lovers, but there are some whose names, once on many lips, have regrettably slipped into oblivion. More's the pity, for a number of them produced some fine songs. Victor Massé is such a composer.

Born in Brittany, Victor Massé (1822–1884) was one whose success seemed assured following a brilliant record as a student at the Paris Conservatoire which he entered at the age of twelve and from which he graduated with first prizes in accompaniment, piano, harmony, counterpoint and fugue, gaining the coveted Prix de Rome in 1844. Even before he had set out for the Villa Medici for his two years residency there he had published three songs: *Te voir*, *Le muletier de Calabre*, and *Chante Madeleine*, the last two being sung so frequently in the salons that they were regarded, together with Morel's *Le fils de Corse*, as among the greatest successes of the 1845 season. In addition, his cantata submitted for the Prix de Rome was performed three times that year at the Opéra.

Returning from Rome, by way of Germany, Victor Massé settled back in Paris to attempt a career, publishing a collection of songs in 1849 called *Chants d'autrefois* using texts from Renaissance poets. The musical language, however, was of his own time, and they fail to live up to the title which suggests that the songs might evoke something of the style of earlier times. Nor, unfortunately, do they exert much musical personality. However, it was not this that a critic complained of, but the texts themselves. It was difficult enough, he said, to understand what singers were singing about at the the best of times, but when they had to sing songs to texts from the period of the Renaissance – full of obsolete words, latinisms, inversions and so on – it was impossible for the listener to follow them, suggesting that this gifted young composer had done such a bizarre thing merely to draw attention to himself.[1] Far from following the critic's advice to set poetry of a more conventional

119

kind, Massé chose for his next collection of songs folk-like poetry, incorporating scenes and tales from his beloved Brittany and incorporating words and phrases peculiar to its culture.

Some of the texts for *Chants bretons* were anonymous, some were by Michel-Florentin Carré, but most were by Auguste Brizeux, a poet inspired by the landscape and lore of his native Brittany. Brizeux published a number of collections of folk-like poetry including *Marie*, *La fleur d'or* and *Histoires poétiques*, all of which provided Massé with his texts – although the composer seemed to have had no hesitation in altering some of the poet's lines. In fact, the language employed in these poems is not that of Brittany. Certainly there are Breton words sprinkled through it and we meet folk-types like the young peasant Loïc, but there it ends, prompting one literary critic of the day to declare that this poetry was too Breton for the Parisians and too parisian for the Bretons.[2] Massé's settings cast aside musical sophistication and catch, if not the stylistic inflections of folk music, an engaging simplicity completely at one with the words.

Naturally, Massé sought (and found) early success as an opera composer, mostly in the genre of opéra comique of which *Les noces de Jeannette* (1850) and *Galatée* (1852) were the most popular of his twenty-three stage works – not all of which, however, were performed. Saint-Saëns felt that Massé's remarkable facility led him to write too quickly – a charge that would also later be laid at both Gounod and Massenet – but of his songs Saint-Saëns believed that they showed 'a penetrating sentiment, a striking colour, a prodigious vitality and irresistible charm.'[3] He wrote 119 of them, his later ones published in 1874 (which were probably composed earlier, their appearance delayed by the Franco-Prussian War and the Commune which followed it), undoubtedly being the finest. His setting of Musset's *Adieux à Suzon* (Example 8.1) and of Hugo's *Dieu qui sourit et qui donne* are amongst the best of the many songs inspired by these two delightful poems. The performance directions at the head of the former might be said to characterize French romantic song as a whole: *passioné, con eleganza*.

Another composer whose once formidable reputation has been largely washed away by time and fashion was Ernest Reyer (1823–1921). Unlike Massé, his early studies were not crowned with glittering prizes – in fact, what musical studies he might have had as a boy at Marseille, near where he was born, were interrupted when he was sent at the age of 16 by his father to work in business with an uncle in Algeria where he kept up his music as best as he could (a depressingly familiar story). When the Revolution of 1848 broke out the electrifying event seemed to spark Reyer's decision to study in Paris. Like his fellow Marseillais Auguste Morel, who two years earlier had tried to enrol at the Paris Conservatoire, Reyer was at 25 too old to be accepted as a student

Example 8.1   *Adieux à Suzon* (Massé)

(Adieu, Suzon, my blonde rose, who have loved for a week; the shortest
pleasures of this world often make the best loves. Do I know as I leave you,
where my wandering star is leading me? Yet I go away, my little one, very far,
very fast, ever on the run.)

there, but he had the great good fortune to have an aunt who was on the staff. Louise Ferrenc, a highly esteemed composer of symphonies and chamber music, had studied piano with Moscheles and Hummel and composition with Reicha, and under her guidance Reyer began to make up for the deficiencies of his late start. Revealing a gift for quite powerful dramatic expression, Reyer's most obvious outlet was opera. But it was also the most difficult genre to break into, and Reyer had little experience in handling large-scale works.

His first published song appeared even before his arrival in Paris; *Romance-bolero* was a setting of words by Alexander Dumas (the son), and was dedicated to the singer Mlle Sabatier. *Le Monde musical* prophesied popular success for it,[4] but Reyer's songs did not seem to do the rounds of the salons – or, at least, were not often reported upon, even though he was a well-known figure in the Parisian artistic and literary scene, particularly the latter. One of his closest friends was the poet Théophile Gautier (whom he staunchly defended from the charge of being 'unmusical'),[5] and Reyer himself established a good reputation as a writer and critic. Perhaps it was his literary involvement that sapped his energies for musical composition for a time, but, whatever the reason, he seems to have gone through a very fallow period during the late 1860s and early 1870s, alarming his friends. To galvanize him into activity the conductor Pasdeloup encouraged Reyer to take up songwriting again, resulting in *La Madeleine au désert* (1874). It seems to have set off Reyer's creative urge once again, for the following years saw the production of his two most important works: the operas *Sigurd* (1884), based on a French translation of the *Nibelungenlied,* and *Salammbô* (1890) based on Flaubert's novel of ancient Carthage. These drew from him music of considerable originality for the time. Indeed, Lalo was to say of him that Reyer was 'amongst the rare number of composers who have a horror of formulae, of practices which bring easy success'.[6] It is not at all unexpected, then, that Reyer thought highly of both Berlioz and Wagner and championed their cause in France through his writings in leading musical and literary periodicals, including the *Journal des débats*, to which Berlioz had been attached. His thirty-one songs were composed mainly during the 1850s and 1860s. Some are marked by fashionable 'orientalism' – such as *Pantoum*, described as a 'chanson indienne' and *Le goum* (to words by Gautier) – but they are not his best songs. More characteristic of his style is *Les gouttes de pluie* (Drops of Rain), which despite its sentimental text rises to eloquent musical expression.

Exactly contemporary with Reyer was Edouard Lalo (1823–1892). A man whose desire to protect his privacy was such that he refused even to disclose the date and place of his birth to Arthur Pougin, then preparing the supplementary volumes to Fétis' great *Biographie universelle des musiciens,* some of the details of his life are still obscure. Born at Lille he studied violin at the Conservatoire there, but in the face of parental opposition to a career in music he left home at the age of 16 and entered the Conservatoire in Paris where he studied composition and violin. It was, indeed, as a string player that Lalo was best known in Paris for some years, particularly as viola player in one of the finest quartets in Paris. The Armingaud Quartet, founded in 1855 by Jules Armingaud, specialized in the classical repertoire, and provided an ambience congenial to a young musician noted for his uncompromising artistry and reserve.

His earliest published works were songs, including a collection entitled *Six chansons populaires* to words by Pierre Jean de Béranger (1780–1857) that came out in 1849. Béranger's poetry was for many people the voice of social conscience that sang its way into their hearts through the popular melodies of the day upon which his poems were based. Lalo set *La pauvre femme*, *Beaucoup d'amour*, *Le suicide*, *Si j'étais petit oiseau*, *Les petits coups*, *Le vieux vagabond*, all of which have some social message: charity to the poor (the impoverished old woman praying in front of the church as the icy wind whistles through her threadbare clothes was once a famous opera singer); love is more important than money; the pathetic case of two young men (personally known to Béranger) so disillusioned with life that they committed suicide; an old tramp who, had he been given the means to earn a livelihood would have called men 'brothers', but instead will die their enemy, and so on, including what must be the strangest drinking song of all, urging one to avoid drunkenness by drinking in small sips! Béranger's poems could be sung to a simple, popular tune (the name of which was usually given at the head of each one). The same musical simplicity lies at the heart of Lalo's settings, resulting in a sentimental romance style that one scarcely expects from the composer of *Symphonie espagnole* or his later songs. Béranger would probably have heartily approved of them.

In 1865 Lalo married Julie Bernier de Maligny, an excellent contralto singer to whom he was to dedicate many of his songs, the finest of which are his settings of six poems by Victor Hugo, settings which seem, to embody those qualities that we have come to associate with French song at its best – a limpid flow of melody, a beautifully conceived accompaniment sufficient to support the vocal line without obtruding on it, a passionate expression that borders on the sentimental, yet escapes it (Example 8.2).

Of composers born in the next decade of the century, i.e. the 1830s, the names of Camille Saint-Saëns (1835–1921) and Georges Bizet (1838–1875) need no introduction. A child prodigy who before the age of eight had studied piano, organ and composition, Saint-Saëns became a towering figure in French music as composer, pianist, organist, conductor and writer.[7] Song

Example 8.2   *L'aube naît* (Lalo)

(Dawn wakes and your door is closed; my lovely one, why are you sleeping? At the hour when the rose stirs, are you not going to wake up? O my charming one, listen to me, the lover who sings and also weeps.)

writing occupied him throughout his long career and he produced over a hundred of them. His very youthful songs are simple romances, but from the age of about twenty he began to produce works that are amongst the finest in the French romantic repertoire. One of the earliest of these was *La cloche*. Hugo's poem, which likens the poet's soul to a solitary bell in the vault of its tower, is embraced by a rich sonority set in motion by the rolling resonance of the accompaniment, both voice and piano reaching a magnificent climax in this truly great song. Another poem by Hugo inspired Saint-Saëns' creative spark in a fascinating way. Each line of *Extase* (Ecstasy) begins with the word 'Puisque', which the composer matches by beginning each musical phrase with the same note in the bass of the accompaniment. Yet the flow of harmonies is seemingly uninhibited by the constraints imposed by this bass-note repetition, Saint-Saëns exploring the very boundaries of harmonic possibilities to produce a rich variety of chordal progessions – while not forgetting, of course, the singer! Other works show flashes of the future, *L'attente*, for example, foreshadowing by twenty years the opening of Duparc's *L'invitation au voyage*.

It seems extraordinary that for all his brilliance and precocity Saint-Saëns had failed to achieve the Prix de Rome while at the Conservatoire. Not so, Georges Bizet, who after a brilliant record as a student, gained it in 1857. Like Victor Massé before him, Bizet enjoyed a degree of public atttention as a composer before leaving for the Villa Medici, having entered a competition organized by Offenbach to set the libretto of an opéra comique called *Le Docteur Miracle*, the prize being a performance of the work at the Bouffes-Parisiennes. Seventy-eight composers entered, two were declared equal winners: Charles Lecocq and Georges Bizet. Neither of the two operas gained much attention, but at least Bizet, aged nineteen, was now not an unknown name.

Prodigious gifts as a pianist together with an ability to sight-read the most complex orchestral scores at the instrument led to Bizet's engagement with various publishers who wanted someone to play through the many manuscripts submitted to them, as well as to make piano transcriptions of orchestral and operatic works. He was also in great demand in the salons as a solo pianist, making a considerable reputation for his performances of Chopin. It was in the salons that his songs also began to be heard for the first time.

It was perhaps only natural that Bizet should have been drawn towards writing songs early in his career, for his father was a well-known singing-teacher whose understanding of vocal technique was clearly passed on to his son, all of whose songs are most sensitively written for the voice. They range from simple, rather sentimental romances to powerful utterances such as *L'esprit saint*, while *Adieu de l'hôtesse arabe* strongly foreshadows the

Example 8.3   (a) Opening of *L'Attente* (Saint-Saëns); (b) Opening of
L'Invitation au voyage (Duparc)

(a)
Opening of L'Attente (Saint-Saëns)

(b)
Opening of L'Invitation au voyage (Duparc)

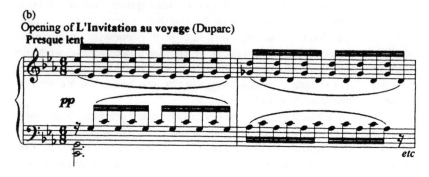

brooding sensuality of *Carmen*. His collection published in 1867 entitled
Fueilles d'album contains some of his loveliest songs.

   Two of Bizet's songs – *La rose et l'abeille* and *Petite Marguerite*, published
when he was only sixteen, were originally composed to texts by Olivier
Rolland, but some years later were re-arranged, re-named and re-published
with different texts provided by a minor writer whose poetry, however,
became popular with a number of composers: Armand Silvestre (1837–1901).
Born in Toulouse, most of his life was spent in the whirl of Parisian literary
and musical life. A prolific writer of poetry, short stories, stage works and
libretti (including Saint-Saëns' *Henri VIII*) which he always wrote in
collaboration with other writers, Silvestre became associated with that group
of poets called the Parnassians. Named after the journal to which many of
these poets contributed – *Le parnasse contemporain* which appeared in 1866
– this group, led by Leconte de Lisle, reacted against the excesses of the highly
personal and emotional style of romanticism, rejecting, as well, the technical
liberties taken by Hugo and his school, and set about writing poetry that was
restrained, objective and impeccable in form. They also subscribed to the
concept of 'art for art's sake', rejecting any 'social' role that literature might
be seen to have. Not surprisingly, the symbolist poets of the 1880s –

Baudelaire, Mallarmé, Verlaine and Rimbaud – were influenced by it. Silvestre was, however, only a minor figure in this movement, writing in a variety of styles that suited the need of the moment. Amongst the composers who were friends of the writer and who were attracted to his poetry were Massenet and Castillon.

Jules Massenet (1842–1912) was a naturally endowed musician whose gifts were nurtured from an early age by his mother. In 1847 financial problems caused the family to move to Paris from an industrial town near Lyon (where his father had worked as a master founder), the boy being good enough to have lessons at the Conservatoire, progressing through its courses eventually to win the Prix de Rome. His teachers had included Reber and Ambroise Thomas with whom he studied composition. During the later years of his period at the Conservatoire he earned money by playing percussion and piano in cabaret and pit orchestras, but the award of the Prix de Rome with its generous student stipend and fully-financed sojourn at the Villa Medici put material problems behind him for a while. Unlike Berlioz and even Gounod before him, Massenet worked unflaggingly while in Italy – a habit that never left him and which partly explains his enormous output. After his return to Paris in 1866 he married Louise Constance de Gressy, who like Clara Schumann, inspired in her husband an outpouring of song. Friendship with two others also encouraged his songwriting. The first was Armande Silvestre and the second was George Hartmann. The latter had just opened his publishing house in Paris, which for ten years was instrumental in assisting the work of new French composers, Massenet being one of his earliest. As both publisher and entrepreneur, Hartmann worked hard for the cause of French music, but his business foundered and bankruptcy led to it being taken over by Heugel. It was Hartmann who published Massenet's first songs which included two song cycles *Poème d'avril* (April Poem, 1866) and *Poème du souvenir* (Poem of Remembrance, 1867), the latter containing one of Massenet's most deeply-felt and eloquent songs. Thirty-five of them come from the four-year period leading up to the Franco-Prussian War, and – not surprisingly given the composer's youthful age at this time – they owe a debt to Gounod and others who were bringing French romantic song to its maturity at this time. This is seen perhaps at its most enchanting form in the song *A Mignonne* where the styles of romance and mélodie are so entwined as to render definition meaningless (Example 8.4).

Six songs may seem a very slender thread to tie Alexis de Castillon (1838–1873) to significant developments in French romantic song, even more so considering that his name is hardly known even to French singers, let alone those outside the country. Yet his settings of six of Armande Silvestre's poems are not only indebted to the romantic past, but look ahead to those

Example 8.4 *A Mignonne* (Massenet)

(For whom will be, Mignonne, the undulating crown of your chestnut hair? For
whom your smile, your eyes wherein I read with pleasure, your tiny mischievous
feet?)

developments in French song which are beyond the scope of this study.

His total output, including chamber music and orchestral works, as well as
his six songs, is small not only because of his tragically short life (he died at
the age of 35), but also because he destroyed all his early works. He came from
an aristocratic family and followed its military tradition by enrolling at the

famous Academy of Saint-Cyr near Versailles becoming a member of the
Imperial Guard, from which he resigned at the age of 24 to devote himself to
music. He studied first with Victor Massé and then with César Franck, forming
a close friendship with Saint-Saëns and Duparc amongst others. The outbreak
of war in 1870 demanded his services as an officer in the army, and after it,
with the creation of the Société Nationale de Musique by Saint-Saëns, with
which Castillon was closely associated, some of his music was performed:
Cinq pièces dans le style ancien for piano solo in 1871, and his Piano Concerto
the following year, conducted by Pasdeloup with Saint-Saëns as soloist. Its
forward-looking style puzzled the audience and it was not well received. On
his untimely death Saint-Saëns declared that Alexis de Castillon had
represented some of the best hopes for the future of French music.[8]

Castillon's *Six poésies d'Armand Silvestre* is a collection of songs rather
than a song cycle and not conceived with one type of voice in mind,
comprising as it does songs for mezzo-soprano/baritone, contralto/baritone
and for tenor. That they are somewhat uneven in style may have been because
the first two, *Le bûcher* and *Le semeur* were written earlier than the other four
and published by Hartmann in 1869. A maturing of Castillon's style and
technique (and perhaps the effect of the war on the composer) is evident in the
later ones, which includes the masterpiece of the collection, *Renouveau*
(Example 8.5). Issued as a collection of six by Heugel (who had taken over
Hartmann's firm in 1891) the publication is undated but it probably appeared
in 1892, eleven years after the composer's death.[9]

As the postlude to *Renouveau* so clearly shows, Castillon was deeply
influenced by Schumann, a composer championed by Castillon's close friend
Saint-Saëns, but whose music met with a degree of hostility in France for
many years. It began to be heard from the 1850s onwards mainly through
organizations such as the Société allemande and Société Schumann founded
by the composer and pianist Delahaye in 1869. Pasdeloup sometimes included
Schumann's works in his orchestral concerts and Saint-Saëns played his piano
music from time to time. Nevertheless, the widespread cultivation of
Schumann's music had to wait until after the Franco-Prussian War.

Despite its debt to Schumann – especially in the postlude (not reproduced
in Example 8.5) – *Renouveau* nevertheless sounded an individual note in
romantic French song from which it sprang, while also catching something of
those qualities of sensuous beauty, tenderness and regret, of mystery tinged
with sadness, of enchantment and passionate longing that marked French song
in the later years of the century in the hands of Duparc, Fauré and Debussy.
Yet the early songs of these three composers owe everything to the romantic
tradition – even to the simple romance with which they all began. The songs
of Gabriel Fauré (1845–1924) commenced in 1861 with a romance-like setting

Example 8.5 *Renouveau* (Castillon)

(Soft awakening of the woods and fields, of variegated gold and of purple, sweet
forgetfulness of gloomy days. Welcome, Spring, father of Roses.)

of Hugo's poem *Le papillon et la fleur* (set by a number of composers, including Reber), but the early songs give only a hint of the individuality to come, this fully revealed only from the 1880s onwards. Of the thirteen songs upon which rest the reputation of Henri Duparc (1848–1933) four were published before 1870 and include two romances (*Chanson triste* and *Soupir*). All of Debussy's songs come from after the period covered by this book, but the earliest of them (such as *Beau soir* and *Fleur des blés*) are steeped in the romance style. Yet even though in his mature songs the once simple lines of melody are blended with richly suggestive harmonies and often so sensitively moulded to each nuance of the text that one might gain the impression of recitative, through its suave contours the lyrical impulse is unmistakably linked to the romantic tradition of romance and mélodie.

No attempt at a roll-call of those who contributed to the large repertoire of romantic French song has been offered in this book. It would have to include César Franck, Delibes, Chausson, Weckerlin and others who contributed excellent songs to the repertoire without changing the course of its development – except perhaps for Chabrier whose piquant songs like *Villanelle des petits canards* look ahead to the satirical works of the next generation. As well as these composers of stature, of course, it would have to include a much greater number of mediocre composers who flooded the salons with their uninspired romances to the despair of fine musicians and reviewers. Their many names are inscribed in the catalogues and the columns of the music journals of the period, and there they should remain. Inevitably then, the more significant repertoire – that which might have a chance of survival were it better known – was a mere trickle.

It is usual to associate the Second Empire with a taste for luxury and opulence, ephemeral pleasures and gaiety, and this cannot be denied. But it was also the period in which education, medicine and science were revolutionized, not least by the towering figure of Louis Pasteur. In music it was certainly the period of Offenbach and the Bouffes-Parisiens. Yet at the same time there was much orchestral music of fine quality to be found in Paris for those who wanted it and chamber music flourished as never before. Certainly, there had been fine artists such as Urhan and Baillot who had given Parisians a taste of this kind of music at the beginning of our period, but it was towards the end of it when it truly burgeoned. The Armingaud Quartet (Jules Armingaud, Edouard Lalo, Mas and Léon Jacquard) was established in 1855 and in the fifteen years that remained before the Franco-Prussian War there also emerged the Société de musique de chambre, Société de quatuors (devoted exclusively to Beethoven), Société populaire de musique de chambre, Société de quatuors français, Société de trios anciens et modernes, and Société Schumann (mainly for that composer's chamber music). The many reviews of their recitals, together with those given by musicians not belonging to those established chamber music organizations, reflect an ever-widening circle of serious music lovers in Paris. There can be little doubt that the enthusiasm shown for music in France during the nineteenth century was driven by the momentum it had gained during the reign of Louis-Philippe, in no small part due to the revival of the salon tradition and through the pages of the many musical journals which rode on the back of this enthusiasm. It is not surprising that much of what was performed was from vocal repertoire, for not only did this lend itself to amateur performance, but a preference for combining music with words has had a long history in France. Given the rise of romantic poetry there it was inevitable that songwriting would flourish, especially with a ready audience to hear the latest romance in the salons. The combination of salons, singers and songs was indeed a fruitful union.

Notes

1. 'Nos chanteurs, si clairement qu'ils prononcent, ont assez de peine déjà à rendre avec netteté la langue contemporaine, sans aller compliquer encore la difficulté par l'adjonction d'un dialecte surchargé de mots hors d'usage, d'inversions, de latinismes et trés-peu familiers à l'immense majorité des auditeurs.' *RGM*, 1 July, 1849.
2. Talvart and Place, *Bibliographie des auteurs modernes de la langue français* (Paris, 1801–), entry on Brizeux.
3. '... un sentiment pénétrant, une couleur éclatante, une vitalité prodigieuse, un charme irrésistible.' Camille Saint-Saëns, *Portraits et souvenirs* (1899), 139.
4. *MM*, 25 April, 1847.
5. Ernest Reyer, *Notes de musique* (1875), 412.
6. 'Vous êtes du rarissime petit nombre des compositeurs qui ont horreur des formules, des procédés qui appellent facilement le succès, et quant à moi, le seul succès que j'envie, c'est l'appui des gens qui ont votre tempérament.' Letter to Reyer from Lalo, 29 October 1880, and quoted in H. de Curzon, *Ernest Reyer: sa vie et ses oeuvres* (1924), Frontispiece.
7. For a recent and comprehensive account of Saint-Saëns's life, times and music see Brian Rees, *Camille Saint-Saëns – A Life* (London, 1999).
8. Société Nationale de Musique (*Proceedings*, 1873).
9. The date is estimated from the Heugel *cotage* for this publication (no.7639).Δ

Postscript

Like a scene so brightly lit that the surrounds are obscured in shadow, the glittering world of fashionable Second Empire Paris hid in its dark edges the appalling misery of at least half the population of the city. While the initial years of Napoleon III's reign, like that of Louis-Philippe's, were marked by burgeoning prosperity, this was paid for in part by an exploited working class, that sector of society which had already fought for social justice in three revolutions, only to see prosperity remain the privilege of the bourgeoisie. Long and arduous working hours for men with pay that never seemed to reach the ever-rising cost of living, and for women an even smaller pittance, most usually for the endless needlework required for the elegant clothes of fashionable society. No wonder that so many working men turned to the opiate of alcohol, often absinthe, and so many women turned to the more profitable profession of prostitution, which at one extreme at least gave the demi-mondaine a taste of luxury, but at the other offered only a vile life on the streets and in the taverns. Even one of the greatest and most beautiful accomplishments of the Empire – Haussmann's reconstruction of Paris – hid a darker side. If Balzac's earlier description of Paris as the 'intimate alliance of splendour and squalor' was less noticeable after Haussmann's work, this was only because many of the poor, no longer able to afford the rents demanded by the acquisitive landlords of the new buildings, had to move to the outskirts of Paris – and in dangerous concentrations of disaffected and discontented workers and the unemployed. Many of these now lived at Belleville and, ironically, at what had once been the centre of the Saint-Simonian experiment in social justice – Ménilmontant. The next such experiment was far from the pacific message preached by Saint-Simon and Enfantin. It was that of Karl Marx whose *Das Kapital* appeared in 1867. These large groupings of malcontents were to be the 'danger within' during the trauma of 1870–1871. But if this was largely unperceived or ignored until too late, the danger from outside – from Germany – had been recognized with growing alarm for a few years.

The King of Prussia and his Chancellor Bismarck had visited Paris in 1867 to attend, like all crowned heads were doing, the Great Exhibition where, amongst other things, French military hardware could be compared with the latest offerings from Krupp, including an enormous cannon. The Germans had every reason to be pleased with what they saw. French political concern at the imminent power of a unified Germany rose to urgent alarm when at the beginning of July in 1870 the prospect of France being surrounded by German power became obvious, Bismark having put forward a Hohenzollern candidate to fill the vacant throne of Spain. The protest from France was so strong and so violent that the candidacy was withdrawn, yet even this did not satisfy those who felt that Germany should be taught a lesson and feel the sting of French anger. A provocative message delivered to the Prussian King by the French Ambassador insisted that a Hohenzollern candidate must never be put forward again. The refusal to comply led the French Emperor (goaded on by the Empress and various members of the government) to declare war on Germany on July 15, 1870, leading to the bloodiest and most terrible catastrophe in the history of the highly civilized, yet turbulent French capital.

Indignation at the Prussian slight whipped up a patriotic fervour that found one of its outlets in music – through a virtual explosion of performances of Musset's *Le Rhin allemande* in its many settings (see Chapter Eight). As *Le Ménestrel* was to report

> Everywhere to right and left, the *Rhin allemand* has been sung. Each theatre chose its own musician: at the Opéra, it's Delioux; at the Opéra-Comique, Félicien David; at the Vaudeville, Vaucorbeil. Why, we say with M Jules Prével, of *Le Figaro,* does no-one sing anywhere the music that Loïsa Puget has composed on the lines of Alfred de Musset? It was to Loïsa Puget that the poet gave the first look at his national song. Other musicians only got hold of it after her. Vaucorbeil was one of the first to write his, which already dates back a long time; he published it at his own expense for his friends. Then MM Félicien David, Charles Delioux and twenty others lay hold of it, for every musician writes his own *Rhin allemand*. Our former Marcel from *Les Huguenots*, M Obin, is publishing one; Faure, our valiant *Guillaume Tell*, has also improvised a new song on the lines of Musset. When we get to a hundred, we'll stop perhaps. In the provinces there is the same fervour: the *Rhin allemand* inspires every musician; at Metz and at Strasbourg our regiments are received to the cry of the Rhine; and the same applies at Bar-le-Duc, where the choral society sings morning and evening the popular tune of M Alfred Yung. In our sea ports the river celebrated by Alfred de Musset ranks before the ocean, before the Mediterranean; only *Le Rhin* is sung. From Dover one hears resonating in Calais the song by M F. Boutenjean, who has also picked up the popular note; everywhere, everywhere, the *Rhin allemand* ... We read in *Le Gaulois*: 'Roger is doing his utmost for our relief fund: the eminent artist went to Raincy to sing the *Rhin allemand* by Vaucorbeil which he had to sing three times: the audience nearly carried him aloft in triumph; as he was escaping from this enthusiasm, a carriage nearly knocked him down. The singer was struck in the side by a shaft,

winding him. Despite this accident and this fatigue, in the evening he once again sang the *Marseillaise* and the *Rhin allemand*, at the Vaudeville. Always hard at it, this Roger! It's the same *Rhin allemand* by Vaucorbeil that *Le Gaulois* published, which is going to be sung at the théâtre de Lyon'. ... Our friend Dorante, from the *Le Journal-Paris* announces that 'M Vachot, director of the théâtre de la Monnaie, in Brussels, has just engaged Roger to go and sing the *Marseillaise* and the *Rhin allemand* by Vaucorbeil in the main towns of our Northern frontiers'.[1]

On 28 July, the ageing and corpulent Emperor rode out of Paris to lead his troops into battle against a Prussian army well trained and disciplined, equipped with the latest weaponry and led by a King who was also a first-rate professional soldier and with him General Moltke, a brilliant strategist. Six weeks later at Sedan, a town near the French border with Luxembourg, the Emperor was defeated and held prisoner before being allowed to leave for exile in England. The Second Empire was over and on 4 September the Third Republic was proclaimed in Paris amidst panic and chaos.

The reaction of the Parisians and the new republican government to the news of the defeat at Sedan was to revile the Emperor and all that he stood for, and to continue the war, holding on to Paris no matter the cost. Thus it was that the German armies began fighting their way through the provinces in order to surround Paris, completing their encirclement of the city by 20 September. The siege of Paris now began.

To maintain civil order in the city the new government revived what Napoléon III had dissolved shortly after his coup d'état in 1851. This was the National Guard, which had been created at the beginning of the French Revolution, reinstated by Napoléon I, and called upon by both Louis-Philippe and Louis-Napoleon during the revolutions of 1830 and 1848. Unlike the earlier ones in which membership was restricted to those who owned property, as many citizens as possible were encouraged to join the new National Guard through the enticement of pay, small though it was at one-and-a-half francs a day. Thus into its ranks came those from different social levels and forming, not a cohesive group, but two mutually antagonistic ones: one from the middle class, the other from the working class (mainly from Belleville and Ménilmontant), both armed with weapons supplied by the army. In addition to the National Guard there was the Garde Mobile into which men of military age were called. With the addition of various forces such as the Francs-tireurs ('guerilla' fighters), and that part of the regular army which had not been sent to the front, as well as some 10000 soldiers who had escaped from the battle of Sedan – many of whom returned badly wounded – there was an estimated half-a-million defenders within the walls and some 3000 cannon.[2] With more decisive leadership the outcome of the siege might have been very different.

The city had at least the advantage of being surrounded by an ancient and largely unbroken wall thirty feet high, a moat ten feet wide and, further out, sixteen powerful forts. On this encircling band of masonry and iron, as well as cannon fire from the forts, two million inhabitants placed their hopes. The German strategy, however, was to starve them into surrender. The populace was also starved of news from the outside, for communication could only take place through pigeon-post and balloon, the latter highly dangerous for pilot and passenger, and both forms notoriously unreliable. Thus, boredom was one of the most difficult burdens for many Parisians to bear and it was here that music was able to provide some distraction. We catch a glimpse of this through a series of articles written by the musician and critic Arthur Pougin who lived through the four months of the siege and the ensuing civil war. Largely unnoticed by modern historians they were published by *Le Ménestrel* in 1872 and describe the part played by musicians, artists and women during those desperate times. Much of the following detail is indebted to them.

When war was declared in the middle of July the concert season had already ended, and most of the theatres were closed for their annual break, although a dozen of them were still offering entertainment to their patrons. The other theatres, including the Opéra and Opéra Comique were still expecting to open their doors as usual at the beginning of September, but when the horrifying news of the disaster at Sedan and the surrender of the French army reached Paris any hopes of a new season were dashed. Six days later the new government issued a decree closing all theatres and demanding that their scenery, curtains, furnishings and anything that could help spread fire be removed within forty-eight hours All firefighters employed by the theatres would now be serving the city itself. In any case, the compulsory call-up of all men of military age into the Garde Mobile was going to have a big effect on the theatres. As one writer put it

> The new law which calls up into the army all Frenchmen between the ages of 25 to 35, is going to make compulsory the closing of our main theatres. Most of our singers, our choirs, and our orchestral musicians are affected by this mass levying. It's virtually a musical expropriation order, in the interests of state security. The *Marseillaise* will not be short of singers at the frontier.[3]

The curtailing of operatic performances and the suspension of the government subsidy to the theatres meant, of course, that even those artists not affected by the call-up no longer had employment. By forming themselves into a Société des concerts de l'Opéra, the aim of which was to present works from the stage of the Opéra, without scenery or costumes, they managed to raise money to support themselves, as well as to donating profits to the war effort. Its committee, under the presidency of Emile Perrin, included Léo Delibes and the singers Villaret and Caron. A system of payment for the operatic 'stars' was worked out which the socialist periodical *Le siècle* noted with approval.[4] Their salaries were reduced (as was also that of the conductor), some singers refusing to take any fee at all.

Described as a *soirée musicale*, its first concert was given on 6 November at the Opéra, profits (presumably after the artists had been paid) going to the town of Châteaudun. The programme consisted of Rossini's overture to *Guillaume Tell*, extracts from Gluck's *Alceste*, Meyerbeer's *Le prophète* and *Les Huguenots*, Auber's *La muette de Portici*, finishing with Méhul's *Le chant du départ*. This series of concerts at the Opéra attracted such a following that they continued every Sunday and Thursday almost throughout the entire siege, the last being held on 26 February, 1871, a month after the siege had finished. During the course of its activities the Société des concerts de l'Opéra performed extracts from a large number of operas and other works – by Berlioz, Gounod, Haydn, Verdi, Wagner, and many others. A complete performance was given of Félicien David's *Le Désert*.

Two weeks before the Société des concerts de l'Opéra had begun their series, the conductor Pasdeloup re-commenced his famous Concerts populaires at what had once been called the Cirque Napoléon, now the Cirque Nationale. Pasdeloup was already a member of the National Guard in the 9th battalion which included a number of excellent musicians: Emile Durand, a teacher at the Conservatoire; Villebichot, composer of light operas; Valdejo, twice prize-winner at the Conservatoire two years before; Roussel, a gifted young tenor; and Arthur Pougin, the eminent music critic and writer. At each of these concerts a stirring oration was also given by a prominent citizen, and the proceeds went to the war effort. Six programmes were presented, the last on the 27 November. On 13 November Beethoven's Seventh Symphony was performed and, with delicious irony, the proceeds went towards the making of a cannon, dubbed 'Beethoven'.

The performance of German music at the Concerts populaires may have struck some Parisians as treacherous, and perhaps this was the reason for inviting the Protestant minister Alphonse Coquerel to give the oration at the third of these concerts at which was performed the overture to Weber's *Euryanthe*, the adagio from Beethoven's Septet, Berlioz's *Marche Hongroise* and Mendelssohn's 'Reformation' Symphony. Some 3000 people attended this concert and many had to be turned away. An Englishman caught in Paris, Nathan Sheppard, was there and in his diary he recalled the stirring oration, the topic of which was 'Mendelssohn and the Reformation'. The orator began

While they enclose us with a girdle of artillery, and with great trouble bring their enormous Krupp cannon from afar and put them in place against us, what do we do here? We play their music (laughter). You come to hear and applaud the grand works of Beethoven, of Weber, and of Mendelssohn – Germans all three. Is this, on our part, an infidelity to our country, a complicity somewhat with those who have so cruelly invaded her? Not in the least. These illustrious dead are not our enemies. The domain of the ideal into which they introduce us has no frontier. Their great works are a part of the universal patrimony of humanity.[5]

The speaker then went on to his main topic. Sheppard believed that the main object of the discourse was to impress upon his listeners that if they wanted honours they had to deserve them by their actions, which could include giving generously to the fund to which this particular concert was directed – to help the wounded. His final words were drowned in the tumult of applause: 'If our ambulance beds are empty [for lack of funds], we are no longer men, we are no longer Frenchmen, we are no longer anything ...'[6]

Not all orators reached this pitch of eloquence. Another Englishman in Paris during the siege was the Special Correspondent of the English newspaper *The Morning Post*, Thomas Bowles. He had been to the first of the events in the Théâtre Français where extracts from Molière's *Le Misanthrope* and other classical repertoire were given by actors and actresses in day-clothes and with no scenery. On this occasion the orator was Ernest Legouvé, well known, as we have seen, in musical circles for his translation of some of Schubert's songs and for his reviews and criticisms, but who certainly didn't impress Bowles. 'That boring old gentleman, M Legouvé, favoured us with a *conférence*, which means that he sat down behind a table and spoke to us a speech of the feeblest description, interlarded with small jokes and pointless anecdotes'.[7] The evening was rescued by Mlle Agar who sang the *Marseillaise* with such fervour from her burning black eyes and wild gestures that she seemed to Bowles to be 'the very impersonation of that spirit which Rouget de l'Isle [sic] first translated into melody'.

The profits from concerts and other presentations went towards a variety of causes, including the making of cannon (each costing 5000 francs), uniforms, ambulances, as well as helping families in need, not least the thousands of refugees from the provinces who had streamed into Paris at the outbreak of hostilities. Support of ambulances (which included the field hospitals as well as the vehicles) was one of the major objectives. From the time of the earliest struggles of the war, they had been kept busy on the battlefields and in Paris as thousands of the dying and wounded were brought back to the capital. In the last weeks of the siege, when the Prussians lost all patience with the inhabitants of the invested city and began bombarding it, using the monstrous cannons once shown at the 1867 Exhibition and hitting any target within range, the role of the Paris ambulances widened to take in the civilian population – although, in fact, deaths from bombardment were surprisingly few.

Because of the space within their foyers many of the theatres became 'field hospitals'. Wives, sisters and mothers of musicians and other artists, as well as actresses, singers and dancers devoted endless hours to nursing and comforting patients who, carried to one of the many field hospitals in the city might find themselves in a vast and opulently decorated foyer of one of the great theatres like the Comédie-Française, Odéon, Théâtre-Italien, Variétés, Porte Saint-Martin, Châtelet, Gymnase, Cluny and others. During the bombardment one of the most powerful shells landed on the front of the Odéon, killing several people and destroying the entrance, so that the field-hospital had to be moved into the auditorium itself. It was at this theatre that patients were comforted and nursed by an actress who had only recently made her début – the young Sarah Bernhardt.

A field hospital was also set up in the Conservatoire, its classes and musical activities having to be suspended, although many of its staff continued teaching their students in their own homes. Some, however, felt it more prudent to take in the country air. The result was that during the siege and what followed the Conservatoire was closed, and unlike the Opéra was unable to contribute to what little musical life there was in Paris at this time.

And what of fashionable society and those who had been the hostesses of those salons of the kind that we have glimpsed in earlier chapters? Those who remained in Paris now busied themselves with charitable work and many devoted their money and their energy to the care of the wounded, some aristocratic women filling their houses with these suffering men.[8] The head of the Ladies Ambulance Committee was the Countess de Flavigny. Bowles noted that elegant women, once attired in splendid gowns, now dressed, without exception, in sombre and modest clothes which gave them the appearance, he said, of refined upper-housemaids.

> They pass their time in mixing tisanes, administering medicines, carrying about trays full of surgical appliances at the heels of doctors, whom they would have considered in former times by no means sufficiently well-bred even to be admitted to acquaintance ... They are delighted with this life, which for the first time brought out the woman in them.[9]

Having often expressed despair at the mercurial behaviour of Parisians in the earlier part of the siege, Bowles felt that the bombardment brought out the best in them. It was therefore doubly agonizing that towards the end of January there was no way out but defeat, the end announced on the 27th day of that month. To the loss of Alsace and Lorraine to Germany, and to the crushing war reparations levied against France was added the humiliation of a triumphal march through the Arc de Triomphe and down the Champs-Elysées by the victorious Prussians.

This took place some four weeks after the end of the war, on 1 March and passed without major incident. But a few days later there was serious confrontation, not between French and Germans, but between French and French – between the government forces of law and order and those of the National Guard who came from the Belleville, Ménilmontant and other poor areas. Now armed like those in the National Guard from middle-class areas, but in greater numbers and with an ever-increasing crowd of sympathizers, the 'Reds' or the 'Communards' (as they were called) held the balance of power in Paris, and Government and army retreated for safety to Versailles. It was to be a second siege of Paris, with food supplies again cut off, and cannon bombardment as the army gradually took over the forts around the city. Within the city walls the clock was turned back to the days of the Revolution three-quarters of a century before, with the creation of a Committe of Public Safety reminiscent of the Directorate and (soon) the unleashing of a reign of terror. Once again churches and priests were a target, and the calendar went back to Revolutionary terminology: 'floréal' instead of 'mai', 'citoyen' instead of 'monsieur'. Yet as government military forces pounded the city and its surrounding villages, communard leaders at the Hotel de Ville were concerning themselves, amongst other things, with re-organizing some of the city's cultural organizations like the museums and the Opéra. They attempted to re-instate the Société des concerts de l'Opéra which had raised money during the first siege, its programme including – besides the Overture to *Der Freischütz* – patriotic works such as Gossec's *Viva la liberté*, a setting of Hugo's *Patria* and a piece by the communard conductor Raoul Pugno (Perrin having been replaced for not co-operating with the authorities) – his *Hymne aux immortelles* sung by Mlle Ugalde. It was billed for Sunday 22 May, but destined never to take place.

Yet in the last days of the Commune the most spectacular, if the least musical, concerts took place in the Tuileries Palace, home to the celebrated Concert Spirituel since 1725 and many other musical events in its long history. Dr Rousselle, a communard sympathizer and head of the Republic's ambulance service, suggested a grand concert in the Tuileries to raise funds for widows and orphans, an idea taken up with enthusiasm by the central authority of the commune. It took place on the evening of Sunday 7 May, the crowds so great that even many of those who had bought tickets in advance were unable to get into the main hall (the Salle des Maréchaux) and had to be put into an adjoining one (the Gallerie de Diane) where they were neither able to see or hear anything. Nor was the occasion improved when the second orchestra, made up from the National Guard and placed at the entrance to the main hall, inexplicably began playing in the middle of a song being sung from the platform; nor when a member of the audience shouted out for the orchestra to stop while he remonstrated against a collection being taken up, claiming that the entrance fee was sufficient for the charitable cause. Nevertheless, despite all this the concert was judged such a success that a second concert should take place under Dr Rousselle's planning four days later. It was on an even grander scale than before – three concerts at the same time – and on this occasion the public was assured of scrupulous organization.

The evening of the 11 May was balmy, and the gardens took on something of their former magic. Coloured lights hung from every tree and shrub, and the lawns and flowerbeds glowed under the Chinese lanterns. Many of the patrons lingered here under the clear skies to take in the scene and listen to the military band give its concert. Another programme of music came from the Tuileries theatre, while the main concert was held in the Salle des Maréchaux. Here there were poetry recitations, songs, duets, violin solos and orchestral music. Carried away by his success, Dr Rousselle planned yet another, still grander concert, this one to be free and to take place on Sunday, 21 May in various venues in Paris: at the Théatre Populaire, Cirque National, the Place de la Concorde (the new 'privileged' class offered seats on the Terrace of the Tuileries Gardens overlooking it), with the entire musical forces of the National Guard joining an orchestra there estimated to comprise 1500 performers. And in the apartments of the Tuileries still more music. But it was the last note of music ever to be heard there. For by the end of the concert the army from Versailles was breaking through the walls enclosing Paris and a week of bloody slaughter was about to begin.

In a mad frenzy the communards began burning Paris. Whole streets were set on fire, and the Tuileries and the Hôtel de Ville were reduced to ashes. A pyre was prepared in the cathedral of Notre Dame, but Verlaine – a communard sympathizer – distracted the crazed insurrectionist from lighting it.[10] Only by a miracle did the Louvre and its priceless treasures escape the planned conflagration. After a week of bloodshed and unimaginable savagery wreaked by both sides, during which it is believed that some 20000 to 25000 people were killed,[11] the madness came to an end.

Yet, writing only a matter of months after these terrible events Arthur Pougin, who had witnessed both the siege and the civil war at first-hand, was still able express belief in the future:

> ... science, the arts and literature will acquire a new lustre, and the thinking person will once again take up his work with that enthusiasm of spirit, that serenity of soul, which, in nations as in individuals, manifests itself at the end of a great crisis, when the energy of temperament succeeds in overcoming the onslaught of illness. France, at last – alas! not everywhere, but be patient – will be renewed, and through its vigorous and fertile exertions will impart a new vitality to the pulse of the human spirit.[12]

Pougin's hopes and aspirations were amply fulfilled.

*   *   *

Most amply were they fulfilled in the arts, for the period which followed saw the great flowering of symbolist poetry, and of impressionist painting, which before 1870 had been ridiculed and ostracized by the Establishment. The tide of musical romanticism was still strong enough to reach the shores of the next century, bringing with it more songs by Gounod, Saint-Saëns and Massenet and many others, as well as those by Fauré, Duparc and Debussy and that generation of composers who, taking the pre-1870 repertoire as a starting point, led French song into paths hitherto unexplored. And although, through new resources, a wonderfully intimate relationship between text and music was established, nevertheless it was still imbued with that gallic gift for tender and mellifluous lyricism that lies at the heart of romantic French song.

Notes

1. Partout, à droite, à gauche, on a chanté le *Rhin allemand*. Seulement chaque théâtre a choisi son musicien: A L'Opéra, c'est Delioux; à l'Opéra-Comique, Félicien David. au Vaudeville, Vaucorbeil. Pourquoi, disons-nous avec M Jules Prével du *Figaro*, ne chante-t-on nulle part le musique que Loïsa Puget a composée sur les vers d'Alfred de Musset? Ce fut à Loïsa Puget que le poëte donna la primeur de son chant national. Les autres musiciens ne s'en emparèrent qu'après elle. Vaucorbeil fut l'un des premiers à écrire le sien, qui date déjà de loin; il le publia à ses frais pour ses amis. Puis s'emparèrent du *Rhin allemand* MM Félicien David, Ch. Delioux, et vingt autres, car tout musicien écrit son *Rhin allemand*. Notre ancien Marcel des *Huguenots*, M Obin, en publie un. Faure, notre vaillant *Guillaume Tell*, a aussi improvisé un nouveau chant sur les vers de Musset. Quand nous serons à cent, on s'arrêtera peut-être. En province, même élan: le *Rhin allemand* inspire tous les musiciens: à Metz, à Strasbourg, on reçoit nos régiments au cri du Rhin, de même à Bar-le-Duc, où la société chorale redit matin et soir l'air populaire de M Alfred Yung. Dans nos ports de mer, le fleuve célèbre, par Alfred de Musset, a le pas sur l'Océan, sur la Méditerranée; on ne chante que le Rhin. De Douvres en entend résonner à Calais le chant de M F. Boutenjean, qui lui aussi a trouvé la note populaire; partout, partout, le *Rhin allemand* ... Nous lisons dans le *Gaulois*: 'Roger se multiplie pour notre caisse de secours; l'éminent artiste est allé au Raincy chanter le *Rhin allemand* de Vaucorbeil qu'il a dû redire *trois fois*; le public l'a presque porté en triomphe; comme il se dérobait à cet enthousiasme, une voiture a failli le renverser. Le chanteur a reçu dans le côté un coup de timon qui lui a fait perdre la respiration. Malgré cet accident et cette fatigue, le soir il chantait encore la *Marseillaise* et le *Rhin allemande*, au Vaudeville. Toujours sur la brèche ce Roger! C'est le même *Rhin allemand* de Vaucorbeil, que le *Gaulois* a publié, qui va être chanté au théâtre de Lyon.' *M*, 14 August, 1870.
2. These figures are given in two classic studies: Michael Howard, *The Franco-Prussian War* (London, 1961) and Alistair Horne, *The Fall of Paris* (London, 1965).
3. 'La nouvelle loi qui appelle à l'armée tous les Français, de 25 à 35 ans, va rendre

obligatoire la fermeture de nos principaux théâtres. Nos chanteurs, nos choristes, nos musiciens d'orchestre se trouvent pour la plupart sous le coup de cette levée en masse. C'est presque une expropriation lyrique, pour cause de salut public. La *Marseillaise* ne manquera pas d'interprète à la frontière. *M*, 14 August, 1870.

4. Oscar Comettant, *Le siècle*, 15 November, 1870, and quoted by Pougin.
5. Nathan Sheppard, *Shut up in Paris* (London, 1871), 136–7.
6. Sheppard, 138.
7. Thomas Gibson Bowles, *The Defence of Paris* (London, 1871), 164–5.
8. Sheppard, 267.
9. Bowles, 227.
10. Edmond and Jules Goncourt, *Journal* (Paris, n.d.), vol. 5 (1870–71), 227.
11. Horne, 497.
12. '... les arts et les lettres vont acquérir un nouveau lustre, et tout être intelligent va se reprendre au travail avec cette vigueur d'esprit, cette sérénité d'âme qui, chez les nations comme chez les individus, se font remarquer à la suite des grandes crises, lorsque l'énergie du tempérament réussit à dompter les efforts de la maladie. La France, enfin, – pas tout entière, hélas! mais patience – va renaître à la vie, et son activité laborieuse et féconde va imprimer un nouvel élan au mouvement de l'esprit humain.' *M* (p. 339).

List of private salon recitals in Paris 1834–1870 compiled from reports in the *Revue et Gazette musicale, Le Ménestrel* and *Le Monde musical*

This list includes only the vocal works and singers in salon recitals in the homes and reception rooms of the fashionable world of Paris and of members of the musical profession. It does not include recitals given solely by the students of leading teachers, nor those given for charitable purposes.

Where names of composers have been mentioned in the above journals they have been placed in round brackets after the work(s), but where omitted from the journals they have been placed in square brackets, even if the works are very well known. If composers have not been traced, a question mark has been placed in square brackets after the work. Orthographical errors in the journals have been corrected without notice. The name of the composer Weckerlin was invariably spelt Wekerlin in the nineteenth century although later changed to Weckerlin, but it has been decided to retain the original as it would have meant also changing the professional name of his wife Wekerlin-Damoreau. The name of the singer Géraldy was sometimes spelt Geraldi, but for consistency we have retained the former spelling. An asterisk after a name in the first column indicates the home of a professional musician. (For further description of Appendix A see the Introduction.)

Salons	Singers	Songs
February 1834 'Dans les salons fashionables'	Mme Stokhausen & Mlles Pixis, Ungher, Julie Grisi, MM Rubini, Tamburini, Ivanoff, Santini	romances by Dessauer: *Le ciel est pur*; *Romance italienne*; *Le nozze di Figaro* (Mozart); extracts from *Der Freischütz* (Weber)
'Une société brillante du Faubourg Saint-Germain'	Mme Ida Bertrand	no details
December 1834 M. Zimmerman* (held every two weeks)	Mlle Falcon; MM Nourrit, Dupont, Piog, Prévost & Derivis	unnamed duets; vocal quintet (Clapisson)
January 1836 Mme la comtesse de Merlin	Mlle Merlin [countess's daughter], M Lablache & unnamed singers, with chorus made up of 'gens du monde'	excerpts from *Il degonda* (Marliani); *Torquato Tasso* (Donizetti); final quartet from *Beatrice di Tenda* (Bellini)
February 1836 M. Frédéric Soulié	M Monpou	no details
March 1836 Mme la comtesse de Merlin	Mmes Crescini (from Venice – first appearance in Paris), Merlin, Mlle Merlin, MM Rubini, Tamburini, Puig [Piog?]	air (Balfe); trio from *Maometto* (Rossini); excerpts from *Ildegonda* (Marliani)

Salons	Singers	Songs
December 1836		
M. Zimmerman*	MM Jansen, Oudot	duo (Donizetti); romance by Doche: *L'insensée*; songs by Schubert, Grisar, A. Thomas
M & Mme Coche (first of the season)	MM Jansenne, Achard, Chaudesaigues, Mlle Castellan	romances by Clapisson, A. Thomas, Grisar
M Decourcelle	M Huhner	romances
Mlle Millin	MM Achard, Huhner, Chaudesaigues	no details
Mlle Berlot	MM Alexis Dupont, Chaudesaigues, Ed. D'Alembert, Zerezo and some women singers (the names forgotten by the reporter)	vocal quartet (Flotow); romances: *Le mauvais-oeil*; *Le guet et les cloches* (Clapisson)
M le baron Delmar	MM Rubini, Lablache	romances by Alary: *Il lago di Como; I contrabandieri*
January 1837		
M Zimmerman*	Mlle Panel & M Géraldy	unnamed duo
M Bodin*	Mlle Bodin	romance: *Juive et Chrétien* [?]; chansonette: *Naïs*
Mlle Dupont	Mlle Nau, MM le comte Adhemar, Vogel, Dupont	[?] duo: *Le chalet* [Adam?]
Mme Or…	Mme Dub…	songs by Schubert
March 1837		
Mme Amélie Boulet	Mme Boulet, Mlle de B…	duo from *Norma* [Bellini]
December 1837		
M. Zimmerman*	MM Lanza, Ed. d'Alembert, Levassor,	songs by Masini & chansonettes by Levassor

January 1838		
Mlle Laure Brice	Mmes Demoreau, Bazun M Ponchard	air from *Mazaniello* [Schira]; romances by Brice; and unnamed vocal quartet
M S…	MM Ferrugini, Ruggiero, Marras, Negri (Italian singers)	excerpts from: *Belisario* (Donizetti); *I puritani* (Bellini); duo bouffe by Donizetti
Mme de Rigni	MM Rubini, Lablache, Tamburini, Mme Persiani	no details
M S…	MM Rossi, Serda, Mlles Bazin, Drouart	excerpt from: *L'elisir d'amore* [Donizetti]; *Robert le Diable* [Meyerbeer]; romance by Meyerbeer: *Le moine*
February 1838		
M Zimmerman*	MM de Caix, Panel, Mlle Méquillet	songs by Concone; duo from *Jeanne d'Arc* [Carafa?]; *Madone* (Flotow), romance: *Le brigand calabrais* [?]
M Mitouflet	Mlle Drouat, Mme Sainville-Gay	excerpt from *La juive* [Meyerbeer]
M Jules Janin	M Roger	no details
'dans nos salons aristocratiques: Mmes La baronne Delmar, Pontalka, de Rigny, M William Hope'	no details	no details
Mme la comtesse Merlin	MM le prince de Belgiojoso, le comte	final quartet from *Lucia di Lammermoor*

Songs	Singers	Salons
M le duc d'Orléans	Poniatowska, Lablache, Mme la comtesse de Sparre	[Donizetti]; romance by Alary: *Il lago di Como*
M Maurice Schlesinger (his sixth salon for the season)	MM Perrugini, Ruggiero, Marras, Negri Mlle Assandri (Théâtre-Italien), Mmes Basin, Gay-Sainville, M Lafont	no details; unnamed Italian airs; romances by Strunz: *Prière de la jeune proscrite*; *Le gitano*; romance by Lafont: *Le marin*

March 1838

Songs	Singers	Salons
M Maurice Schlesinger	Mlles Brambilla, Drouart, MM Serda, Levassor	romance by Alary: *Eloïsa nel chiostro*; *Ave Maria* (Schubert); excerpts from *Die Zauberflöte* (Mozart); 'plusieurs bouffonneries'
M. Zimmerman*	M Ponchard, Miss Keble (from England), Mlle d'Hennin	no details
Mme la comtesse Merlin	Mmes Gentien, le comtesse Sparre, M le prince Poniatowski, Lablache	*Le pirate* (with choir); finale from *Beatrice di Fendi* [Bellini]; airs by Mercadente & Marleau; cantata by Alary; air from *Niobe* [Pacini]
M Maurice Schlesinger	Mlle Drouart; M Géraldy	excerpts from *Nitocri* (Mercadante); *Don Giovanni* [Mozart]; romances by Maria Malibran
Mme Th ... 'qui habite un des plus beaux hôtels de la rue Petits Augustins'	Mlle d'Hennin, MM Rémusat, Rignault, Walknaer, Chaudesaigues, Huner, Pantaléoni, Lecorbeiller	romances: *Deux familles*; *Le brigand calabrais* [?]; unnamed chansonnettes
Mme Rinaldi	Mlle Guichard, M Achille Oudot (Belgian tenor)	romances by Mercadente, Clapisson, Masini, Merlé

April 1838

Mlle Dupont*	Mme Wideman (Opéra), MM Dunat, Trinquart	romances by Vimeux: *Madeleine; Brigite; Ave Maria; Revenant*; romance by Fourcy
M Rinaldi*	Mme Wideman, Mlles Barthélemy, Guichard, MM Espinasse, Walkenaer, Trinquart	duo from *Norma* (Bellini); chansonnettes & romances by Amédée de Beauplan
M de la Bouillerie	no details	songs and arias by Flotow

December 1838

M Zimmermann	Mlle Dombrée	excerpt from *Fernand Cortez* [Spontini]
M Zimmerman	Mlle. Pauline Garcia, Mlle … (a pupil of Bordogni)	no details
M L…	M Ancemot	romance by Toury; cavatina from *Zaïre* [Bellini]; *La sonnambule* [Bellini]
M Bodin*	MM Bodin, Vogel	songs by Vogel
Mlle Amsler	MM Verroust, Schwederlé, Chaudesaigues, Mme Mens	no details
Mme la comtesse de Gr… (every two weeks)	Mme Wideman, Mlle Bodin, MM Albrecht, Haas, Gentille	romances by Haas: *Mal du pays; Un coeur de jeune fille*
M Traullé	Mme Wideman, MM Dubart, Achille Oudot	aria from *Lucia di Lammermoor* [Donizetti]; *Nestor le coiffeur* [?]
M Tressoze	Mlles Drouart, Wideman	nocturne by Concone: *Les orphélines égarées*; scène by Gheret: *Le souvenir*; excerpts from: *La reine de Saba* (Elwart); *Piquillo* [Monpou]; romances by Puget

Songs	Singers	Salons
February 1839		
Mme la marquise du Vi… Mme la princesse de B[elgiojoso]	Mme Baptiste Quiney, M Clemenceau MM Rubini, Lablache, Mme Grisi	romance by Meré: *L'accusée* no details
March 1839		
Mme la comtesse Grabowska	Mme de Sparre	*Ave Maria* [?]
'Dans plusieurs salons de Paris,'	MM Chaudesaigues, Charles Dufort	nocturne by Dufort: *Le pont des soupirs*
M Zimmerman*	MM Géraldy, Duprez, Rubini, Mlles Pauline Garcia, Rivière, Mme Henry Potier	excerpts from: *I puritani* [Bellini]; *Norma* [Bellini]; *Crociato in Egitto* [Meyerbeer]; *Orphée* [Gluck]; *Lucia di Lammermoor* [Donizetti]
M Bodin* (monthly recitals)	Mme Quiney	no details
Mme la comtesse Grabowska	Mmes Vigano, Wideman	no details
April 1839		
Mme la comtesse Grabowska	Mme Laty, Mlle Bodin, M Ghys	excerpts from a Mass by Charles Dufort
M Rinaldi*	Mlles Guichard (Opéra-Comique), Bodin, MM Deloffre, Pilet	no details

December 1839		
Mlle Dupont*	Mmes Médard, Baptist Quiney	duo from *Lucia di Lammermoor* [Donizetti]
Mlle Rinaldi	no details	no details
M. Zimmerman*	Mlle Pauline Garcia	no details
January 1840		
M Zimmerman	Mlles de Rivière, Hennin, Levoye, M Roger	excerpts from: *La sonnambula* [Bellini]; *Le château de Kenilworth* (Concone); romances by Clapisson: *S'il faut douter de toi; C'est une coquette*
Mme Gloux (the first of her series)	MM Rignault, Decourcelle, Oudot, Mme Dubart	operatic excerpt (unnamed) and romance by Haas
M Van Nuffel	Mlles d'Hennin, Lavoie	romances by Concone: *Elisabeth et Amy Robart; La jeune fille et la page; Vive l'hiver*
M Rinaldi*	Mlles d'Hennin, Darcier, MM Lefebure, Triebert, Clemenceau, Triquart	unnamed chansonnettes
Mme Gloux	M Roger, Mme Dubart	airs by Flotow: *La fiancée; Dormez, noble dame;* romances by Beauplan: *Sois à moi; Le secret*
M Rinaldi*	Mme Dubart, Mlle Barthélemy	no details
M le duc d'Orléans	Mme Dorus, Mlle Garcia, MM Duprez, Géraldy	excerpts from: *Bianca et Falliero* [Rossini]; *Le Pré aux Clercs* [Halévy]; *Capuletti ed i Montecchi* [Bellini]; *Guillaume Tell* [Rossini]
February 1840		
Mme Gloux	M Inchinid, Mme Dubart	no details

Songs	Singers	Salons
M Rinaldi*	M Oudot	chansonnettes by Oudot
Mme la comtesse Grabowska	M Ponchard, Mme Widemann	no details
Mme Gloux	Mmes Gloux, Dubart, MM Fleury, Girard	no details
Mlle Pauline Dussand*	Dussand	excerpts from *Guillaume Tell* [Rossini]; *Fernand Cortez* (Spontini)
Mme la comtesse Grabowska (the last of her salons for the season)	Mme Widemann, M Boulanger	romance by Haas: *Le mal du pays*
March 1840		
M Zimmermann*	Mlles Pauline Garcia, Loïsa Puget	Heine lieder by Lachner (with cello obbligato played by Batta); romances by Puget works by Handel (solo & choral)
M E…R…	no details	
December 1840		
M Zimmerman*	MM Roger, Balfe, Peyronnet, Haas, Albrecht, Gardet	romances & trios by Clapisson; two Italian airs by Balfe; excerpts from: *Falstaff* (Balfe); *Le postillon* (Balfe)
January 1841		
M & Mme Bodin	no details	no details
Mlle Traullé*	Mmes Chamazetti, Dubart	excerpts from: *La sonnambula* [Bellini]; *Zampa* [Hérold]; *Semiramide* [Rossini]

M Thys*	M Lac	romance by Thys: *Pense à moi*; vocal quartets
Mme Orfila. ('Tous les représentants de la haute fashion parisienne assistaient à cette magnifique soirée')	Mme la comtesse de Sparre, Mlle Fodor Mainvielle, MM Peyronnet, Haas, Albrecht, Gardet	
Mme Panckouke, M Moineran, Mme Gloux have each begun their series	no details	no details
M & Mme Rondonneau	M Rondonneau	no details
February 1841		
M Mens*	Mmes Mens, Marchand	romances: *La rose bretonne* (Puget); *Fais qu'il ne m'aime pas* (Masini)
M Zimmerman*	MM Wartel, Peyronnet, Haas, Albrecht, Gardet	songs by Schubert, vocal quartets by Masset & Thys
'Parmi les soirées musicales qui vont lutter cet hiver contre les concerts publiques'	Mlles de Moret d'Erlo, Drouart, Pauline Jourdan, Moret, Pollet, Thys, MM Euzet, Chaudesaigues	no details
Mme Mens*	Mlle Nau	no details
March 1841		
Mlle de Moret d'Erlo*	Mlle d'Erlo	romance by Niedermeyer: *Le lac*

153

Songs	Singers	Salons
December 1841		
M Montal	Mme Dubart, M Chaudesaigues	romances: *L'enfant naufrage* (Beauplan); *La demande en mariage* (Puget); unnamed romances by Thys
M Hyppolyte Arnaud*	M Arnaud	no details
1841 (undated in *MM*)		
Mme T… (Chausssée d'Antin)	M…	aria from *Roberto Devereux* [Donizetti]
Mme T… 'comme toujours d'élite de la Chaussée-d'Antin'	no details	no details
M Crém[ieux]	Mlles Dorus, Nathan, M Duprez	unnamed romance by Morel
M Branca (weekly salons)	Donizetti	no details
January 1842		
M & Mme Orfila	Mme la comtesse de Sparre, M Bonjour	romance by Puget: *Je veux que vous n'aimez que moi*
M le duc & Mme la duchesse d'Orléans (two soirées)	artists from the Opéra; Italian artists	no details
M Ponchard*	MM Ponchard, Balfe, Levasseur, Poultier, Mlle Puget	romances by Puget: *La demande en mariage*; *Véritable amour*
Mme Mélanie Waldor	Mme Anais Ségalas	romance by Waldor: *Blanche colombe*
M & Mme Géraldy 'dans	M Géraldy (with other unnamed artists)	excerpt from *La dame blanche* [Boïeldieu];

154

son petit appartement de la rue Richepance'		romance by Monpou: *Gastibelza*; new ballade by Morel [*La fille de l'hôtesse*]
February 1842 M Félix Le Couppey*	MM Ponchard, Erkel, Dorus, Lecointe, Mlle Dobrée	no details
March 1842 Mme la comtesse C…	Mme Mens	romance by Masini: *Veux-tu mon nom?*
April 1842 M Hyppolyte Arnaud*	Mlle Lici Duport, MM Tagliafico, Arnaud	no details
January 1843 M Thys*	M Lincelle	chansonnettes; scène bouffe: *Les petits mystères de Paris* (Bourget & Marquerie)
M Baumès-Arnaud	Ponchard, Sabatier, M Baumès-Arnaud	romances by Baumès-Arnaud: *Berthe la folle; Au départ; Au retour*
Mme Janvier	Mlle Jane Bianchi	no details
M Perronet*	M Duprez, Perronet, Perronet fils	songs by Duprez; air from *Piquillo* [Monpou]; romance: *Le savalier et le financier* (Offenbach); excerpt from *Lucrezia Borgia* (Donizetti)
M & Mme Girardin	Mme Labarre, MM Corelli (Théâtre-Italien), Porto, Balfe	unnamed air by Balfe; excerpts from *Roberto Devereux* [Donizetti]; *Bélisario* [Donizetti]; two romances by Labarre

155

Salons	Singers	Songs
M Peyonnet	M Duprez	no details
Mme la duchesse de Cazes	no details	no details
M Hoppe [Hope?]	M Corelli	no details
February 1843		
Mme la comtesse de Latour	D Fournier	*Hourrah!* (Fournier)
Mme la vicomtesse de Ker...	D Fournier	*Hourrah!* (Fournier)
M Beaumès-Arnaud*	no details	no details
Mme la duchesse de C... 'Le faubourg Saint-Germain a ses soirées et ses artistes de prédilection'	Mme Mens	romances by Vimeux & Puget
M Zimmerman*	Mme Pauline Viardot, MM Duprez, Géraldy, Balfe	romance by Duprez: *Gastibelza*; unnamed German song
M & Mme Boulanger-Kunzé*	Mmes Rouconi, Boulanger, MM Duprez, Géraldy	unnamed air allemand
Mlle Korn	Mme Sabatier	two romances by Thys [including *La follette*]
March 1843		
Mme Taverne	M Amat	romances by Clapisson
M & Mme Magnin	MM Marié [Mario?], Saint-Denis	romance by Niedermeyer: *Le lac*

Mme la comtesse Pozzo di Borgo	Mme Sabatier	romance by Thys: *La follette*
Mme la comtesse de Nerval	Mme Sabatier	romance by Thys: *La follette*
Mme la comtesse de Ségur	Mme Sabatier	romance by Thys: *La follette*
English Embassy	Mme Brambilla, Mlle Grisi, MM Mario, Ricci	excerpts from: *I puritani* [Bellini]; *Semiramide* [Rossini]; Neapolitan songs by Ricci; songs by Schubert
Mme la comtesse L…	Mlle Reccio, Mme Henir Potier	romance by Puget: *Mort d'amour*
April 1843		
Mme la comtesse de Merlin	Mme Merlin, M le prince de Belgiojoso	excerpts from: *Il corrado d'Altamura* [Ricci]; *Il prigione d'Edinburgo* [Ricci]
April or May 1843		
Mme M…L…	no details	songs by Niedermeyer: *Scène dans l'Appenin*; *Isolement*; *L'automne*; duo from *Stradella* [Flotow]
December 1843		
English Embassy	Mlle Grisi, M Mario	songs by Schubert
January 1844		
M Trollé [Traullé?]	Mmes de Garaudé, Sabatier, Mlle Massey, MM Géraldy, Roger	romance by Puget: *La petite bergère*

157

Salons	Singers	Songs
Mme la duchesse de Galliéra	no details	Italian music only
Mme la marquise de las Marismas	no details	no details
M & Mme Alexandre Dumas	MM Lablache, Fornasari, Ronconi, Balfe, Porto, Géraldy, Nicoli, Ricci, Alary Mlle de Richemont, Mmes Ronconi	programme mainly of Italian music
February 1844		
Mme de la Fosse*	M Saint-Denis	romances by Morel: *Le fils du Corse; Les adieux dans la nuit*; romance by Vimeux: *Le cavalier Hadjouté*
March 1844		
Mme la comtesse Fleury	Mme Mens	no details
Mme Legrand	M Treunthal	*Un coeur brisé* (Marmontel)
M F Delsarte	M Camille Delsarte (tenor)	no details
Mlle Vény	Mme Potier	*Les amours de Michel et Christin* [?]
'Un des riches salons de la Chaussée-d'Antin'	MM Barroilhet, Salvi, Inchindi, Mmes Manara, Belloni	no details
April 1844		
M & Mme Orfila	Mlle Falcon, M Tagliafico	no details

158

December 1844		
Mlle Barrault	Mme Labardie, MM Sarniquet, Baron, Canonville, Mlle Julien Bouché	romances: *Les yeux bleus*; *La mère au bal* (Arnaud); *Fais tinter la clochette*; *Fleur de l'âme* (Vimeux); unnamed romance by Thillon; duo from *Le Comte Ory* [Rossini]
January 1845		
'Un de nos salons aristocratiques du faubourg Saint-Germain'	Mlle de Bockholtz	no details
Mlle Duport		
Mlle Joséphine Laguesse*	Mlle de Reccio	romance by Thys: *Madelinette*
M Roger* (rue Rochechouart)	Mme Potier, MM Révial, Albertini	romance by Potier: *Le moine mort*
	M Roger	mélodie by Massé: *La feuille du chêne*
February 1845		
MM Perronet* (père & fils)	MM Herman Léon, Abadie, Mmes de Garaudé, Masson	no details
M & Mme Boulanger-Kunzé*	MM Tagliafico, Boulanger, Mlle Cotti	trio from *Maître de chapelle* [Paer]; romances by Thys: *Madelinette*; *L'amour et la musique*
M Ropicquet	Mme Desaint, MM Mengal, Albertini, Amat, Ropicquet	no details
March 1845		
Mme d T…	no details	*L'âme delaissé* (Rossini)

159

Salons	Singers	Songs
M Lincelle	Mlle Emma Chevalier	romances by Henrion, Arnaud & Clapisson
April 1845		
M & Mme Boulanger-Kunzé*	Mme Dorus Gras, Mlle Bochkoltz, M Tagliafico	romance by Massé: *Tayant*
M de Saint-Phil	Mlle Henry	no details
M Amat*	M Amat	romances by Amat
December 1845		
M le marquis de Louvois	MM Meyerbeer, Halévy, Adam, Pillet	no details
February 1846		
Le docteur…	Mme Emmanuel Gonzalès, M Henelle (Opéra)	unnamed romances and duos
March 1846		
M Peronnet	MM Poncard, Peronnet	extracts from opera and some romances
December 1846		
Mlle Dupont*	Mme Vaillant	excerpts from *L'eau merveilleuse* (Grisar)
M & Mme Orfila	Mme Sabatier, M Tagliafico	excerpts from: *Il barbiere di Siviglia* [Rossini]; *Don Pasquale* (Donizetti); romance by Puget: *Beneditta*
Unnamed salon in the Faubourg Saint-Germain	Mme Mens	romances by Arnaud: *S'il pouvait revenir; Les fleurs arrivées*

January 1847		
Mlle Porte*	M Audran (Opéra-Comique)	romances by Arnaud, Morel, F David
Mlle Joséphine Laguesse*	Mlle Julie Daniel, M Lamazou	unnamed romances and duos
M & Mme Lefébure-Wély*	Mmes Cinti-Damoreau, Iweins-d'Hennin, MM Tribert, Gauthier, Chaudesaigues, Lefort	unnamed romances and airs
Mme la princesse M[athilde]	no details	'… la partie vocale, qui est toujours italienne, a fait exception, ce soir-là en faveur de la romance d'Auguste Morel, *La plainte du pâtre*'
February 1847		
M le baron R…	M Mezia	excerpt from *Gemma di Virgy* [Donizetti]; romances: *Premier crime* (Bonoldi); *Chant du Carrousel* (Abadie)
March 1847		
Mme Phédora Lottin*	M Ponchard, Mme Iweins-d'Hennin	no details
Mlle Joséphine Martin*	Mlles Julie Vavasseur, Marin, M Lamazou	no details
January 1848		
Mlle Joséphine Laguesse*	MM Menghys (ex-tenor from the Opéra), Dervès, Mlle Julie Daniel, Mme Lefébure-Wély	extracts from opera and romances
	MM Ponchard, Géraldy, Lefébure-Wély	
M Henry Ravina		duos and romances

Salons	Singers	Songs
February 1848		
M de L...	Mmes Allard Blin, Mme Campan	romances by Arnaud
Mme la comtesse de B...	Mlle Marie Henry	no details
(Faubourg Saint-Germain		
Mme de S...)	M Amat, Mme Elise M...	romances by Amat
March 1848		
chez M le président de la	Mme Mulder (Théâtre de la Nation),	excerpts from: *Torquato Tasso* [Donizetti]; *Actéon*
République	Mlles Lavoye (Opéra-Comique), Naldi,	(Auber); *Cantilène* (Martini)
	MM Masset (Théâtre de la Nation),	
	Bataille (Opéra-Comique)	
March 1849		
M & Mme Louis Perrée	M Barroilhet	romance by Arnaud: *Soldat du Roi*
January 1850		
Mlle Joséphine Laguesse*	Mme Lefébure-Wély	various romances
M Massart	Mme Cabel	*Jenny la blonde* (Léon Kreutzer)
February 1850		
M Massart	Mme Cabel	excerpt from *Idomeneo* (Mozart); *Cantatrice*
		(Bourges)
M Duprez (rue Turgot)	MM Duprez, Portheaut, Mlles Duprez,	unacc. vocal quartet by Duprez; duo: *Le chalet*
	Miolan	(Duprez); excerpts from: *Il barbiere di Siviglia*
		[Rossini]; *Les mousquetaires de la reine* [Halévy];
		Danse des sylphes [?], acc. by Godefroid on harp

162

M le ministre de l'Intérieur	Mlles Vera, Mainville, MM Lablache, Lucchesi, Boudié	Italian vocal pieces; aria from *Niobe* (Pacini)
March 1850		
Mlle Emma Uccelli	M Ronconi	romances and chansonnettes
Mlle Joséphine Martin	M Lamazou	no details
Mlle Joséphine Laguesse*	Mlle Perrini	no details
Mme D[ubignon?]	Mlle Stephanie Del Pino	no details
M la comtesse de M[erlin]	Mlle Stephanie Del Pino	no details
M la marquise d'A[lbuféra]	Mlle Stephanie Del Pino	no details
December 1850		
Turkish Embassy	Mme Ugalde, M Géraldy	no details
February 1851		
Mme Warte[l]*	M Delsarte (brother-in-law of the pianist), Mlle Werthember	no details
M Boulanger-Kunzé	MM Géraldy, Mme Gaveaux-Sbatier	no details
Mme Lefébure-Wély	no details	salon opera by Poizot
Mme Charles Ponchard*	Mme Ponchard	romances: *Tu mens* (Arnaud); *Miroir et souvenir* (Hocmelle)
M Georges Mathias	Mlle Dobré	excerpt from *Der Freischütz* [Weber]
March 1851		
Mlle Joséphine Laguesse*	M Montigny, Mlle Duëz	romances: *Le rêve du coeur*; *Ce que mon fils sait*

163

Salons	Singers	Songs
M & Mme Massart	no details	*dire* (Arnaud); *Près d'un berceau* (Dupont) no details
April 1851		
Mme la comtesse de W…	Mlle Henry	romances by Potharst: *La mer se plaint toujours*; *Dieu vous la rendra*
M Dubochet	M Lionnet	romances by Abardie: *Le réprouvé*; *Le malheur*
Various unnamed salon recitals	Mmes Gavaux-Sabatier, Lefébure-Wély, Allard-Blin, MM Ponchard, Poitier, Rabi, Géraldy, Lamazou, Ribes, Chaudesaigues, Malézieux, Sainte-Foy, Lincelle, Sudot (etc)	no details
February 1852		
Mme la comtesse de W… ('parmi les nombreuses soirées')	Mlle Henry, M Gozora ('ces deux artists sont très recherchés dans le monde musical du faubourg Saint-Honoré')	romances by Potharst & Abadie
M le vicomte d'Arlincourt	M Duprez	romances by Potharst & Abadie
M & Mme Mutel	Mlle Nau, M Mutel	excerpts from *Maria di Rudenz* (Donizetti); *Torquato Tasso* (Donizetti)
Le général M…	Chaudesaigues	no details
December 1852		
M Chaudesaigues*	Mmes Ponchard, Duvall	romance: *La forêt de Sénart* (Michel)
M & Mme Lefébure-	no details	no details

164

Wély* (the beginning of their salon recitals)		
January 1853 M & Mme Deloffre*	Mmes Petit-Brière, Gaveaux-Sabatier, MM Jolivet, Chaudesaigues	no details
M le vicomte & Mme la vicomtesse Mahé de Villeneuve	Mlle Molidoff (from Germany)	German songs (no details)
January 1853 M le comte de Niewerkerke (at the Louvre)	M Alexis Dupont	no details
February 1853 Unnamed private salon in the rue Hauteville	Mme Nissen-Saloman, M Ferranti	no details
M & Mme Deloffre*	Mme Petit-Brière, MMHenrion, Chaudesaigues	no details
M Hesselbein*	Mlle Leserre, M Lyon	romance from *Les mousquetaires de la reine* [Halévy]
M Boulanger-Kunzé	MM Ponchard, Géraldy, Boulanger, Nadaud, Mmes Ponchard, Oberlin, Brousse	romance by Wekerlin: *Fleur des Alpes*; air from Galathée [?]

Salons	Singers	Songs
M Lacombe*	unnamed German singer	lieder by Schubert
Mlle de Courcelles	Mme Dancla, M Ribes	excerpts from: *La muette di Portici* [Auber]; *La poupée de Nuremburg* [Adam]; various romances
M Roger (rue Turgot)	Mmes Frezzolini, Iweins d'Hennin, MM Cambardi, Masson, M Roger	excerpts from: *Don Giovanni* [Mozart]; *Le comte Ory* [Rossini]
January 1854		
Le comte Nieuwerkerke (has just re-commenced his weekly salons at the Louvre)	M Lefort, Lionnet frères	chanson by Nadaud: *Le voyage aérien*
La princesse Mathilde/Prince Murat	no details	included dramatic scenes
M & Mme Lefébure-Wély (their new season of salon recitals)	MM Lionnet frères, Lefort, Malézieux, Mme Lefébure-Wély	romances & chansons by Nadaud and others
[M Mme?] Sénat	Mmes Gaveaux-Sabatier, Lefébure-Wély, M Lefort	no details
March 1854		
Mme Rinaldi	Mmes Iweins d'Hennin, Albini, M Brian	excerpts from *Semiramide* [Rossini]; romances and chansonnettes
M Paul Dollingen	MM Roger, Lionnet, Mlles Bruce [Brousse?], Worms	no details
April 1854		
M Boulanger-Kunzé*	Mme Gaveaux-Sabatier, Mlles Brousse,	various romances

M Duprez (rue Turgot)	Maria Boulanger-Kunzé, MM Wartel, Guyot, An. Lionnet; Mlles Duprez, Mira, MM Duprez, Roger, Mocker, Rauch	opera by Duprez: *Jeliotte*
M Massart*	Mme Marie Cabel and other unnamed singers	no details
Mme Mennechet de Barival	Mlle B…	mélodie by Mme Mennechet
March 1855		
M Duprez (rue Turgot)	MM Duprez, Gueymard, Euzet, Stockausen, Rauch, Cluas, Mlles Duprez, Charry, Charles	unpublished opera by Duprez: *Samson*
M le préfet de la Seine	Mme Borghi-Mamo, M Gardoni	excerpts from *Il trovatore*
December 1855		
Mme la baronne de L…	M Jules Lefort	romance by Collin: *Le rappel des chèvres*
January 1856		
M & Mme Deloffre*	MM Lionnet, Malézieux, Mlle Penetrat	excerpts from *Semiramide* (Rossini)
M le comte Nieuwerkerke (at the Louvre)	MM Ponchard, Levassor	excerpt from *Tarare* (Salieri)
'Dans un élégant réunion de la Chaussée-d'Antin'	Mlle Marie Martin (pupil of Wartel)	excerpts from: *Le favorite* [Donizetti]; *Le Pré aux Clercs* [Hérold]

Salons	Singers	Songs
February 1856		
M & Mme Orfila ('… toujours le centre aristocratique des arts.')	Mmes Viardot, Miolan-Carvalho, Arnould Plessy, Ponchard, Mlle Brousse, MM Poncard, Lyn	no details
Mlle Laguesse*	Mmes Sabatier, Labadie, MM Jouet, Euzet	romance by Wekerlin
M & Mme Deloffre*	Mlle Pauline Thys	romances by Thys
M Leverrier ('sénateur & directeur de l'Observatoire')	M Ed. Lyn & Mme Lefébure-Wély	extracts from unnamed opera
Mlle Ida Boullée	M Jules Lefort	no details
M & Mme Pfeiffer*	Mme Iweins d'Hennin	excerpts from Le prophète [Meyerbeer]
M & Mme Boulanger-Kunzé*	MM Jules Lefort, Boulanger-Kunzé, Mlle Caroline Duprez	no details
M le préfet de la Seine	Mmes Borghi-Mamo, Miolan Carvalho, MM Gardoni, Bonnehée	no details
March 1856		
M le docteur Bouland	Mme Gaveaux-Sabatier, M Jules Lefort	salon opera by Manni: La bourse ou la vie
M Goria	Mmes Wekerlin-Damoreau, Meillet, MM Bataille, Malézieux, Lionnet frères	oratorio by Gounod: Jésus de Nazareth
M Duprez	Mme Pauline Viardot, Mlle Duprez (and others)	act four of Duprez's opera: Samson

168

January 1858		
M Devinck, membre du corps législatif – at his home	Mlle Sulzar, MM Belart, Douai, Malézieux	no details
February 1858		
Le comte Nieuwerkerke (at the Louvre)	Mme Stockhausen, M Roger	no details
Le comte Nieuwerkerke (at the Louvre)	M Duprez	Excerpt from *La juive* [Halévy]; romance: *Gastibelza* [Duprez?]
M Marmontel*	Mme Stockhausen, MM Roger	mélodies by Vaucorbeil
March 1858		
Mme Massart*	Mme la baronne Vigier, Mlle Sophie Cruvelle	lieder by Schubert (sung in German)
M Bertall – dessinateur	MM Berthelier, Saint-Foy	*Les deux aveugles* (Offenbach)
M le préfet de la Seine	Mlle Lefèvre, M Barbot	excerpt from *Psyché*; unnamed romance: *Guido et Ginevra*
April 1858		
Mme Mackenzie de Dietz*	Mlle Bosc, M Fleury	excerpt from *Zampa* [Hérold]
unnamed private salon	M le comte de…	mélodie by Meyerbeer: *Près de toi* (cello obbligato played by Séligmann)

Salons	Singers	Songs
December 1858		
M & Mme Herwyn*	Mlle Grange & M. Portehaut	unnamed romances
M & Mme Herwyn*	M & Mme Herwyn, Mlle de Saptes, MM Boutines, Aubel, Nadaud	no details
M Rossini*	Mlle Mirca, M. Bréval	salon opera by Wekerlin: *La laitière de Trianon*
January 1859		
unnamed private salon	M Prudent (accompanying at piano)	romances by Prudent
Mme Orfila	Mlles Boulanger-Kunzé, Thys	romances by Pauline Thys: *Le vieux portrait; Le charmant oracle; Les larmes sans soeurs*
M & Mme Herweins	Mlle de Saptes, M Nadaud	chansons by Nadaud: *Les projets de jeunesse; La cuisine du château; Le sultan; Le message; Pandore*
M Lebouc*	Mlle de Ruppelin	four mélodies by Schubert; romances by Grétry
February 1859		
M & Mme Delangle	Mme Wekerlin-Damoreau	excerpts from *Le Pré aux Clercs* [Hérold]; lieder by Schubert: *Sérénade; La truite*
M & Mme Billaud (municipal councillor & financier)	Mme Nantier-Didiée, MM Varesi, Galvani, Nadaud	unpublished [vocal?] quartet by Flotow; Spanish airs; chansons by Nadaud
M Pereire (Faubourg Saint-Honoré)	Mme Alboni, Frezzolini, MM Graziani, Miraglia	excerpts from *Robert le diable* [Meyerbeer]; *La sonnambula* [Bellini]
M Becker	no details	*Paradis perdu* (Ritter)
'Plusieurs salons dans le	Mmes Sabatier, Barthe, M Lefort	opéra comique by le comte Wilfrid d'Indy

Host / Venue	Performers	Works / Details
Faubourg Saint-Honoré' M. H. Herwyn*	Mmes Wilson & Grangé, MM Wartel & Potel	[uncle of Vincent d'Indy]: *Les deux princesses* pastoral operetta by H Saloman: *Au printemps*
Mmes Orfila & Mosnerons de Saint Preux M Novarre	Mme Ponchard, MM Lavasseur, Prat M Jourdan (Opéra-Comique)	no details romance by L'hote: *Le soir* (text by Lamartine)
M & Mlle Martin	M Gardoni	no details
March 1859 M Rossini* Le comte Nieuwerkerke (at the Louvre)	Mlle Mira, MM Bussine & Biéval MM Géraldy & Ciosti	salon opera by Wekerlin: *Mariage en poste* *Paradis perdu* (Ritter); operatic airs
M Pereire M & Mme Boulanger-Kunzé*	Mme Frezzolini, MM Graziani Mme Boulanger, Mlle Obelin, Mlle Boulanger-Kunzé, MM Boulanger-Kunzé, Berthelier	no details unnamed sacred trio; mélodie by Offenbach: *Si j'étais petit oiseau*; chansonnettes by Berthelier
M & Mme Billaud (their second of the season) 'Plusiers salons dans le Faubourg Saint-Honoré'	Mlles Saint-Urbain (Théâtre-Italien), Dorus, M Tagliafico Mlle Desmaisons	no details (includes performance by 12-year-old Sarasate) *Souvenir-mélodie* (Desmaisons)
M & Mme Crémieux	Mmes Borghi-Mamo & Ugalde, Mlles Monrose, Bruni (pupils of Duprez)	excerpt from *Die Freischütz* [Weber]
M & Mme Paul Bernard*	Mmes Coches, Iweins-d'Hennin	chansons by Nadaud: *Le sultan*; *Le pays natal*; *Au callon de la jeunesse*; *A Rose-Claire-Marie*; Unnamed compositions by Bernard

Salons	Singers	Songs
Mmes Orfila & Mosnerons	Mme Bertrand, MM Géraldy, Varesi, Galvani	chansons by Nadaud: *Le sultan*; *La cuisine du château*; *L'étudiant à l'étudiante*; *L'aimable voleur*
Le comte Nieuwerkerke (at the Louvre)	Mmes Gaveaux-Sabatier, Barthe, M Jules Lefort	opéra-comique by le comte Wilfrid d'Indy: *Les deux princesses*
Mlle Joséphine Martin*	MM Morachetti, Bellouet, Wekerlin, Mlle Thys	vocal quartets by Wekerlin; romances by Thys
M Isaac Peireire (royal hôtel du faubourg Saint-Honoré)	Mlle Marimon (acc. by harpist Félix Godefroid)	no details
Mme Eugénie Garcia*	MM Varesi, Galvani, Lefort, Lamazou (together with Garcia's most gifted pupils)	no details
M & Mme Herwyn* (quai de la Tournelle)	Mmes Bockholtz-Falconi, Mlles Huet, Darjou, Wilson, MM Lyon, Paulin, Herwyn	no details
January 1860		
Mlle Virgine Huet*	M Nadaud	chansons by Nadaud: *Le fou Guillau*; *Le nid abandonné*; *Le sultan*; *Bernique*
M Jules Beer	Mme Sabatier, M Lefort	no details
Lionnet frères (inaugurating their weekly salons)	MM Gounod, Nadaud, Delsarte, L'Epine, Lionnet frères	excerpts from: *Philémon et Baucis* (Gounod); *Iphigénie en Tauride* [Gluck]; romances, chansons & mélodies: *Le nid abandonné*; *Les adieux à un ami* (Nadaud); *Cousine Marie*; *Sous les tilleuls* (L'Epine); *Le matin* (Massé); *Les cloches de*

172

M & Mme Herwyn*	Mlle Acs	*Saint-Loup* (Delsarte); *Fanchette* (Hignard); *Les gardes françaises* (Delioux)
Mme Eugénie Garcia*	Mme Trélat, Mlles Bertraut, Reiss, MM Jules Lefort, Gustave Garcia	no details
Mlle Joséphine Laguesse*	Mme Mancel, Mlle Laguesse, MM Luchesi, Marochetti	romance by Niedermeyer: *Le lac* no details

February 1860

M Marmontel*	M Roger	*mélodies* by Vaucorbeil
Mme Orfila	Mme Ugalde, Mlle Marie Sax (Théâtre-Lyrique), M Roger	excerpts from: *La traviata* [Verdi]; *La dame blanche* [Boieldieu]; *mélodies* by Vaucorbeil: *La ballade serbe*; *Les chèvres d'Argos*; *Le rondel*
M & Mme… (rue Taitbout)	Mlle François, MM Barbot, Lefort	*scène lyrique en quatre chants*: *La fée des eaux* (Léon Gastinel); romance: *Le bonheur est un songe!* [?]; chanson by Nadaud
M Pigeony (rue d'Amsterdam)	Mlle Mira, M Biéval	two salons operas: *L'Accord parfait* (Bernard); *Loin du bruit* [Bernard?]
Mmes Ofila & Mosneron de Saint-Preux	Mmes Plessy, Ugalde, Ponchard, Berthelier, Mlle Marie Sax, MM Sainte-Foy, Orfila, Laborde, (Mme Taglioni & Mlle Livry – her student – danced in one of the pieces)	Two salon operas: Parody on Gluck's *Orphée* (M P.…); *Il matrimonio empetreto* [sic] (Wekerlin)
M & Mme Peigné	Mme Ponchard, MM Renié, Crémieux (acc. By Mme Crémieux)	salon opera: *Jobin et Nanette* (Wekerlin)

Salons	Singers	Songs
March 1860		
unnamed 'soirée intime' Mlle Bochkoltz-Falconi*	Mme Pellegrin Mlles Falconi, Maillard, de Dufresne, Wiesen	some works by Kruger *Psaume 23* (Schubert); vocal quartets by Mendelssohn; mélodie by Litolff: *Douleur*
'Un des plus beaux salons de la rue Hauteville'	Mlle de Pommeraye (Opéra), Mme Pellegrin, M B …	songs by unnamed composers: *Air valse; Santa Lucia;* romance: *Deux et deux font deux; Ave Maria* (Bach/Gounod)
Le Couppey*	Mme Caroline Barbot	excerpts from *Iphigénie en Aulide* [Gluck]; chansons by Berthelier
M & Mme Anais Ségalas	Mmes Ségalas, Sabatier, MM Le Bressant, Malézieux	*Les femmes terribles* (Dumanoir), chansons by Nadaud
M & Mme W … (de la rue Lafitte)	MM Géraldy, Pagauza (student of Géraldy), Lafont, Mlle … (from Rio-Janeiro)	excerpts from: *Il barbiere di Siviglia* (Rossini); *L'elisir d'amore* [Donizetti]
M & Mme de L… 'Un splendide salon du faubourg Saint-Germain'	MM Malézieux, Lespaire Mlle Alphonsine Lemit (student of Damoreau & Sontag), MM Gardoni, Dancla, Nathan	no details excerpts from *L'elisir d'amore* [Donizetti]; *Voitures versées* (Boïeldieu)
Le Couppey*	Mme Caroline Barbot, MM Barbot, Lafont	excerpts from Lully, Gluck, Handel, Pergolesi
Mlle Ida Bertrand* ('avait réunit l'élite de l'aristocracie russe')	Mmes Bertrand, MM Graziani, Varesi, Pagans	excerpt from *Orphée* [Gluck]

174

April 1860 M Ravisy*	Mlle François, MM Ravisy, Balanqué	excerpts from: *Le nozze di Figaro* [Mozart]; *Masaniello* [Carafa?]; mélodie by Alary: *L'étranger*
Mmes Orfila & Mosnerons de Saint Preux M Marmontel* M Disderi	Mme Caroline Barbot, MM Barbot, Lafont Mlle Durand, MM Troy, Archainbaud Mlle Darcier, MM Anatole Lionnet, Malézieux	excerpts from: *Iphigénie en Aulide* [Gluck]; *Armide* [Gluck]; *La favorite* [Donizetti] no details chansons by Nadaud: *L'aimable voleur; La bûche de Noël; La cuisine du château; Bernique; Le roi boiteux; Les côtes d'Angleterre*
Le comte Nieuwerkerke (at the Louvre)	M Trcy (Opéra-Comique)	scène bouffe: *Romance sans paroles au musique de l'avenir* (words by de Courcy)
December 1860 M & Mme Rossini*	Lionnet frères, M Badiali (Théâtre-Italien)	duos and scenes from opera (including *Le nozze di Figaro*); chanson by Nadaud: *La promenade*
Mmes Orfila & Mosnerons de Saint Preux	Mme Gaveaux-Sabatier, Ponchard, MM Lourdel-Belval, Géraldy, Levasseur	salon opera: *La perruque du bailli* (Thys); romances & chansons: *Voitures versées* (Boïeldieu); *Les côtes d'Angleterre* (Nadaud); excerpt from *Le Philtre* [Auber]
January 1861 M Trouvé (at Passy)	Mmes Denizet (pupil of Ugalde), Ponchard, MM Levasseur, Ponchard, Petit (young baritone, 1st prize	salon opera by Canoby: *Les sabotiers*; excerpts from: *La fausse magie* [Mouret]; *Le nouveau Seigneur du villages* [Boïeldieu]; *La dame blanche*

Salons	Singers	Songs
Mlle Gabrielle Colson* (every Wednesday)	Conservatoire) Mmes Labadie, Mme C..., MM Altavilla, Audubert, D'Herment	(Boïeldieu); *Le Philtre* [Auber] no details
M & Mme Rossini* (every Saturday)	Mlle Grisi, Mme Conneau, MM Badiali, Naudin	no details
M & Mme Rossini*	MM Graziani, Zucchini, Malézieux, Castellani frères	duos bouffes; chansons by Nadaud
'Une soirée particulière' at Passy	MM Ponchard, Petit, Gourdin, Capoul	opéra-comique by Gustave Canoby (maître de Chapelle at Passy); *Je chanterai*; *Les quatre âges du coeur* [?]
M le prince... ('un des salons princiers du faubourg Saint-Honoré')	MM Guidon frères, Ducros, Mlles Méa, Huet	chanson by Nadaud: *Voyage aérien*
M & Mme Dubois (rue d'Antin)	Mlle Reeves	no details
M R...	Mme Gaveaux-Sabatier, M Lourdel [-Belval]	salon opera by Paul Bernard: *Bredouille*
Mme la princesse...	Mlle Angèle Cordier (Opéra-Comique)	no details
M & Mme Ernest Lévi-Alvarès (every fortnight on 1st & 3rd Saturdays)	Mme Alard, Mlle Marville (Jacob), M Lafont	no details
M & Mme Jules Beer*	Mlle Mira, MM Gourdin, Capou	opéra-comique by Beer: *Les roses de M de Malesherbes*
M Rev... ('riche financier	MM Géraldy, Saint-Foy	*Le médecin tant pis*; *Le médecin tant mieux*;

ce qui ne l'empêche pas d'être excellent musicien') Mlle Laguesse*	Mme Gaveaux-Sabatier, Mlles Marville, Laguesse*, MM Guidon frères	*La montagne qui accouche* (words by La Fontaine, music by Thy Ymbert), romance by Membrée: *La colombe*
M Félix Godefroid*	Mme Lyon, MM Lyon, Michot (Opéra)	no details
M & Mme Rossini*	Mlle Mira, MM Gourdin, Capoul	opéra comique by Beer: *Les roses de M de Malesherbes*
February 1861 M & Mme Rossini	Mme la vicomtesse Grandval, MM Berthelier, Badiali	excerpts from: *Guillaume Tell* [Rossini]; *Vêpres siciliennes* [Verdi]; unnamed Mozart opera; chansonnettes and romances
M Bergson* M & Mme Rossini*	Mme Mancel, MM Lucchosi, Marochetti Mlle Mira, MM Capoul, Gourdin	excerpt from *Le pardon de Ploërmal* [Meyerbeer] opéra-comique by Beer: *Les roses de M de Malesherbes*
M & Mme Rossini*	MM Duprez, Brasseur (singer and dancer from Palais-Royal)	no details
M Bazzoni* M & Mme Crémieux	Mlle Caroline Strauss, M Tagliafico Mme Viardot-Garcia, MM Duprez, Duprez fils, Le Franc, Gardoni	duo from *La fille du régiment* [Donizetti] excerpts from: *Orphée* [Gluck]; *Il trovatore*; *Rigoletto* [Verdi]; *Il matrimonio segreto* (Cimaroso)
M & Mme Rossini*	MM Duprez père & fils, Lefranc, Mme Vanzenheuvel, Mlles Brunetti, Godfrend	two opéras bouffes by Duprez: *Les trois étoiles chez un directeur; Les trois ténors*
M Félix Godefroid* (his third salon for the season)	M Dufrène (Opéra), Mme Iweins-d'Hennin	romance from *Martha* [Flotow]; *Plaisir d'amour* (Martini)

177

Salons	Singers	Songs
M & Mme Charles Sebault (Pauline Thys)	Mme Gaveaux-Sabatier, MM Lourdel, Jules Lefort	opéra comique by Thys: *La perruque du bailli*; proverbs and romances by Thys: *Quand Dieu est dans le mariage*; *Dieu le garde*; *La France*; *Les vingt-ans*; *La sirène*
M & Mme Rossini*	Mlles Marchiso soeurs, Trio Gordigiani, MM Bonheur, Badiali, Montaro (Neapolitan tenor)	Spanish duo (Rossini), duo from *L'Italiana in Algeri* [Rossini]
Ottoman Embassy	MM Frères Lionnet, M Gounod	mélodie by Gounod: *Le soir*; chanson by Béranger: *Le vieil habit*; chansons by Nadaud: *La promenade*; *Florimond l'enjôleur*
Corps-Législative	MM Lionnet frères, Félicien David, Edmond Membrée, Ernest Lépine	no details
M & Mme Ponchard*	MM Lionnet frères, Levasseur, Montaubry, Ponchard père	new romance: *Je n'ai plus vingt-ans* [?]; duo: *La fausse magie* [Mouret]
Mme la princesse Mathilde	M Reichardt	*Poèmes de la mer* (Wekerlin)
March 1861		
Son Excellence M le président du Sénat [M Troplong]	Mmes Viardot, Tardieu	excerpts from: *Armide*; *Orphée* (Gluck); arias from Haydn & Mozart
M & Mme Rossini*	no details	no details
M & Mme Rossini*	MM Badiali, Montanaro, Mme la vicomtesse de Grandval	grand duo from *Semiramide* [Rossini]
Son Excellence le ministre	Mlles Marchiso soeurs, Mme Wekerlin-	no details

178

M Delangle	Damoreau, M Faure	no details
M le Directeur-générale de la Caisse des dépots & consignations	Mme Wekerlin-Damoreau	
M Duprez	Mme Vanderheuvel-Duprez, Mlles Brunetti, Godfrend, Kestemond, Schlesinger, MM Duprez fils (Léon), Le Franc, Agniez, Muller	excerpts from: *Moïse* [Rossini]; *Samson* (Duprez); *Les trois étoiles du directeur* (Duprez); *Tout est bien qui finit bien* (Duprez)
M Bénezat ('dans un magnifique hôtel de la rue de la Ville-l'Eveque') – one of many soirées	Mmes Rasa Kastner, Servais, Herman, Vanderheuvel-Duprez, Mlle Battu, M Saint-Foy	unpublished opera by Rillé: *Au fond du verre*
M & Mme Rossini*	M Badiali, Mlle Marie Brousse	*Sérénade* (Estienne); cavatina from *Tancredi* [Rossini]
le grand référendaire au Sénat, M d'Hautpoul	M Gourdin	excrpt from *Le pardon de Ploërmel* [Meyerbeer]
Mme Erard	Mme Ida Bertrand, MM Graziani, Montanaro	no details
Mmes Orfila & Mosnerons de Saint Preux	Mme Ida Bertrand, Mlle Marimon[t], MM Montanaro, Badiali	*Chanson du chien* (Barkhouff)
M & Mme Piereire	Mlle Marimont	*Chanson du chien* (Barkhouff)
M & Mme Ernest André	Mlle Marimont	*Chanson du chien* (Barkhouff)
S A I la princesse Mathilde	Mlle Marimont	*Chanson du chien* (Barkhouff)

Salons	Singers	Songs
M Marmontel*	Mme Oscar Commettant	La calabraise [?]
Le Couppey*	Mme Duprez Vandenheuvel	no details
M & Mme Rossini*	Mlles Barbara Marchisio, Mira, Mme Iweins d'Hennin, MM Castellani frères, Badiali, Solieri, Berthelier	no details
M & Mme Alvarès-Levi	M Guyot (Bouffes-Parisiens)	Credo des quatres saisons; David devant Saul; Le maître chanteur (some by Limnander)
April 1861		
Mme Alphonse de Rothschild	no details	Chant pour orgue, piano, violoncelle (M le prince de Metternich)
M Schnieder, vice-président du Corps Législatif	Mlle Trebelli, Lorini, MM Badiali, Gardoni, Zucchini	excerpts from: Il matrimonio segreto [Cimarosa]; Le nozze di Figaro [Mozart], L'Italiana in Algeri [Rossini]
Le comte Nieuwerkerke (at the Louvre)	MM Duprez père & fils, Lefranc	trios bouffes
M de Rothschild	M Berthelier	Chansonnettes by Berthelier
December 1861		
Mme Antonin Prévost-Rousseau	MM Ch. Archainbault, Bussine jeune, Mme Blanche Peudefer (pupil of Ponchard)	Unnamed salon opera by M O'Kelly; new chansons by Nadaud
Mlle Laguesse*	Mmes Gaveaux-Sabatier, Tillemont, MM Lafont, Bellouet, Guidon frères	no details
Mlle Gabrielle Colson	Mme Borgogni-Bolton, Mlle Estell	unpublished salon opera by Lecoq

Frasey, MM Tayau, Walter Bolton (English tenor), de Helcel, Audubert

January 1862

M & Mme Orfila	Mme Gaveaux-Sabatier, Ugalde, MM Jules Lefort, Del Sedie. (Violin obbligatos played by Sarasate)	excerpts from: *Le Pré aux Clercs* [Hérold]; *Maître de chapelle* [Paer]; mélodies by Gounod: *Sérénade*; *Le vallon*; two Italian romances by Donizetti; unpublished Spanish chanson by Delioux
M Damcke* (the first of his series)	no details	*Salve regina* (for unaccompanied voices) by Damke
Mme Pfeiffer*	Mme Ernest Bertrand, MM Lafond, Pagans (pupil of Géraldy)	chanson by Nadaud: *Le nid abandonné*, duo from *Il barbiere de Siviglia* [Rossini]
Mmes Orfila & Mosnerons de Saint Preux	Mme Bertrand, Mlle Trebelli, MM Engel (English organist & singer), Archaimbaud, Anthiome, Saint-Germain	excerpt from *Il barbiere di Siviglia* [Rossini]; romances by Godefroid: *Gouttes de rosée*; *Le vieux menuet*; *Le rêve*; air from *Jeannot et Colin* [Isouard?]; chansons by Nadaud & Thys
M Paul Bernard*	Mme de Rosaven (pupil of d'Hennin), MM Guidon frères	romance by Bernard: *Pleurs*
M & Mme Ernest-Lévi Alvarès	Mmes Alard, Mme Ernest-Lévi Alvarès, MM Guidon frères	*Miserere* from *Il trovatore* [Verdi]; romances & mélodies: *Le billet de Marguerite* [?]; *Sérénade* (Gounod); *Le chant des feuilles* (Bernard)
S Exc M le ministre de la justice, M Delangle	Mme Wekerlin-Damoreau, M Léon Lecieux	no details
M le maréchale Regnault-	Mme Gaveaux-Sabatier, M Géraldy	no details

Salons	Singers	Songs
Saint-Jean d'Angely M & Mme Varcolier	Mlles Trebelli (Théâtre-Italien), Agar (Odéon), Mmes Ugalde-Varcolier (Opéra-Comique), Mme Gaveaux-Sabatier, MM Jules Lefort (Théâtre-Lyrique), Lionnet frères, Berthelier, Fauvre	scene from *Lucrèce* (Ponchard)
M Tinant, sculptor, Avenue Dauphine ('le nobiliare du faubourg Saint-Germain & faubourg Saint-Honoré')	Mlle Amélie Faivre, M Petit	unpublished opera by M le comte Raoul de Lostanges: *Le valet poëte*
M Peireire (organized by Rubini)	Mlle Amélie Farvre, MM Petit, Legrand, Girardot (all from the Opéra-Lyrique)	no details
S Exc le Ministre de justice (organized by Rubini)	MM Delle-Sedie, Gardoni, Zucchini	no details
Mme…	M Delle-Sedie, Mme Damoreau-Wekerlin	excerpts from: *Il barbiere di Seviglia* [Rossini]; *Le nozze di Figaro* [Mozart]; *Un ballo in maschera* [Verdi]; *Le mauvais oeil* [?]; *Faust* [Gounod]; Spanish chanson: *Ay chiquita!* [?]; chansonnettes by Saint-Germain
Son Exc le ministre de la justice, M Delangle	no details	no details

M le président Troplong	no details	aria from *La sonnambula* [Bellini]; mélodie by Gounod: *Le Printemps*
M le Baron de la Banque de France	M Gardoni, Mme Frezzolini	unnamed airs and duos
Mme Wartel*	Mme Wekerlin-Damoreau, M Levasseur	no details
M & Mme Paul Bernard*	Mme Iweins d'Hennin	no details
March 1862		
M & Mme Delangle (at the Ministry of Justice)	Mmes Carvalho, Penco, MM Delle-Sedie, Gardoni, Zucchini	no details
M & Mme…	Mmes Miolan-Carvalho, Wekerlin-Damoreau	duo from *Le nozze di Figaro* [Mozart]
M & Mme B…	Mme Wekerlin-Damoreau (violin obbligato played by Sarasate)	air by Clapisson; mélodie by Gounod: *Sérénade*
Mme Pfeiffer*	MM Géraldy, Biéval, Mlle Baretti (Théâtre-Lyrique)	rehearsal of salon opera by Pfeiffer: *Capitaine Roche*
M & Mme Ernest Lévi-Alvarès*	M Vincent (tenor), Mlles Van den Berghe, Nina Polak	mélodie by Gounod: *Sérénade*; romance from *Si j'étais roi!* [Adam]; grand air from *Zampa* [Hérold]; romance by Godefroid: *Réveil des fées*
M & Mme de St-Chaffreid (faubourg Saint-Germain)	Mme Frezzolini	no details
Mme Osmont du Tillet ('son élégant hôtel de l'avenue de Saint-Cloud')	MM Bonnehée (Opéra), Géraldy, Capoul, Mlle Vestris	excerpts from: *Les mousquetaires de la reine* [Halévy]; *Le chalet* [Adam]; *Il trovatore* [Verdi]

183

Salons	Singers	Songs
M le baron de Montour	Mme Penco, MM Lucchesi, Tagliafico, Zucchini	*Il bacio* [Giordani]; *Tarantelle* (Rossini)
Ministère de l'Etat	Mmes Viardot, Gueymard, MM Gueymard, Obin	French & Italian repertoire
Mlle Joséphine Martin*	Mme Trélat, Mlle Martin soeur, MM Lyon, Lévy	chansons by Malézieux
Mmes Orfila & Mosnerons de Saint Preux	Mme Bouland, MM Coulons, Marochetti, Pagans, Guidon frères	no details
M & Mme Paul Bernard*	Mmes Peudefer, Iweins-d'Hennin, MM Vincent (tenor), Guidon frères	romance by Bernard: *Le réveil des fleurs*; *Plaisir d'amour* [Martini?]
M Le Couppey*	Mme Bouland, M Bataille	duo from *Caïd* (Le Couppey)
	MM Brasseur, Pellerin (both from Palais-Royal)	salon opera by Chautagne: *Jean qui rit et Jean qui pleure*
M L…	M Alatavilla	excerpts from *Martha* [Flotow]; romance by Stanzieri: *Io t'amerò*
M Pitre-Chevalier* (faubourg Saint-Honoré)	Mlles Rousseil, Dupont, Mme Ugalde, M Delle-Sedie	proverbe by Pitre-Chevalier
Mmes Orfila & Mosnerons de Saint Preux	Mlles Baretti (Théâtre-Lyrique), Dorus, MM Géraldy, Biéval, Naudin (Théâtre-Italien)	salon opera: *Capitaine Roque* [*Roche*] [see Mme Pfeiffer above]
Mmes Orfila & Mosnerons de Saint Preux	Mme Charton-Demeur, Mlle Trebelli, MM Naudin, Standley [Stanley?], Petey (both from 'the English Opera')	Quartet from *Rigoletto* [Verdi]; Spanish chansons [?]; aria (Mercadante)

April 1862

Le comte Nieuwerkerke (at the Louvre)	M Cazaux (Opéra)	no details
M & Mme Crémieux (two salons in the same week)	Women's Choir (cond. Membrée), Mmes Grisi, Wekerlin-Damoreau, Nantier-Didiée, Brunetti, MM Duprez (père & fils), Levasseur, Mario, Delle-Sedie, Géraldy, Standley [sic], Petey	excerpts from La reine de Saba [Gounod]; Moïse et Pharaon [Rossini]; mélodies by Membrée
M le président Troplong (au Sénat)	no details	no details
M le préfet de la Seine	Mme Penco, M Graziani	excerpts from Il trovatore [Verdi]; Il bacio [Giordani]; Ave Maria [Gounod]
M le comte & Mme la comtesse de Morny (au Corps législatif)	Mme Corani (Spanish singer)	no details
Other salons during the week: S A I la princesse Mathilde; Son Exc le comte de Walewski; M le ministre d'Etat	M & Mme Gueymard, M Obin (Opéra) – no other details	no details
M & Mme Rossini*	Mlle Marie Battu, MM Badiali, Frizzi	unpublished boléro by Rossini
M & Mme G H...	Mlle de Marville, M Vincent	air from Le concert à la cour [?]; duo from Les mousquetaires de la reine [Auber]
Le comte Nieuwerkerke	MM Duprez (père & fils)	excerpt from La juive (Halévy)

Salons	Singers	Songs
(at the Louvre) M & Mme Paul Bernard*	Mme Iweins d'Hennin	romances: *Les saisons* (Massé); *Ce que femme veut* (Lhuilier)
Mme Ida Bertrand*	Mmes Bertrand, Wekerlin-Damoreau, MM Roger, Graziani, Samson	excerpts from: *Semiramide; Tancredi* [Rossini]; air by Géraldy: *Le toréador; Le chalet* [Adam]
Mme Osmond du Tillet (at Villa du Passy)	Mm Graziani, Bettini, Capoul	excerpts from: *La fille du régiment; La favorite* [Donizetti]; *Le prophète* [Meyerbeer]
December 1862 M & Mme Rossini* (have begun their winter salons)	no details	no details
M & Mme Rossini*	MM Géraldy, Nadaud	chansons by Nadaud: *La maison blanche; Le prince indien*
January 1863 M Pitre-Chevalier* (rue des Ecuries d'Artois [rue d'Artois] faubourg Saint-Honoré)	Mme Comettant, MM Géraldy, Delle-Sedie, Anthiome père & fils, Comettant	'comédie en wagon' by Pitre Chevalier: *De Pont l'Eveque à Trouville, ou la question du cigare* [see also below]
M & Mme Rossini*	Mlle Trebelli, MM Badiali, Delle-Sedie	excerpts from: *Semiramide; Il barbiere di Siviglia* [Rossini]
M & Mme Orfila	Mlle Marie Battu, Mme Charles Ponchard, M Delle-Sedie	no details
unnamed salon in the Chaussée-d'Antin	no details	mélodies by Mutel: *Clair de lune; Il suffit d'aimer; Le réveil du printemps*

M & Mme Rossini*	Mlle Adelina Patti, M Delle-Sedie	duo from *Il barbiere di Siviglia* [Rossini], *La calesera* [Yradier]
Mmes Orfila & Mosnerons de Saint Preux	Mlles Battu, Trebelli, MM Naudin, Zucchini, Delle-Sedie, Levassor, M & Mme Ferranti	Italian (vocal) quintet [?]
Mme Chaudesaigues*	MM Triebert, Jacourt, Michiels, Guidon, Fauvre, Guidon frères, Mlle Louise Chaudesaigues	air from *La muette de Portici* [Auber]; chansonnette by Plantade
M Bergson*	Mmes Marchesi, Guery-Fleury, Mlle Lindo	works by Bergson: *Berceuse*; *Barcarolle*; *Styrienne*
M & Mme Rossini*	Mme Trebelli, Mlle Battu, MM Badiali, Gardoni, Zucchini, Caponi	aria and duo from *Tancredi* [Rossini]
M Pitre-Chevalier*	Mlle Rousseille, MM Berthelier, Malézieux	music for a charade by Pitre-Chevalier: *Le cigare en wagon* (ouverture, cavatine, romance & chansons)
Mme Orfila	Mlles Balbi, Géraldine (Opéra-Comique)	bolero from *La chanteuse voilée* [Massé]; [vocal] variations by Rode
M Billault (two soirées given in his 'bel hôtel', rue de la Michodière)	Mlle Trebelli	no details
February 1863 M & Mme Pereire	Mlle Adelina Patti (who had appeared in this salon in 1862), Mme Méric-Lablache, MM Mario, Delle-Sedie	no details

Salons	Singers	Songs
M le président Troplong (every Sunday)	no details	no details
M le duc de Morny (every Wednesday)	no details	no details
M Marmontel	Mlles Rey, Lée, M Vincent	no details
Mme Erard ('dans son splendide appartement dans la rue du Mail' – her 2nd private salon for the season)	Mlle Trebelli	airs: *Giuramento* [?]; *Voi che sapete* [Mozart]; *Echo des îles* [?]
M Moreau, l'agent de change	Mme Trebelli, Mlle Battu, MM Delle-Sedie, Zucchini, Naudin, Gardoni, Capponi	no details
Mme la comtesse Lowenthal	Mme Viardot, M Delle-Sedie	various operatic intermèdes from the Théâtre-Italien (in costume)
M Haussman (at the Hôtel de Ville)	Mlle Battu, M Zucchini	excerpts from *Stradella* [Flotow]
M & Mme Rossini*	Mlle Battu, MM Badiali, Géraldy	music preceding a comédie (no details)
Mme Orfila	MM Duprez, Naudin, Mlles Brunetti (pupil of Duprez), Rives (pupil of comtesse Sparre)	duo from *Rigoletto* [Verdi]
M & Mme Rossini	Mme la vicomtesse de Grandval, Mlle Trebelli, MM Badiali, Tagliafico, Berthier	no details

M & Mme Billaud	Mlles Trebelli, Brunetti	no details
Lady Cowley	Mme Emma Wernik (Drury Lane, London)	excerpts from *Lucrezia Borgia* [Donizetti]
Mme Erard	Mlle Brunetti, M Jules Lefort	mélodies: *Chanson d'amour* (Membrée); *Le vallon* (Gounod)
M Paul Bernard*	MM Nadaud, Vincent, Guidon frères	chansons by Nadaud
M & Mme Billaud	MM Tagliafico, Berthelier, Mlle Rousseille	three comédies: *La leçon de chant*; *Le cigare en wagon* (Pitre-Chevalier); *L'école des vieillards* [?]
M & Mme Rossini	Mlles Dinah Félix, Battu, Mme Alboni, MM Delle-Sedie, Solieri	*Le cigare en wagon* (Pitre-Chevalier)
M & Mme Rossini	MM Levassor, Berthelier, Brasseur	comédie/vaudeville: *Carabinier et Fantassin* [?]
March 1863		
M & Mme Haussmann (at the Hôtel de Ville) – their second private concert	Mlle Batu, M Zucchini	excerpts from *La bohémienne* (Balfe); *Colinette à la cour* (Grétry)
Le comte de Nieuwerkerke (at the Louvre)	M Naudin	excerpts from *Robert d'Evreux* [Donizetti]; *Così fan tutti* [Mozart]
M & Mme Isaac Pereire (organized by Rubini)	Mmes Frezzolini, Nantié-Didier, MM Naudin, Graziani, Capponi, Tamberlick, (with choir)	excerpts from: *Così fan tutti* (Mozart); *Ernani* (Verdi); *Il Desiderio* (Gordigiani); *Guillaume Tell* (Rossini); *Rigoletto* (Verdi); *Lucia di Lammermoor* (Donizetti); *Norma* (Bellini); mélodie by Pinsatti; Valse by Ciardi

Salons	Singers	Songs
Mlle Joséphine Martin*	Mlle Trebelli, M Bettini	excerpts from: *Tancredi*; *La Gazza Ladra* [Rossini]; lieder by Schubert, arr for two voices by Mlle Martin: *Dis-le-moi* [Die vier Weltalter]
Mme Ernest Lévi-Alvarès* (every Saturday)	Mme Sébaut (Mlle Pauline Thys), Mlle Camille Labarr, MM Vincent, Alfred Guyard, Jules Bosquin	no details
M le préfet de la Seine (M Haussmann) at the Hôtel de Ville	Mlle Trebelli [Mme Bettini], M Bettini, (with orch & choir cond. by Pasdeloup)	excerpts from: *L'elisir d'amore* (Donizetti); *Sapho* (Pacini); *La cenerentola*; *Semiramide* (Rossini)
La marquise d'Aoust (in Faubourg Saint-Germain)	Mme Ribault, Mlle Lapommeraye, MM Jules Lefort, Biéval (with choir and orchestra cond. by the composer)	opéra comique by le marquis d'Aoust: *Une partie de dominos*
M le Grand, référendaire marquis d'Hautpoul (at the Palais de Luxembourg every Wednesday)	Mlle Marie Sax, M Caron	no details
M de Royer, at the Palais de Luxembourg	no details	no details
M & Mme de L…	Mlle Balbi, MM Félix Lévy, de Boislisle, Levassor, Malézieux	*Poème de la mer* (Wekerlin); chansons by Nadaud
M & Mme Crémieux	MM Duprez (father & son), Naudin, Delle-Sedie, Mmes Vandenheuvel-Duprez, Laborde	no details
M & Mme Mathieu	Mmes Miolan-Carvalho, Faure-Lefebvre,	no details

Host	Performers	Details
M & Mme Seydoux	MM Battaille, Capoul Mme Trebelli-Bettini, MM Delle-Sedie, Ravina, Braga	no details
Mme Alexandre (Charlotte Dreyfus)*	Mmes Oscar Comettant, Bertini	excerpts from: Lalla-Roukh [F David]; Il Bacio [Giordani]; Robin des bois [arr of Weber's Die Freischütz]
M Rossini*	Mlle Trebelli	La farfalletta [Giordani]; unpublished [vocal] polka-mazurka [?]
Mme Erard	Mme Viardot	excerpt from Orphée (Gluck)
M Ettling (his second matinée musicale for the season)	Mme Gaveaux-Sabatier, Mlle Labarre, M Tagliafico	opéra comique by Maquet: Les dragons de Villars; chansonnettes by Ettling
M Rossini*	Mlle Gris, Mmes Ferranti, Trebelli (with choir)	settings of Stabat mater by Pergolesi, Haydn & Rossini
Mlle Gabrielle Colson (every month)	Mlle Samary, MM Paul Briand, Lionnet frères	no details
Mme Orfila	M & Mme Bettini-Trebelli, MM Lévy, Marochetti, Mlle Marie Bailly (pupil of Wartel)	no details

April 1863

Host	Performers	Details
M & Mme Rossini*	M & Mme Bettini-Trebelli, Mme Ferranti, MM Gardoni, Badiali	no details
M le préfet de la Seine (M Haussmann) at the Hôtel	Mlle Sax, MM Gardoni, Colomb	Inflammatus (Rossini); sacred aria by Stradella; Sanctus (Gounod); excerpts from Elie

Salons	Singers	Songs
de Ville M Pitre-Chevalier*	M & Mme Tagliafico, Levassor, Mme Comettant	(Mendelssohn) no details
M Pitre-Chevalier* (this salon event involving painting, declamation and music)	M & Mme Bettini-Trebelli, Mmes Méric Lalande, Garait, Paër, Mlle Clara Lemonnier, M Coquelin, Dubois	duo: Mira la bianca luna (Morin); arias by Rossini; romance from Aladin [?]; duo bouffe from Les tourtereaux (Vizentini); new chanson by Nadaud; salon opera by Barbier: Le loup et l'agneau
M & Mme Pfeiffer*	Mme Bertrand, MM White, Lebouc, Pagans	no details
M & Mme Ernest Lévi-Alvarès* (the first of their fortnightly salons for the season)	M Vincent	no details
M Nadar (in his atelier in the boulevard des Capucines)	M Gossier	excerpt from Il barbiere di Siviglia [Rossini]
December 1863 Mlle Laguesse* (the first of the season for her salons in the Chaussée-d'Antin)	MM Saint-Foy, Guidon frères	two romances by Lhuillier: L'enfant prodigue; La lettre d'un chinois
'une soirée intime'	Mmes Gagliono (Spanish singer), Allard-Guerette, MM Faure, Guidon frères	no details

January 1864

various salons at the homes of M & Mme Pereire, M & Mme Jules Beer, Mmes Orfila & Mosnerons	Mme Charton-Demeur, MM Nicolini, Giraldoni, Sighicelli, Berthelier	no details
M & Mme Bernard*	Mlle Ducasse, MM Henri Le Roy, Nadaud ('le chansonnier parisien')	no details
M le ministre des travaux publics (à ses invités')	Mme Frezzolini, M Severini	no details
Mlle Laguesse*	Mme [Mlle?] Tillemont	aria from *Il barbiere di Sivigli* [Rossini]; [historiette musicale] by Lhuillier: *La tante Julie*
Mme Pfeiffer*	Mmes Bertrand, Pfeiffer	no details
Mmes Orfila & Mosnerons de Saint Preux	M & Mme Bettini-Trebelli. M G Duprez & Mlle Marimon unable to appear because of illness, their places taken by members of the invited audience: Mme Cagliano, MM Lyon, Duprez (fils)	two unnamed mélodies; aria by Mozart; *L'hiver* (Offenbach), *Le géant* (Delioux)

February 1864

M & Mme Haussmann (at the Hôtel de Ville – their first for the season)	Mme Trebelli-Bettini	excerpts from: *Tancredi*; *L'italiana in Algeri* (Rossini); *Les Huguenots* (Meyerbeer)
M & Mme Naudin*	Mmes Sax, Frezzolini, Lanari, Tilmant, MM Naudin, Lefort, Saint-Foy	excerpts from: *Jérusalem* [Verdi]; *Martha* [Flotow]; *Linda* [?]

Salons	Singers	Songs
Son Exc M & Mme Boudet at the hôtel de la place Beauvau	Mme Miolan Carvalho, MM Gardoni, Faure, Braga	excerpts from: *Le nozze di Figaro* (Mozart); *Philémon et Baucis* (Gounod); *L'étoile du nord* (Meyerbeer); mélodie by Faure: *Les rameaux*
M & Mme Rossini*	Mme Adelina Patti, Mme de Méric-Lablache, MM Gardoni, Delle-Sedie, Scalese	excerpts from: *Moïse et Pharaon*; *La cenerentola*; *Tancredi*; *Semiramide*; *La gazza ladra* [Rossini]; *Un ballo in maschera* (Verdi); some unpublished songs by Rossini
M Lebouc* (every Monday)	M Jules Lefort	three new mélodies by Durand
M le président Troplong (at the Petit-Luxembourg)	Mme Vandenheuvel, MM Gardoni, Tagliafico	excerpts from: *Otello*; *Il barbiere di Siviglia* [Rossini]; *Don Giovanni* [Mozart]; *La traviata* [Verdi]; *Lalla-Roukh* [F David]
M & Mme Haussmann (at the Hôtel de Ville)	Mlle Battu, Lévy, MM Faure, Villaret	excerpts from: *Don Giovanni* (Mozart); *Jérusalem* (Verdi); *Le chamelier* (Auber); *La cenerentola*; *Moïse* (Rossini); *Euranthe* (Weber); *Les rameaux* (Faure)
M & Mme Orfila	Mme Tillemont, MM Saint-Foy, Eugène Guidon	salon opera: *A deux pas du bonheur* (Godefroid); two chansons by Godefroid
Son Exc le ministre de l'interieur	M Faure	excerpt from *L'étoile du nord* (Meyerbeer); *Les rameaux* [Faure]
Mlle Joséphine Martin*	Mme Oscar Comettant, Mlle Martin, MM Bonnehée, Nadaud	duo from *Lalla-Roukh* [F David]; *La colombe* (Membrée); *Agnus Die* (Godefroid); aria from *Les saisons* (Haydn); three chansons by Nadaud
M & Mme Melchior	Mlle Girard, MM Goudin, Nadaud	chansons by Nadaud

Mocker*

March 1864

	Performers	Details
M & Mme Paul Bernard*	Mme Tillemont, M Sainte-Foy	no details
M & Mme Ettling*	Mlles Bodin, Lee, M Lutz (Théâtre-Lyrique)	excerpts from *Rigoletto* [Verdi]; vocal variations (Rode); mélodie (Schumann); *Sérénade* (Braga); unpublished opera by Ettling: *Un jour de noce*
M & Mme Paul Bernard*	Mme Gagliano, M & Mme Tagliafico, M Nadaud	no details
M le comte Nieuwerkerke (at the Louvre)	M Naudin	no details
M & Mme Pereire	Mmes Carvalho, Battu, MM Faure, Gardoni & choirs	no details
M le directeur général Guillemot (Hôtel de la Caisse des dépôts et consignations)	Mme Peudefer, M Lamazou	no details
M & Mme Paul Bernard*	Mme Marie Damoreaux	unpublished songs by Mme Amélie Perronnet; two chansons espagnoles by Dessauer
M le docteur Mendl	M Gardoni, Mlle Dorus	no details
M le président du Sénat [M Troplong]	Mmes de Taisy, Trebelli-Bettini, MM Tagliafico, Gardoni	excerpts from: *Kruschmann*[?]; *La gazza ladra* [Rossini]; *Les diamants de la couronne* [Auber]; *Ermione* [Rossini]; *Il barbiere di Siviglia* [Rossini]; *Le pierre de Médicis* [Poniatowski]; *Le*

195

Salons	Singers	Songs
M le comte & Mme la comtesse Pepoli (at their home in the Cours-la-Reine, Champs-Elysées)	Mlle Hebbe	comte Ory [Rossini]; L'italiana in Algeri [Rossini]; Rigoletto [Verdi]
M & Mme Paul Bernard* (the conclusion of their season)	MM Saint-Foy, Nadaud, Mmes Tillemont, Gagliano, M & Mme Tagliafico	no details
M Marmontel* (the conclusion of his Wednesday salons for the season)	MM Lyon, Guidon frères, Mme Lagnier, Mlle d'Oram	no details
M & Mme Lévi Alvarès* (Place Royale in the Marais)	M Lafont, Mlle Nina Polak, Mme Lévi Alvarès	Félicité de ma misère (Durand)
M le docteur Trousseau	Mmes de Caters, Méric-Lablache, MM Delle-Sedie, Gardoni	no details
April 1864		
M & Mme Rossini*	Mlles Marchisio soeurs, MM Gardoni, Delle-Sedie, Agnesi, Frizzi	no details
M & Mme Lévi-Alvarès (their final salon for the season)	Mmes Pothin-Labarre, Lévi-Alvarès, MM Thys, Guidon frères	Le cor des Alpes [?]; romances by Thys

M Marmontel*	Mme Oscar Comettant, Crépet-Garcia, Mlle Darans	air from *Lalla-Roukh* [F. David]; air from *Robert le diable* [Meyerbeer]

January 1865 ('Les salons officiels et privés s'ouvrent sur toute la ligne')

M le ministre des travaux publics (à ses invités')	Mme Frezzolini, M Severini	no details
La princesse Mathilde (the first of her Sunday receptions)	Mmes la vicomtesse Grandval, Boucher, M Naudin	no details
M & Mme B…	MM Marochotti, G Duprez, Mme B… (Duprez's pupil)	excerpts from: *Il trovatore* [Verdi]; *L'elisir d'amore* [Donizetti]; scene: *Gastibelza* (Duprez); chansons by Duprez
Various salons at the homes of 'le président Troplong, le ministre du commerce et des travaux publique, M & Mme Benoit-Champy, M & Mme Legouvé, les docteurs Trélat & Mendl et dans bien d'autres salons …	MM Naudin, Gardoni, Delle-Sedie, Agnesi, Mmes Frezzolini, Crépet (daughter of Manuel Garcia), T…, Mlle Battu	*L'âme du purgatoire* (Silny); chansons by Nadaud
M Cordier ('célebre statuaire')	Mmes Michaeli, Lagnier, Pothin, MM Tissérand, Henry	excerpt from *Un ballo in maschera* [Verdi]; quatuor bouffe by Duprez: *Les trois étoiles*;

Salons	Singers	Songs
M & Mme Naudin* (every Wednesday)	Mmes Sax, Domenich-Bardoni (Turin Opera), M Naudin	unnamed operetta by Godefroid; excerpts from *Robert le diable* [Meyerbeer]; *Rigoletto* [Verdi]; 'air di bravura'; several Italian romances
Château de la Rocheville, Saint-Germain	Mmes Mackenzie (Catinka de Dietz); David Villers	three 'morceaux de caractère'
February 1865		
mention of salons in the homes of le Prince Metternich; la duchesse Riaro de Sforza; la princesse Troubetzkoï	no details	no details
M & Mme Isaac Pereire	Mme Adelina Patti	music by Rossini, Donizetti, Verdi, Auber (*Manon Lescaut*), Gounod (*Ave Maria*)
M le président Benoit-Champy	Mmes Bouchet, Crépet-Garcia, M de Saint-Julien (with choir composed of 'femmes du monde')	Act 1 of *Mireille* [Gounod]
Mme Linger	la princess B…, Mme S… (with choir composed of 'femmes du monde')	Act 1 of *Mireille* [Gounod]
M & Mme Naudin	Mmes Sax, Frezzolini, M Naudin	excerpts from: *Jérusalem* [Verdi]; *Il trovatore* [Verdi]; *Martha* [Flotow]
Mme Erard (every Sunday)	Mme Vandenheuvel-Duprez	no details
Mme Camille Dubois	Mme T…, M Silny	*L'âme du purgatoire* (Silny); chansons by Nadaud

Host	Performers	Program
M le comte Nieuwerkerke (at the Louvre)	M Naudin	no details
M Lebouc*	Mme Serre de Bonne	no details
M Rinaldi fils (rue Favart)	MM Guidon frères, Agnesi, Mlle Baretti	no details
M Pigeory	no details	no details
March 1865		
M le comte Nieuwerkerke (at the Louvre)	M Naudin	excerpts from: *Cosi fan tutti* [Mozart]; *Rigoletto* [Verdi]
M Troplong, président du Sénat	Mme Lanari	excerpts from *Semiramide* [Rossini]
M le marquis et Mme la marquise d'Aoust	Mlle de Lapommeraye (Opéra), MM Bach, Marochetti	salon opera by Peruzzi: *L'Amour voleur* (orchestra conducted by le marquis d'Aoust)
Mme Erard ('l'élite des artistes, des littérateurs & des gens du monde')	Mlle Nilsson (Théâtre-Lyrique), M Delle-Sedie (Théâtre-Italien)	excerpts from: *Rigoletto* [Verdi]; *Don Giovanni* [Mozart]; *Un ballo in maschera* [Verdi]; *Il maggio de canto* [Campana]; romances and melodies: *Hai luli* (Reber); *Pauvre Jacques* (Garat); air from *Betty* [A. Thomas]
M le préfet de la Seine	Mme Rudersdorff	excerpts from: *La clemenza di Tito* [Mozart]; *La création* [Haydn]
M & Mme Isaac Pereire	M Graziani, Gardoni, Mme Frezzolini, Mlle Nilsson	excerpt from *Don Giovanni* [Mozart]
M Pozzo di Borgo (organized by Rubini)	Mme Bertrand, Mlle Battu, MM Faure, Gardoni, and choirs from the Conservatoire	excerpts from *Moïse* [Rossini]

Salons	Singers	Songs
M & Mme Billaud	Mmes B…, C…, M L…, Agnesi	chansons by Nadaud
M & Mme Billaud	MM Capoul, Caron, Mme Pascal (Opéra)	no details
M & Mme T…	Mmes Frezzolini, Bertrand, Crépet-Garcia, MM Agnesi, Nadaud, and female choir	no details
M Rossini	M Agnesi, Mme Bemberg	excerpts from: *Il barbiere di Siviglia* [Rossini]; *La sonnambula* [Bellini]
Mme la marquise d'Aoust	Mlle de Lapommeraye (Opéra), MM Bach, Marochetti	opéra comique by d'Aoust: *L'amour voleur*
Mlle Joséphine Martin*	MM Tamburini, Gardoni, Nadaud, Mlle Cordier	chansons by Nadaud
Mme Osmond du Tillet (in rue d'Eylau)	Mlle de Maësen (Théâtre-Lyrique), M Arsendeau	no details
M le comte de Nieuwerkerke (at the Louvre)	M Graziani	no details
M Rossini	Mme Méric-Lablache	romance from *La Duchessa di San Giuliano* (Graffigna)
M & Mme Naudin*	Mmes Frezzolini, Naudin, Mlle Tillemont	no details
M & Mme Billaud	Mmes Marie Cinti-Damoreau, Pascal, MM Capoul, Caron	no details
M & Mme Crémieux	Mmes Duprez-Vandenheuvel, Nantier-	no details

200

Host	Performers	Details
	Didiée, MM Tamberlick, Delle-Sedie	
M Melchior Mocker*	Mlle Joly, MM Lebouc, Lebrun, Nadaud, Mocker	no details
M & Mme Naudin	Mmes Frezzolini, Castelmary-Sax, Mlle Taisy, MM Naudin, Steller (Théâtre-Italien, Moscow)	excerpts from *La reine de Saba* [Gounod]; *Le siège de Corinthe* [Rossini]; *Linda* [?]
Mme Erard ('à sa société intime')	Mlle Nilsson	excerpts from *Die Zauberflöte* [Mozart]
M & Mme Castelmary-Sax*	Mlle Taisy (Opéra), M Villaret	excerpts from: *Jérusalem*; *Les vêpres siciliennes* [Verdi]; *Norma* [Bellini]; *Il sogno* [?]; unnamed mélodie by Massé
Mme la duchesse Pozzo di Borgo	Mme Bertrand, Mlle Battu	excerpts from: *Moïse* [Rossini]; *Mireille* [Gounod]; *La reine de Chypre* [Halévy]; *Le chalet* [Adam]

April 1865

Host	Performers	Details
M & Mme Naudin*	Mlle Cruvelli, MM Jules Lefort, Naudin	excerpts from: *Lucrezia Borgia* [Donizetti]; *Tannhaüser* [Wagner]; *Belisario* [Donizetti]
M Marmontel*	Mlle Fioretti, M Jules Lefort	no details
M & Mme Benoit Champy	Mmes Frezzolini, Crépet-Garcia, MM Tamburini, Graziani, Nadaud	*Ave Maria* (Gounod)
M le préfet de la Seine	Mlle Lemmens-Sherrington (English singer)	*Il pensiero* (Handel); *Variations* (Rode); *Agnus dei* (A. Thomas); *Inflammatus* (Rossini)
M le comte Nieuwerkerke (at the Louvre)	M Petit (Théâtre-Lyrique)	no details
M & Mme Beynac*	Mme Beynac; Mlle Martin, MM Beynac,	excerpts from: *Mireille* [Gounod]; *Moïse*

Salons	Singers	Songs
(rue Jacob)	Nadaud	[Rossini]; *Le Pré aux clercs* [Hérold]; chansons by Nadaud
M & Mme Lévi-Alvarès* (their last for the season)	Mme Alard-Guerette	chansonnettes by Bloch
Mlle Joséphine Martin*	MM Roger, Lafont, T..., Mme Lanari, choirs from the Conservatoire	romance by Roger: *Oiseaux légers*
Le comte et la comtesse Pillet-Will	Mlles Marchisio soeurs	*Petite messe solennelle* (Rossini)
December 1865		
'Soirée musicale du grand monde officiel dans les salons du ministre des travaux publics'	Mme Battu, M Fraschini	excerpts from: *Martha* [Flotow]; *La gazza ladra* [Rossini]; *Les vêpres siciliennes* [Verdi]
Mme Eugénie Garcia*	MM Gardoni, Nadaud, Mmes T..., C...	romances & chansons: *Les jaloux* (Bériot père); *Lorsque j'aimais* (Nadaud); *La prière du barde* (Godefroid); various chansons espagnoles
January 1866		
M & Mme Béhic (in the salons of Ministère du Commerce & des Travaux Publics)	Mlle Nilsson, M Delle-Sedie	lieder by Schumann
S A I la princesse Mathilde	Mlle Nilsson, M Delle-Sedie	excerpts from *Il barbiere di Siviglia* [Rossini]; *Die Zauberflöte* [Mozart]; *Il sogno* [?]

M & Mme Orfila	Mme Cabel, Mlle Astieri, MM Delle-Sedie, Agnesi, Jules Lefort	excerpt from: *Maometto* [Rossini]; romances, chansons & mélodies: *Chanson d'amour* (Membrée); *Adieu à l'hôtesse arabe* (Vaucorbeil); *Insomnie; Ma maison; Le prince indien; Les chaussettes; Le fantassin* (Nadaud)
Mlle Mosneron ('qui habite la maison Orfila')		no details
Mme la princesse Mathilde ('La musique règne en souveraine aux réceptions du dimanche')	Mme Carvalho	no details
M Rossini		
Docteur Trélat	M Faure, Mme de Grandval	scène-mélodie Mme Grandval: *Le bohémien; Les regrets* (Mme de Grandval)
	M Pagans (Théâtre-Italien), Mlle Anaïs Roulle	works by Italian, French and German composers
Docteur Mandl	MM Gardoni, Tamburini	new chansons by Nadaud
M & Mme Béhic (in the salons of Ministère du Commerce & des Travaux Publics)	Mlle Nisson, MM Delle-Sedie, Zucchini	excerpts from Rossini, Donizetti, Verdi, Gounod, Meyerbeer
M Rossini	M Tamburini, Mlle Battu	excerpt from *Il barbiere di Siviglia* [Rossini]; *romance à une seule note* (Rossini)
February 1866 Mme Gunzberg ('dans	Mme Carvalho (replacing Mme Patti),	excerpts from *Martha* [Flotow]; *Il barbiere di*

Salons	Singers	Songs
ses salons magnifiques')	Mlle Grossi, MM Naudin, Delle-Sedie	Siviglia [Rossini]
Le ministre d'Haïti (arranged by M Bazzoni)	Mmes Sylvie, Débrosse (pupils of Bazzoni)	no details
M Ernest Nathan*	MM Marachotti, Nadaud, Puget	unpublished new opera by Nathan fils
Mlle Joséphine Laguesse*	Mme Gaveaux-Sabatier, M Nadaud	no details
Hôtel de Ville	Mlle Nilsson, M Naudin	excerpt from L'africaine [Meyerbeer]
M & Mme Orfila	Mme Damoreaux-Wekerlin, MM Ulisse Duwast (Théâtre-Lyrique), Barré	excerpts from L'ambassadrice [Auber]; Le nouveau seigneur du village [Boïeldieu]; chansons by unnamed composers, incl La promesse
Mme J H...	MM Delle-Sedie, Scalese, Sighicelli, Durand, Godefroid, de Bériot, Mme Crépet-Garcia	vocal quintet by Godefroid: La prière des bardes
Le comte Nieuwerkerke (at the Louvre)	no details	no details
M & Mme Pereire	Mmes Carvalho, Nilsson, MM Delle-Sedie, Michot	no details
Mme Gaveaux-Sabatier*	Mme Gaveaux-Sabatier, MM Hermann Léon, Bellouet	new unnamed salon opera by Wekerlin
Mme C... (in the rue de la Chaussée-d'Antin)	MM Nadaud, Félix L..., Mme T..., and 'un groupe d'amateurs excellents musiciens ...')	Oiseaux légers (Gumbert)

March 1866

Salons	Singers	Songs
M & Mme de Forges	Mme Thys-Sébault, MM Ducellier, Doyen	unnamed operetta by Thys-Sébault

M & Mme Achille Fould	Mlles Battu, Rives, MM Delle-Sedie, Gardoni	trio from *Il matrimonio segreto* (Cimarosa)
Le marquis & la marquise d'Aoust	Mmes Grandval, Ronalds, MM Franchesci, Marachetti, Vinay	chansons by Nadaud; work by the marquis d'Aoust
M Revenez (rue du Sentier)	Mme Peudefer, Mlles Lefébure-Wely soeurs, MM Barré (Théâtre-Lyrique), Guidon frères	salon opera: *Pour les pauvres* [?]
M & Mme Jules Beer* (rue d'Aumale)	M Capoul, Mlles Cornélis soeurs, Mme Crépet-Garcia	excerpts from: *La fille d'Egypte* (Beer); *Le lion amoureux* [Beer]; *Die Freischütz* [Weber]; *Adelaïde* (Beethoven)
various salons featuring two visiting artists in the homes of Henri Herz, Marmontel, Heugel, Beer	Mlles Cornélis (from Brussels)	no details
Mme Tarbé des Sablons (rue Boudreau 'où le culte de la musique soit particulièrement en honneur')	Mlle de la Pommeraye, MM Naudin, Pancani	excerpts from *Les noces de Jeanette* [Massé]; *Rigoletto* [Verdi]; *Il sogno* [?]
M & Mme Naudin*	Mlle Méla, MM Tagliafico, Zucchini, Sighicelli, Sainte-Foy	excerpts from *Roberto Devereux* (Donizetti); trio bouffe: *Papatacci* [Rossini]
M Paul Bernard*	MM Nadaud, Sainte-Foy, Coedès, Guidon frères, Mmes Marie Damoreau, Peudefer, Tillemont, Mlles Roulle,	no details

205

Salons	Singers	Songs
	Fauchet	
Le comte Nieuwerkerke (at the Louvre)	Mlle Nisson, M Capoul	excerpts from *Martha* [Flotow]; *Rigoletto* [Verdi]; songs: *Adelaïde* (Beethoven); *Ave Maria* (Gounod)
M Melchior Mocker* (weekly salons)	Mlle Girard, M Nadaud	excerpt from *Le saphir* [F. David]; ancient airs by Wekerlin; chansons by Nadaud
M le docteur Mandl	M Sainte-Foy	unnamed chansonnettes
La princesse Mathilde	Mme Carvalho	mélodies by Mme de Grandval: *L'absence*; unpublished *Valse* (dedicated to Mme Carvalho)
M le comte Nieuwerkerke (at the Louvre)	M Capoul	*Adelaïde* (Beethoven); excerpt from *Marie* [*Maria Stuarda* by Donizetti?]
M & Mme Orfila	Mlles Reboux (Théâtre-Italien at Moscow), Cornélis soeurs (from Brussels), M Lamazou	*Au bal* (Badia)
Le comte Nieuwerkerke (at the Louvre)	Mme Carvalho (accompanied by Bizet)	excerpt from *Mireille* [Gounod]; mélodie: *Vieille chanson* (Bizet)
Mme Elie de Beaumont	M Archainbaud	romances by Mathieu: *Les larmes d'un ange*; *Le chevalier*
Le comte Nieuwerkerke (at the Louvre)	M Delle-Sedie [Liszt was the featured artist at this salon]	arias from *Stradella* [Flotow? Niedermeyer?]; mélodie: *Medjé* (Gounod)
Mlle Joséphine Martin*	Mlle Léonie Martin, MM Géraldy, Puget, Pagans, Lafont, Nadaud, Lecieux, Nathan	no details
M Melchior Mocker* (weekly salons)	Mlle Girard, M Nadaud	excerpts from *Le saphir* [F. David]; ancient chansons arr. by Wekerlin; chansons by Nadaud

Hôtel de Ville	Mme Carvalho, M Gardoni	excerpts from *Le magali* [?]; *Martha* [Flotow]; *Le nozze di Figaro* [Mozart]
M & Mme Lévi-Alvarès*	Mlle Roulle, Mme Pothin, MM Guidon frères	*Nocturnes* [?]; chansons by Nadaud
Mlle Jenny Sabatier	no details	chansons by Nadaud; scènes & Chansonnettes by Levassor & Mme Teisseire

April 1866

M Rossini (in the presence of Abbé Liszt)	MM Delle-Sedi, Gardoni	works by Rossini: *Stabat mater*; *La lazzarone*; *Il povero bambino*
Mme Clara Pfeiffer*	Mme Crépet-Garcia	*La calesera* (Yradier)
M & Mme Paul Bernard*	Mmes Gaveaux-Sabatier, Mme Bigare (her pupil), MM Hermann-Léon, Le Roy	excerpts from: *Le rouet* [?]; *Martha* [Flotow]
M Rossini*	Mme Adelina Patti, Mlle Battu, MM Fraschini, Delle-Sedie, Mmes Carvalho, Castelmary-Saxe, MM Faure, Villaret and choir	*Marche vers l'avenir* (Faure); *Tirana; Inflammatus, Adieu* (Rossini); *Le siège de Corinthe* [Rossini]; *Guillaume Tell* [Rossini]; excerpts from: *Le nozze di Figaro* [Mozart]; *Mireille* [Gounod]
Mme la princesse Mathilde	Mmes Carvalho, la vicomtesse de Grandval, Gaveaux-Sabatier, la princesse de Beauffremont, MM Lévy, Hermann-Léon	trio from *Songe d'un nuit d'été* [Mendelssohn]; quartet from *La charité* [?]; duo from *Philémon et Baucis* [Gounod]
M Benou	Mme Gaveaux-Sabatier, MM Hermann-Léon, Henri le Roy	operetta: *La sérénade interrompue* (Wekerlin)

Songs	Singers	Songs
December 1866		
M Lebouc*	Mme Marie Damoreau	La vision de Sainte-Cécile (Lebouc); Les trois pêcheurs (John Hullah); Jeanne d'Arc (Mme de Grandval)
M Rossini*	Mlle Reboux, M Agnesi	romance: Chant du nautonier (Diémer)
M Lebouc*	Mme Marie Damoreau, M Archainbeaud	excerpts from: Mignon (A. Thomas); Faust [Gounod]; Le bouffe et le tailleur [Gaveaux]
Mlle Paule Gayrard*	M Galvani (Théâtre-Italien), M & Mme Tagliafico (Covent Garden, London), Mlle Méla	no details
M & Mme Louis Orfila	Mme de Grandval, M Hermann-Léon, Mlle Hebbé (from Théâtre-Lyrique)	mélodies by Gounod; mélodies by Grandval: Les lucioles; Valse à Mme Carvalho; excerpts from: Mignon (A. Thomas); La juive [Halévy]; various Swedish songs
'Quelques salons de la haute société parisienne'	Mlles Pellini soeurs (Paris début)	Villanella (Schumann); Le départ des hirondelles (Mendelssohn); Les bohémiens (Gabussi); chansons basques
January 1867		
M Lebouc*	Mme Bertrand	Adélaïde (Beethoven)
M & Mme Tagliafico*	Mmes Fiorentini, Méla, Duclos, MM Guidon Frères, Tagliafico	trio: Papatacci (Rossini)
Mme Gaveaux-Sabatier* (every fortnight)	Mme Gaveaux-Sabatier, M Hermann-Léon	unnamed vocal trio by Mozart; excerpts from: L'elisir d'amore (Donizetti); Joseph [?]; Les trois bouquets de Marguerite (Braga); La robe d'azur

Mme Eugénie Garcia*	M Galvani, Mmes Trélat, Crépet-Garcia	(Yradier); *Chanson de l'été* (Delahaye) mélodies by Gounod: *Le printemps*; *Sérénade*; unnamed song by Bériot père; excerpt from *Norma* [Bellini]; romance by Beer: *Mignon*
M & Mme Rossini*	M Guglielmi	*Stabat mater* [Rossini]
Mme A…	M Pagans	*chanson espagnole* [?]
M & Mme Rossini*	MM Delle-Sedie, Armand Barré, la comtesse Alboni	romance from *Don Pasquale* (Donizetti): *O salutaris*; *Le lazzarone* [Rossini]
M Carjat (photographer)	M Lionnet, MM David, Villaret, Castelmary, Capoul (artists from the Opéra & Opéra-Comique)	two mélodies by Gouzien and works from the operatic repertoire
M Trinquart (photographer)	MM Jules Lefort, Tagliafico, Trinquart, Voisy (Opéra-Comique), Mlles Méla, Llanès (Théâtre-Italien), Llanès' soeur	*nocturnes espagnoles* [?]; unnamed chansonnettes
Mme Gaveaux-Sabatier*	Mmes Gaveaux-Sabatier, Anna Favre, M Hermann-Léon	unnamed mélodie by O'Kelly; excerpts from *Les trouvatelles* (Duprato); *Martha* [Flotow]; romance by Yradier: *La robe d'azur*
Mme Clara Pfeiffer*	Mme Pfeiffer	*La plainte* (Mlle Nicolo)
Mme la princesse Mathilde	Mme Carvalho, Mlle Schroeder	excerpts from: *Le nozze di Figaro* [Mozart]; *Semiramide* [Rossini]; lieder by Schumann
M & Mme Rossini*	Mme Conneau, MM Barré, Lionnet frères	*La lazzarone* (Rossini); *Santa Maria* (Gordigiani); romance from *Saul* [?]; *Lorsque j'aimais* (Nadaud); *Les souvenirs du peuple* (Béranger); *Noël* (Lecoq)

Salons	Singers	Songs
Soirée in the faubourg Saint-Germain	Mme de M…	O Salutaris (la comtesse de Beaumont)
Mme Perrière-Pilté	Mlle Hebbé, M Nadaud	excerpts from La juive [Halévy]; Le sorcier (Mme Marcelli)
February 1867		
M & Mme Rossini*	Mme Alboni, Mlle Battu, M Gardoni	duo by Lucantoni: La dichiarazione; songs by Rossini: mélodie sur une note seule: Adieu à la vie; Il stornello (composed for Gardoni)
M Benson	Mme Ferranti, Mlle Jonas (from Berlin), MM Pancani, Mico	excerpts from: La traviata; Les vêpres siciliennes; Rigoletto [Verdi]; Die Freischütz [Weber]; duo by Lacantoni; Italian air by Ciardi
M le comte de R…	no details	extracts from a new opera by Poll da Silva
M Lucas	MM Guidon frères	chanson de pays arr. Guidon frères: Les casseux de cailloux
M & Mme Rossini*	Mmes Grandval, Battu	excerpt from Moïse et Pharaon [Rossini]; two chansonnettes by Malézieux
M Davelouis	Mlle Nilsson, MM Guidon frères	chanson de pays arr. Guidon frères: Les casseux de cailloux
M de Gasperini*	MM Galvani, Agnesi, Pancani, Zucchini, Nadaud, Lionnet frères	no details
Mme la comtesse de Moustier (faubourg Saint-Germain)	Guidon frères	no details
M Boulé	Guidon frères, Mme Peufeder	romance from Mignon [A. Thomas]

Hôtel d'Amérique	Mlle Jonas (from Berlin)	programme of German and Italian songs
Mme Clara Pfeiffer*	Mlle Roulle	no details
M & Mme Rossini*	Mme Conneau, M Alboni	*O salutaris* (Rossini)
Mme la princesse Mathilde	Mmes de Grandval, Bouchet, Mlle Rives	*La serenata* (Braga)
M Legouvé	MM Delsarte, Braga	Two fables by La Fontaine [Delsarte?]; two Neapolitan chansons
M le docteur Mandl	M Ismaël (Théâtre-Lyrique), Saint-Germain, Mlles Groult, Damain	salon opera by Mme Peyronnet: *Monsieur et Madame Scapin*
Mlle Gabrielle Colson	M Manini, Mmes Alard-Guérette, Béraud	no details
Mme la princesse Ladislas Czartoryska (at the hôtel Lambert)	Mlle Marguerite Nicolaï	mélodie by Gounod: *Sérénade*; aria from *Il trovatore* [Verdi]

March 1867

'Une soirée intime'	M Pancani	excerpt from *I lombardi* [Verdi]; unnamed ariette by Ciardi
M & Mme Rossini* (celebrating his 65th birthday)	Mme Adelina Patti, MM Agnesi, Zucchini, Gardoni, Delle-Sedie, Llanes	excerpts from *Il matrimonio segreto* [Cimarosa]; *La traviata; Il ballo in maschera; Rigoletto* [Verdi]; *Semiramide; L'italiana in Algeri* [Rossini]; arias: *Vanne a colei che adoro* (Costa); *Il fanciullo* (Rossini)
Hôtel de ville	Mme Carvalho, MM Troy, Laurent (Théâtre-Italien)	excerpts from *Mireille* [Gounod]; *Die Zauberflöte* [Mozart]; *La reine Topaze* [Massé]
Hôtel de la Présidence	Mme Carvalho; MM Capoul, Zucchini,	excerpts from: *Actéon* (Auber); *Mireille* [Gounod];

211

Salons	Singers	Songs
M l'amiral ministre (ministère de la marine)	Agnesi, Mercuriali Mlle Schroeder, MM Lionnet frères	*Crispino e la comare* [Ricci]; *Joseph* [?] excerpt from *Die Freischütz* [Weber]; unnamed chansons etc
M le docteur Mandl (rue Tronchet)	Mme Rosa Czillag, Mlle Roulle, MM Verger, Ketten, Lamazou, Nadaud	excerpts from: *Ernani*; *Il ballo in maschera* [Verdi]; *Faust* [Gounod]; *Mignon* (Thomas); *Tito Matei* [?]; *Les saisons* (Haydn); romance by Yradier: *La calesera*; chansons by Nadaud
Hotel d'Amérique	MM Morère (Opéra), Troy (Théâtre-Lyrique), Gardoni (Théâtre-Italien), Pancani (Théâtre-Italien), Guerette (Théâtre-Italien), Lamotte, Mlles Praldi, Gastoldi	songs by Rupès, various chansonnettes
Mme Gaveaux-Sabatier*	Mme Gaveaux-Sabatier, MM Hermann, Leroy	salon opera by Wekerlin: *Manche à manche*
M Lebrun*	Mme Talvo-Bedogni (Théâtre-Lyrique), MM Nadaud, Guidon frères	no details
M Hartog*	no details	works by Hartog: *Ave Maria; Chanson du printemps* (four-part vocal canon); *Chant d'amour* unpublished work by Rossini: *La lazzarone chansons béarnaises; La calesera* (Yradier); *Barcarolle* (Offenbach); *Le bouffe et le tailleur* [Gaveaux]; excerpts from *Mignon* [A. Thomas]; *Così fan tutti* [Mozart]
Mme Moiana	M Barré (Théâtre-Italien)	
M & Mme Roulle	Mlle Roulle, M Lamazou	
Mme Viguier*	Mme Talvo-Bedogni, Mlle Anna Regan	*Plaisir d'amour* (Martini); *Chanson de mai*

212

Mme Osmond du Tillet	M Saint-Germain, Mlle Delisle	(Meyerbeer); excerpts from *Orphée* (Gluck); *Stabat mater* (Rossini)
M le du et Mme la duchesse de Mouchy	Mme Carvalho, Mlle Rives, M Capoul	*C'est Gertrude* [?]
Mme la baronne Meyendorff	Mme la marquise d'Aoust, Mlle Rives, M Fraschini	no details
M & Mme Charles Thomas	Mmes Lefébure-Wély, Trélat, MM Capoul, Hermann-Léon (and choir)	'répertoire des grands maîtres'
M & Mme Rossini*	La comtesse Pepoli (Marietta Alboni), M Géraldy	romance from *Mignon* [A. Thomas]; mélodie by Gounod: *L'automne*; *Les ducats* (Bériot)
Mme Jousselin*	Mlle Marie Bourdon	excerpts from: *Il matrimonio segreto* (Cimarosa); *Il barbiere di Siviglia* (Rossini); *Idylle* (Haydn);
M & Mme Lévi-Alvarès*	Mmes Alard-Guérette, Lévi-Alvarès	excerpts from *Les noces de Jeannette* [Massé]; *Martha* [Flotow]; *Mignon* [A. Thomas]
M le président du Sénat [M Troplong]	Mlle Schroeder, MM Capoul, Crost	romance from *Mignon* [A. Thomas]; mélodies by Rupès
M le marquis de Talhouet	Mlle Battu, M Delle-Sedie	no details
Mme la maréchale Regnault de Saint-Jean-d'Angély	Mme Sass, Mlle Battu, MM Faure, Warot, Obin	chansonnettes by Berthelier; excerpts from *Don Carlos* [Verdi]
Mme de Piré	Mme Cabel, Mlle Battu, MM Panconi, Delle-Sedie, Zucchini	Italian repertoire
Mme de …	Mlles Caussemille, Lambert (Théâtre-	no details

Salons	Singers	Songs
	Lyrique), M Delle-Sedie	unnamed song by Schubert; saltarelle from *Fior d'Aliza* (Massé)
April 1867		
M le comte de Nieuwerkerke (at the Louvre)	Mme Vandenheuvel-Duprez	*Zora ou la petite bohémienne* (Rossini)
M & Mme Rossini*	Mlles Rives, Schroeder (Théâtre-Lyrique), M Delle-Sedie	no details
Mlle Adelina Patti*	daughters of Giulia Grisi	
M le ministre de la marine et colonies	Mlles Battu, Rives, MM Capoul, Delle-Sedie	excerpts from: *Ernani* [Verdi]; *Don Pasquale* (Donizetti); *Mireille* (Gounod); *Il barbiere di Siviglia* (Rossini); *Marie* (Capoul); *Le nozze di Figaro* (Mozart); *Adelaïde* (Beethoven); *Le chemin du paradis* (Blumenthal)
Mme la princesse Mathilde	Mme Carvalho, M Delle-Sedie	no details
M Forcade de La Roquette (at l'hôtel du Ministère du Commerce)	Mmes Carvalho, Peyret, MM Faure, Capoul, Neveu	excerpts from: *Die Zauberflöte* [Mozart]; *La reine de Chypre* [Halévy]; *Il ballo in maschera* [Verdi]; *Les rameaux* (Faure)
Hotel de ville	Mmes Vandenheuvel-Duprez, Mlle Formi, MM Laurent, Crosti – with choir	*Athalie* (Mendelssohn); *Stabat mater* (Rossini)
M & Mme Rossini*	Mme Conneau, la comtesse de La Borde, M Gardoni	*Beatrice di Fenda* [Bellini]; duo from *Mireille* (Gounod)
M Hélios (photographer)	Mlle Nilsson	Swedish airs; two romances by Collinet

M & Mme Rossini	Mlles Battu	air sur une seule note: *Adieu, mère, adieu* (Rossini)
Mme la marquise de Saffroy	Mlle Méla	no details
M Lebouc* (his 12th and last matinée musicale of the season)	Mmes la comtesse de Grandval, Marie Damoreau	*Pater noster* (Grandval); air from *La création* [Haydn]
Mme Pellereau*	Mme Blanche Pedeufer, Mlle Berthe R...	romance from *Mignon* (A. Thomas); *Ondine du Rhin* (Wekerlin); *Le voyage de l'Amour et du Temps* [?]; *Les toreros* (Yradier)
January 1868		
M & Mme Garfounkel	artists from the Théâtre-Lyrique	no details
M & Mme Jules Beer*	Mlles Schroeder Maudit (with choir)	*Psaulme CXXXVII* (Beer – 1st performance); duo from *La fille d'Egypte* (Beer)
M & Mme Diémer*	Mme T..., Mlle Derasse (Opéra-Comique), M Malézieux	romances: from *Mignon* [A. Thomas]; *L'apprenti orfèvre* (Membrée); *L'amour qui passe* (Diémer); *Carcassonne* (Nadaud)
Mme Gaveaux-Sabatier*	Mmes Gaveaux-Sabatier, Barthe-Banderali, MM Hermann-Léon, Pagans	no details
M & Mme M...	M Nadaud	chansons by Nadaud
Mme Clara Pfeiffer*	Mme Marie Damoreau, M Géraldy	new mélodie by Damoreau; *Non più andrai* (Mozart); duo by Blangini: *Per valli*; excerpt from *Les voitures versées* (Boïeldieu)
M Wekerlin*	Mmes Barthe-Banderali, Roulle, Peudefer, MM Archainbaud, Hermann-Léon, Idrac, Pagans	works by Wekerlin: *Ballade de Christine de Pisan*; *Les vanneurs de blé*; *Félicité passée*; *Stances de Malherbe*; *Le ghazal indien*; extract from *Poèmes de la mer*

Salons	Singers	Songs
M le docteur Trélat (rue Jacob)	Mme Trélat, Mlle Nilsson, M Delle-Sedie	romance from *Mignon* (A. Thomas); *Les ducats* (de Bériot), duo by Blangini; excerpt from *Don Pasquale* [Donizetti]
M Gustave Doré (painter)	MM Pagans, Nadaud	no details
February 1868		
M le docteur Mandl	MM Jules Lefort, Saint-Germain, Nadaud, Mme Wekerlin-Damoreau	no details
Mme la marquise de Saffroy	Mmes Peudefer, Boudié	works by Mattiozi: *Danse d'amour*, *Polka chantée*
Mme Gaveaux-Sabatier*	Mme Gaveaux-Sabatier, M Hermann-Léon (with choir)	mélodie by Lavignac; unnamed cantata by Wekerlin
M & Mme Trélat	Mlle Jeanne Devriès, Mme Trélat (with choirs directed by Bizet & Délibes)	*La jeune religieuse* [Die junge Nonne] (Schubert); *Les nymphes des bois* (Délibes); *Le Saint-Valentin* [attrib. Bizet]
Mme Viguier*	Mme Godin, M Aubéry	excerpts from: *Le nozze di Figaro* [Mozart]; *Zaïre* (Mercadante); mélodies by Vaucorbeil: *La ballade-serbe*; *Les cloches du soir*
M Pierre Véron (rue des Pyramides) – chief editor of *Charivari*	Mmes Sasse, Barthe (Opéra), Galli-Marié (Opéra-Comique), M Stellar (Théâtre-Italien)	programme includes chansons by Nadaud
M le docteur Mandl (rue Tronchet)	MM Pagans, Alfred Audran, Mlle Marie Marimon	unnamed chansonnettes; aria from *Die Zauberflöte* [Mozart]
Mme Gaveau-Sabatier*	Mme Gaveaux-Sabatier, Mlle Anna Fabre, MM Hermann-Léon, Lévy	salon opera by Wekerlin: *La laitière de Trianon*

M Legouvé	Mlle Battu, MM Delle-Sedie, Capoul	*Variations sur Santa Lucia*
M Le Couppey*	Mme Barthe, M Pagans	vocal works by M le comte d'Indy
M Louis Diémer*	Mme Barthe-Banderali, MM Pagans, Malézieux	no details

March 1868

La marquise de Talhoüet	Mlle Maudit, MM Gardoni, Delle-Sedie	excerpts from: *Roméo et Juliette* [Gounod]; *Don Juan* [Mozart]; *Lucrezia Borgia* [Donizetti]
Louis Diémer*	Mmes Rives, Peudefer, Mlle Battu, M Lévi, Frères Lionnet	no details
M le comte de Nieuwerkerke (at the Louvre)	Mme Adelina Patti, Cordier, MM Vivier, Gardoni, Steller	excerpts from *Le pardon de Ploërmel* [Meyerbeer]
Mme Pierson-Bodin*	Mme Gaveaux-Sabatier, M Pagans	duo from *Les voitures versées* [Boïeldieu]; duo: *La robe d'azur* (Yradier)
Mme la duchesse Pozzo di Borgo	Mlle Harris, MM Gardoni, Vivier	excerpts from: *Joseph* [?]; *Martha* [Flotow]; *Die Zauberflöte* [Mozart]; *Sérénade* (Schubert)
Mme la duchesse de Mouchy	Mlle Rives, M Delle-Sedie	no details
Mme la duchesse de Galiera	Mmes Carvalho, Bloch, MM Faure, Gardoni	excerpts from *Le prophète* [Meyerbeer]; *Martha* [Flotow]; unnamed mélodie by Faure
Mme la princesse Mathilde	Mlle Rives	no details
M Louis Diémer*	Mlle Rives	cavatina from *Ernani* [Verdi]
Mme la marquise de	Mlle Rives, Mme Ophélie-Nilsson	no details

| Singers | Songs
--- | --- | ---
Talhoüet | |
M & Mme Charles Maquet | Mlle Marie Brunetti, MM Gardoni, Géraldy | Angelina della Biondina (Mariani); duo from La traviata [Verdi]; Idylle (Haydn); Villanelle (Reber); L'abeille (Massé); Barcarolle (Offenbach); Ave Maria (Gounod)
Mme la duchesse de Frias | Mlle Battu, MM Scalese, Verger, Gardoni | duo from Don Pasquale (Donizetti); Santa Lucia (Cottreau); Non torno (Mattei); trio: Vieni al Mar (Gordigiani); Miei rampolli (Rossini); M'appari [?] (Flotow); duo from Les voitures versées (Boïeldieu); trio: Vadasi, via di quà (Martini)
M Louis Diémer* | Mmes de Grandval, Gaveaux-Sabatier, MM Gardoni, Hermann-Léon, Nadaud | no details
M Lebouc* mention of Mme la marquise d'Aoust; Mme de Talhoüet; la princesse Mathilde | Mlle Marie Damoreau mention of Mlles Rives, Nilsson | Stances (Damoreau); La source; duo: Le bal [?] no details
M le comte de Nieuwerkerke (at the Louvre) | Mme Sass | excerpts from Il trovatore (Verdi); Betley (Donizetti); Galathée (Massé); mélodie by Gounod: Printemps
Mme la marquise d'Aoust | Mme la marquise d'Aoust, Mlle Rives, MM Gardoni, Verger | excerpts from Martha [Flotow]; Swedish songs
Mme la duchesse de Frias | Mlle Battu, MM Gardoni, Verger | trio bouffe by Martini; barcarolle napolitaine
M le docteur Mandl | Mme Kraus (Théâtre-Lyrique), Mlles | excerpts from: Fidelio (Beethoven); Les djinns

S A I la princesse Mathilde	Marie Roze, Rives, Della-Rocca, MM Gagliano, Verger	(Auber); Il matrimonio segreto [Cimaroso]; several romances; Ave Maria (Schubert)
M le préfet de la Seine	Mme Conneau, MM Gardoni, Hermann-Léon	no details
Ministère de la marine ('grand soirée')	Mme Carvalho, M Gardoni	works by Weber, Gounod, Massé, Flotow
M Garfounkel (in the presence of Auber)	Mlles Battu, Nilsson, Mme Norman-Neruda, MM Faure, Vivier	barcarolle napolitaine; Sancta Maria [?]; romance from Joseph [?]
Mme Abel Laurent	Mmes Sasse, Norman-Neruda, Mlles Nilsson, Bloch	excerpts from Les djinns [?]; Stabat mater [Rossini?]; air from Jaconde [?]
	Mlles Nilsson, Bloch, MM Gardoni, Aubery	excerpts from: Martha [Flotow]; Le prophète [Meyerbeer]; Stabat mater [Rossini?]
Mme Gaveaux-Sabatier*	M Nadaud	chansons by Nadaud: Osmanomanie; Les nouveaux boulevards
Mlle Gabrielle Colson	Mlle Claire Courtois, M Aubery	salon opera by Wekerlin: Tout est bien qui finit bien
Mlle Joséphine Martin	M&M Puget, Lütz (Théâtre-Lyrique), Mlle Léon	excerpts from: La reine de Chypre [Halévy]; Joseph [?]; Mireille [Gounod]
M & Mme Fournier	Mlle Marie Roze, MM Nadaud, Berthelier, Pagans	mélodie by Gounod: Printemps; air from Les djinns [Auber]; chansons by Nadaud
M C…	Frères Lionnet, M Audran, Mlle Meyer	La revanche de Fortunia [Robillard]; chansonnettes
M & Mme Rossini*	MM Gardoni, Delle-Sedie, Mme Alboni, Mlle Battu	songs by Rossini: mélodie sur la gamme chinois; Romance sur une seule note; Il fanciullo smarrito
M le docteur Mandl	Mme Gaveaux-Sabatier, Mlle Marie Roze, MM Hermann-Léon	romance from Les djinns [?]; Les rameaux (Faure)

219

Salons	Singers	Songs
April 1868		
Mme la princesse Mathilde	Mmes Carvalho, Norman-Neruda, M Delle-Sedie	no details
Hôtel de Ville	Mmes Cabel, Roze, M Capoul	works by Auber: *La muette de Portici*; *L'ambassadrice*; *Le premier jour du bonheur*
Mme la baronne de Maistre	M Franceschi	excerpts from *Sardanapale* (de Maistre)
December 1868		
Mme la marquise de Caux	Mme la marquise de Caux, M Agnesis	*L'étranger* (Alard); unpublished mélodie by Osmond
M Charles Lebouc* (his salons recommenced in November)	Mme Marie Damoreau	excerpts from: *Otello*; *Guillaume Tell*; *L'italiana in Algeri* (Rossini)
Mme Pierson-Bodin*	Mlle Carmen Muñez (pupil of Pierson-Bodin), M Taffanel	*La molinera* (Yradier)
January 1869		
M Charles Lebouc*	Mmes Léonard, Barthe-Banderali	aria by Handel; *Les plaintes de coeur* (Lebouc); *Iris* (Wekerlin)
M & Mme Alphand (every Sunday at their Villa Beauséjour)	Mlle Favel	no details
M Emile de Girardin	Mlle Minnie Hauck, M T…	excerpts from: *Hamlet* [Joncières?]; *Rigoletto* [Verdi]

Host/Venue	Performers	Details
M Paul Bernard*	Mme Thuot	no details
M Wekerlin (a private recital in the Salons Pleyel-Wolff)	Mmes Barthe-Banderali, Fobre, MM Archaimbaud, Pagans	works by Pergolesi and other Italians; Psalm by Paër; chansons espagnoles
Mme Clara Pfeiffer*	Mlle Léonard	no details
Mme la marquise de Saffray	Mme Boudier, M Tamburini	no details
M le docteur Mandl	Mlle Caroline Ferni, MM Giraldoni, Melchissédec	excerpts from: *Saulle* [?]; *Le nozze di Figaro* [Mozart]; *Les rameaux* (Faure)
Hôtel de Ville	artists from the Théâtre-Lyrique	no details
M Charles Lebouc*	Mme Peudefer	two mélodies by Durand
Mme Erard	Mlle Krauss	excerpts from: *Die Freischütz* [Weber]; *Le nozze di Figaro* (Mozart); *Mignon* (Spontini); mélodies by Vaucorbeil: *Voix lointaines*; *Les adieux de l'hotêsse arabe*
M & Mme Emile Girardin	Mlles Nilsson, Krauss, Mme Trélat Mme Brian de Bois-Guilbert, Mlles Paradés, de Rionell, MM Franceschi, Coeuilte	no details
Mme la baronne de Maistre	Mlle Nilsson	excerpt from opera by de Maistre: *Ninive*
M Parke-Godwin ('un riche Américain des Champs-Elysées')		Airs suédois [?]
Mme Gaveaux-Sabatier*	Mme Gaveaux-Sabatier, MM Hermann-	romance by Hermann-Léon; duos from *Le*

Salons	Singers	Songs
	Léon, Nadaud	nouveau seigneur du village [Boïeldieu]; Gilles ravisseur [Grisar]; recent chansons by Nadaud
M & Mme Lyon* (rue de la Tour-d'Auvergne)	Mlle Roulle, MM Pagans, Lyon, Nadaud	recent chansons by Nadaud
M & Mme Melchior Mocker	MM Tagliafico, Nadaud	no details
February 1869		
M & Mme Edouard Fournier	Mme Ernest Bertrand, Mlle Boudier, MM Jules Lefort, Nadaud	Félicité passé (Wekerlin); air by Mattiozzi; chanson by Nadaud: Le petit chaperon rouge
M le docteur Mandl	M Alfred Audran	no details
M de B…	M Alfred Audran	no details
M Krüger*	Mme Fumagalli, M Félix Léon	no details
M Langhans	Mme Godin	lieder by Schumann
Mlle Gabrielle Colson	Mlles Delauney, de Rionelli, Courtois, Lehuedé, M Castel	unnamed chansonnettes
Mme de Vallette & Mlle Le Callo	MM Géraldy, Marochetti	no details
Ministère de la marine	Mme Carvalho, M Vivier	no details
M le docteur Mandl	Mme Monbelli, MM Tamburini, Delle-Sedie, Gardoni, Audran	no details
M & Mme Viguier*	Mlle Mira	mélodies by Vaucorbeil
M & Mme Diémer* (Quai d'Orsay)	Mlle Battu, Mme Guillaume, M Lévy	excerpts from: Bianca e Falliero [Rossini]; Armide [Gluck]; mélodie by Vaucorbeil: Adieu la Marguerite, Ninon

222

Host	Performers	Repertoire
Mme Coppa	Mlle Hebbé, Mme Coppa, M Lopez, Mme Monbelli	Benedictus (Grandval); Swedish songs
M le comte de Nieuwerkerke (at the Louvre)		no details
M le duc de Galliera	Mlles Nilsson, Bellaviv [Bellariva?], MM Gardoni, Agnesi, Sivori	Sérénade (Schubert); mélodie by Campana
M Gustav Doré (painter)	Mme B…	O salutaris (Rossini); airs béarnais; chansons by Nadaud
		no details
M Pierre Véron	Mmes Carvalho, Ilma de Murska, MM Nicolini, Capoul, Bonnehée	excerpts from unpublished operetta by Varney: Les coquetteries de Catherine
M Eugène Trouvé (painter)	M Tayau (ténor bouffe)	excerpt from: Herculanum [F David]; Galathée [Massé]
M le docteur Agostini	Mlle Adèle Aimée	

March 1869

Host	Performers	Repertoire
Mme la marquise de Saffray	Mlle Desportes-Bernard, M Mottez	no details
M & Mme Diémer*	Mme de Grandval	Ballade suisse; Sequidille; Offertoire (Grandval)
M & Mme Fournier	Mme Peudefer, MM Bruneau, Lefort, Berthelier	ballade from Mignon [A. Thomas]; chansonnettes
Mlle Joséphine Martin*	MM Gardoni, Pagans, Bonnehée, Nadaud	mélodies espagnoles; chansons by Nadaud
M Magner (every Sunday)	Mlles Hebbé, Magner	excerpts from: Mignon (A. Thomas); Lalla-Roukh (F. David); Hamlet [Joncières]

Salons	Singers	Songs
M & Mme Koenigswarter	Mlle Nilsson, M Bonnehée	excerpts from: *Die Freischütz* [Weber]; *La traviata* [Verdi]; *Jean de Paris* [Boïeldieu]; new mélodie by Mme Rothschild; two Spanish chansons [?]
M le docteur Mandl	Mmes Paule Gayrard, Boudier, Noble, MM Jules Lefort, Pagans, Bruneau, Audran, Lamazou, Tamburini fils	*Les rameaux* (Faure); *Valse* (Mattiozzi); excerpts from: *Don Giovanni*; *Le nozze di Figaro* [Mozart]; various chansons
M & Mme Trélat (rue Jacob)	Mmes Trélat, de Grandval, M Gardoni	excerpts from *Piccolino* [Grandval]
M & Mme Diémer*	Mme Barthe-Banderali, MM Barthe-Banderali, Barré	no details
M & Mme Paul Juillerat (Boulevard Malesherbes)	Mme Bertrand, M Jules Lefort	new chansons by Nadaud
Hotel de Ville	Mlle Battu, Mme Wertheimer, MM Nicolini, Bonnehée, Bosquin	excerpt from *Les Troyens* (Berlioz); *Stabat mater* (Rossini); *Ave Maria* (Gounod)
M Lacombe*	Mlle Nicolai, M Hayet	*La sequidilla*; *air bouffe* (Lacombe)
M & Mme Carminate	M Charles Gautier	*La pauvre hirondelle* (Aviragnet)
M & Mme Lévi-Alvarès*	Mmes Godin, Peudefer, Mlle Leheudé, MM Guidon, Nadaud	no details
April 1869		
M & Mme Koechlin	Mme Carvalho, Mlle Nilsson, MM Faure, Caron	songs by Faure: *Sancta Maria*; *Etoile*; *Que le jour me dure*; *Pourquoi?*; *Les rameaux*
Mlle Joséphine Martin* (two soirées)	Mlle Léonie Martin, MM Lefort, Pagans, Lévy, Tamburini, Nadaud	two mélodies by Joséphine Martin; chansons by Nadaud
M & Mme Edouard	Mmes Bertrand, Boudier, Mlle Marie	*chansons espagnoles* [?]; musical playlet:

Fournier	Dumas, MM Pagans, Bruneau, Nadaud	*Arlequin et Colombine* [?]; *Les femmes qui font des scènes* (Monselet); chansons by Nadaud
M le docteur & Mme Mandl	Mlle Jaraczewska, M Delle-Sedie	comic chorus by Wekerlin: *Les cris de Paris.* (30 performers took part in a programme of music, parodies and a charade)
M Paul Bernard*	Mmes Léonard, Peudeffer, MM Léonard, Magnin, Taffanel, Guidon, Nadaud	chansons by Nadaud
Mlle Nau	M Pagans, Mlle Richard	mélodies & lieder by Gounod, Schumann & Pauline Viardot
M Legouvé*	Mlle Battu, Mme de Meriche Lablache, MM Faure, Gardoni	mélodies by Gounod; *Les lucioles* (Mme de Grandval); *La charité* (Faure)
M le duc de Galliera (programme organized by Rubini)	Mlles Nilsson, Bellariva, M Gardoni	no details
M & Mme Diémer*	Mmes de Grandval, Barthe-Banderali, MM Léon Duprez, Nadaud	*Les lucioles* (Mme de Grandval); *Le grillon* (Bizet); Boléro from *Piccolino* [Grandval]; chansons by Nadaud
December 1869		
Mme Pierson-Bodin	Mme Roussel, Mlle Muñoz	excerpts from *Ariodante* [Handel?]; *Anna Bolena* [Donizetti]; *I puritani* [Bellini]
M le docteur Fauvel	Mlles Sessi, Reboux, MM Lionnet frères; Berthelier	no details
M & Mme A Fabre (have recommenced their	Mme Fabre, M Hermann-Léon	chanson by Jouret & unnamed operetta

Salons	Singers	Songs
winter salons)		
January 1870		
MM Lasserre & Delahaye*	MM Roger, Devoyod (Opéra)	Le roi des Aulnes [Erlkönig] (Schubert); Les rameaux (Faure); duo from La reine de Chypre [Halévy]
M Wekerlin*	Mmes Barthe-Banderali, Bertrand	new works by Wekerlin
February 1870		
'un salon de la rue d'Aumale' (weekly)	Mlle Schroeder, Mme Bemberg	works by Reissiger, Schumann, Handel; chanson havanaise
M Paul Bernard* mention of salons in the homes of le consul des Pays-Bas; M Halphen	Mme Jacques, MM Waldeck Thuot Quatuor vocal (MM Miquel, Levaut, Bertringer, Quesne)	excerpt from L'africaine [Meyerbeer] no details
Mme la vicomtesse de Grandval	Mmes la baronne de Caters, Trélat, MM de Meynard, Hermann	Stabat mater (Grandval)
Georges Pfeiffer	Mme Barthe-Banderali, M Pagans	airs, duos, choruses
M le docteur Mandl (his 'soirées littéraires et musicales' have recommenced)	Mlles Priola (Opéra-Comique), Selvi, MM Gardoni	excerpts from Rienzi [Wagner]; Rêve d'amour [?]; Spanish chanson [?]
Mme la princesse Mathilde	M Gardoni, Mme Moulton (from America)	excerpt from Les djinn [?]; La guitarre [?]
M & Mme Diémer*	MM Jules Lefort, Pagans, Mme Cabel	mainly new works by Diémer

226

MM Lasserre & Delahaye*	Mme Monbelli, M Devoyod	excerpt from *Semiramide* [Rossini]; *Mignon* [A. Thomas]; *Serenata* (Braga)
M Paul Bernard*	Mme Jacques, M Léonce Waldeck	includes new works by Bernard, no details
M & Mme Lyon	MM Roger, Lyon	excerpt from *Don Carlos* [Verdi]; chansons by Nadaud
M Paul Bernard*	MM Audran, Bruneau	chansonnettes
M & Mlle [sic] Mandl	MM Roger, Delle-Sedie, Mme Monbelli	*Oiseaux légers* (Gumbert); excerpt from *Don Pasquale* [Donizetti]; *La Marseillaise!*
M Pierre Véron	Mlles Favart, Krauss, Nilsson, Selvi, M Coquelin, Delle-Sedie, Capoul	excerpts from *Die Freischütz* [Weber]; *Le nozze di Figaro* [Mozart]; *La traviata* [Verdi]; *Mignon* [A. Thomas]
M & Mme Diémer*	Mme Bertrand, MM Delle-Sedie	no details
M Langerock (painter & photographer, Boulevard des Italiens)	Mmes Peudefer, Picard, Gérard, M Audran	*Valse* (Diémer); *Esméralda*; *La meunière de Tréguier* (Wekerlin); various chansons

March 1870

M le Sénateur, le comte de Nieuwerkerke (at the Louvre)	Mlles Stucklé, Couvreur, Verken, Isaac, MM Girard, Müller, Morlet, Reine, Edouard, Léon Duprez	excerpts from *La favorite* (Donizetti); *Ernani* (Verdi); *Les Huguenots* (Meyerbeer); *Il barbiere di Siviglia* (Rossini)
M & Mme Lafontaine (Rue Grenelle-Saint-Honoré)	M Léon Duprez	various unnamed airs and chansonnettes
M & Mme Mandl	Mme de la Grange, MM Pagans, Nadaud, Daniele	*La Marseillaise des Gourdins réunis* (Lavignac)

Salons	Singers	Songs
M & Mme Viguier	M Varesi, Vaucorbeil, Mme N… (his pupil)	songs by Wekerlin: *Voix lointaines*; *Le Rhône*; *Le Rhin allemande*
M Wekerlin*	Mme Peudefer, Gray soeurs, MM Richard, Duffoure	programme devoted to works by Wekerlin
M Paul Bernard*	Mlle de Busk, Gray soeurs, MM Waldeck, Audran, Bruneau	mélodies polonaises; duo: *Les fleurs* (Bernard); excerpt from *Paulus* (Mendelssohn); various chansons
MM Lasserre & Delahaye*	Mme Gaveaux-Sabatier, M Hermann-Léon	excerpts from: *Philémon et Baucis* [Gounod]; *Les trouvatelles* [Duprato]; *Chanson de l'été* (Delahaye); lied by Schumann
M Paul Bernard*	Mmes Meillet, Thuot, MM Meillet, Nadaud	excerpts from: *Le postillon de Longjumeau* [Adam]; *Robert le diable* [Meyerbeer], mélodie by Gounod: *Le vallon*; chansons by Nadaud: *Cousin Charles*; *Le candidat électoral*
M le docteur Trélat	Mmes de Grandval, Trélat, Mlle Krauss, M Léon Duprez (with choirs)	no details
April 1870		
M & Mme Fournier	Mme Bertrand, Boudier, M Aurèle	17th-century brunette and air by Guérou [Guédron]; duo from *Arlequin et Colombine* [?]
MM Lasserre & Delahaye*	Mlle Cécile Dolmetsch, M Lévy	German lieder (in French) by Schumann: *L'heure du Mystère*; *Elle est à toi* (Schumann); duo from *Faust* [Gounod]
Mlle Joséphine Martin (three soirées)	MM Lafont, Nadaud, Pagans, Tamburini, Lefort, Nadaud, Mlles Dolmetsch,	no details

M & Mme Lévi-Alvarèse*	Léonie Martin	no details
	Mme Peudefer, Lehuédé, Pothsin, MM Aurèle, Naudin	no details
M le docteur Mandl	Quatuor vocale	

Schubert's solo songs, published by Richault

LIST A (songs published separately)

German title	Opus, Nachlass etc	French title	Cotage	Year (est.)	Comments
Gretchen am Spinnrade	2	Marguerite	2371	1828	
Die Post	89 no. 13	La poste	3106	1834	Richault's Six mélodies célèbres de Schubert announced in June 1834
Ständchen	Schwanengesang 4	Sérénade	3113	1834	
Am Meer	Schwanengesang 12	Au bord de la mer	3117	1834	
Der Tod und das Mädchen	7 no. 3	La jeune fille à la mort	3120	1834	
Das Fischermädchen	Schwanengesang 10	La fille du pêcheur	3125	1834	
Schlaflied	24 no. 2	Berceuse	3145	1834?	
Die Allmacht	79 no. 2	La Toute Puissance	3159	1834?	
Erlkönig	1	Le Roi des Aulnes	3258	1834?	
Die junge Nonne	43 no. 1	La jeune religieuse	3281	1834?	
Auf dem Wasser zu singen	72	Barcarolle	3290	1834?	

German title	French title	Opus	D	Year	Notes
Geheimes (Lebe Wohl)	Le secret	14 no. 2	3317	1835	trans. dedicated to Nourrit
Adieu			3319	1835	song by Weyrauch misattributed to Schubert
Der Doppelgänger	Vision	Schwanengesang 13	3320	1835	
Dass sie hier gewesen	La verrai-je encore	59 no. 2	3321	1835	trans. dedicated to Nourrit
Nacht und Träume	Nuit et songes	43 no. 2	3322	1835	trans. by D.P*** dedicated to Nourrit
Der Wanderer	Le voyageur	4 no. 1	3323 bis	1835	
Frühlingsglaube	Le printemps (pastorale)	20 no. 2	3324	1835	
Die Forelle	La truite	32	3325	1835	trans. by D.P.*** (Die Forelle was trans. by Bélanger as 'La Péri' for the Octavo Edition)
Wandrers Nachtlied (Über allen Gipfeln ...)	La chanson de nuit du voyageur	96 no. 3	3327	1835	
Alinde	Marie!	81 no. 1	3330	1835	
Das Zügenglöcklein	La cloche des agonisants	80 no. 2	3331	1835	
Der Hirt auf dem Felsen	Le berger sur la montagne	op.post. 129	3332	1835	not included in the Octavo Edition
Ellen's Gesang (Hymne an die Jungfrau)	Ave Maria	52 no. 6	3334	1835	trans. dedicated to Mlle Falcon
Die Krähe	Le corbeau	89 no. 15	3335	1835	trans. dedicated to M. Levasseur
Greisengesang	Le vieillard	60 no. 1	3337	1835	
Sei mir gegrüßt	Sois toujours mes seules amours	20 no. 1	3349	1836	trans. dedicated to Nourrit.

German title	Opus, Nachlass etc	French title	Cotage	Year (est.)	Comments
Des Mädchens Klage	58 no. 3	Les plaintes de la jeune fille	3350	1836	trans dedicated to Mlle Falcon
Der Leiermann	89 no. 24	Le joueur de vielle	3351	1836	
Die Nebensonnen	89 no. 23	Regrets	3352	1836	
Das Wandern	25 no. 1	Le meunier voyager	3370	1836	trans. dedicated 'à son ami Devilliers'
Pax vobiscum	Nachlass 10 no. 1	La paix soit avec vous	3372	1836	trans. by Legouvé, dedicated to Nourrit
Vom Mitleiden Mariae	Nachlass 10 no. 2	De la compassion de Marie	3372	1836	trans. by Legouvé, dedicated to Nourrit
Dem Unendlichen	Nachlass 10 no. 3	A l'Etre infini	3372	1836	trans. by Legouvé, dedicated to Nourrit
Himmelsfunken	Nachlass 10 no. 4	Extase	3372	1836	trans. by Legouvé, dedicated to Nourrit
Das Marienbild	Nachlass 10 no. 5	L'image de Marie	3372	1836	trans. by Legouvé, dedicated to Nourrit
Die Gestirne	Nachlass 10 no. 6	Les astres	3372	1836	trans. by Legouvé, dedicated to Nourrit
Gebet während der Schlacht	Nachlass 10 no. 7	Prière pendant la bataille	3372	1836	trans. by Legouvé, dedicated to Nourrit
Litanei	Nachlass 10 no. 8	Requiescat in Pace	3372	1836	trans. by Legouvé, dedicated to Nourrit
Der stürmische Morgen	89 no. 18	La matinée orageuse	3376	1836	trans. dedicated to Wartel

Der Schiffer (Im Winde, im Stürme ...)	21 no. 2	Le nautonier	3377	1836	trans. dedicated to Géraldy
Meeres Stille (Tiefe Stille herrscht ...)	3 no. 2	Le calme plate (ballade)	3379	1836	trans. dedicated to Géraldy
Suleika (Ach, um deine feuchten Schwingen ...)	31	La colombe	3380	1836	trans. dedicated to Nourrit
Täuschung	89 no. 19	L'illusion	3381	1836	trans. dedicated to Géraldy
Bei dir allein	95 no. 2	Au près de toi	3382	1836	trans. dedicated to Nourrit
Wiegenlied (Schlafe, schlafe, holder ...)	89 no. 2	La jeune mère	3383	1836	
Der Alpenjäger (Willst du nicht ...)	37 no. 2	Laissez-moi partir ma mère	3393	1836	
Liebesbotschaft	Schwanengesang 1	Le message d'amour	3401	1836	trans. dedicated to Géraldy
Frühlingssehnsucht	Schwanengesang 3	Le désir du printemps	3402	1836	trans. dedicated to Alexis Dupont, artiste de l'Académie Royale de musique
Am See	Nachlass 9 no. 3	A l'océan	3403	1836	trans. dedicated to Géraldy
Die Rose	73	La rose	3404	1836	trans. dedicated to Mme Dorus-Gras
Abschied	Schwanengesang 7	Le départ	3406	1836	trans. dedicated to Alexis Dupont
Die Stadt	Schwanengesang 11	La ville	3407	1836	on the cover trans. dedicated to Nourrit; on the 1st page of music to

German title	Opus, Nachlass etc	French title	Cotage	Year (est.)	Comments
Ihr Bild	Schwanengesang 9	Son image	3408	1836	Géraldy
Gute Nacht	89 no. 1	Je dois te fuir	3409	1836	trans. dedicated to Mlle Falcon
Gefrorne Tränen	89 no. 3	Les larmes	3410	1836	trans. dedicated to Nourrit
Wasserflut	89 no. 6	Le ruisseau	3411	1836	trans. dedicated to Nourrit
Morgenlied (Eh' die Sonne …)	4 no. 2	Chant du matin	3412	1836	trans. dedicated to Nourrit
Kolmas Klage	Nachlass 2 no. 2	Les plaintes de Colma	3422	1836	trans. dedicated to Nourrit
Der Wanderer an den Mond	80 no. 1	Le voyageur à la lune	3424	1836	trans. dedicated to M le baron de Stockhausen, attaché à la légation de S.M.B. le Roi de Hanovre
Im Freien	80 no. 3	Nuit d'été	3425	1836	trans. dedicated to Nourrit
Wandrers Nachtlied (Der du von Himmel …)	4 no. 3	Chant du soir	3426	1836	trans. dedicated to E. Devilliers
Kriegers Ahnung	Schwanengesang 2	Pressentiments d'un soldat	3427	1836	trans. dedicated to Géraldy
Aufenthalt	Schwanengesang 5	Mon séjour	3428	1836	trans. dedicated to Géraldy
In der Ferne	Schwanengesang 6	L'exile	3429	1836	trans. dedicated 'à son ami E. Devilliers'
Thekla: eine Geisterstimme	88 no. 2	Thékla ou La voix du fântome	3437	1836	trans. dedicated to Mlle Falcon

Der Atlas	Schwanengesang 8	L'Atlas	3438	1836	trans. dedicated to Géraldy
Die Taubenpost	Schwanengesang 14	L'oiseau messager	3439	1836	trans. dedicated to Nourrit
Dithyrambe	60 no. 2	Dithyrambe	3440	1836	trans by D.P.***
Widerschein	Nachlass 15 no. 1	Le reflet	3454	1836	trans. dedicated to Mlle Falcon
Liebeslauschen	Nachlass 15 no. 2	L'amour aux écoutes	3455	1836	
Du bist die Ruh'	59 no. 3	L'attente	3458	1836	trans. dedicated to Mme de Chambure
Schiffers Scheidelied	Nachlass 24 no. 1	Adieux du matelot	3485	1836	trans. dedicated to M Duvilliers
Das Heimweh	79 no. 1	Le mal du pays	3486	1836	trans. dedicated to Géraldy
see comments	see comments	Amour et mystère	3492	1836	vocal arr. of Waltz for piano, op 9 no. 2
Gesänge des Harfners (Wer sich …)	12 no. 1	Le chant du barde	3493	1836	trans. by D.P.*** (cf 4689). Not in Octavo Edition
Lied der Anne Lyle	85 no. 1	Romance d'Anna Lyle	3494	1836	trans. dedicated to Mlle Falcon
Der Zweig	22 no. 1	Le nain (ballade)	3495	1836	trans. dedicated to Géraldy
Über Wildemann	108 no. 1	Jamais	3496	1836	trans. dedicated to M Zerezo
Todesmusik	108 no. 2	Chant de cygne	3497	1836	
Die Macht der Augen	83 no. 1	Puissance d'un regard	3510	1836	trans. dedicated to M Lablache
Der getäuschte Verräter	83 no. 2	Le rêve du coupable	3511	1836	trans. dedicated to M Lablache
Die Art ein Weib zu	83 no. 3	Je prends femme	3512	1836	trans. dedicated to M

German title	Opus, Nachlass etc	French title	Cotage	Year (est.)	Comments
nehmen					
Wehmut (Wenn ich durch Wald ...)	22 no. 2	Pauvre fleur	3514	1836	Lablache
Lied der Mignon (Heiß mich nicht ...)	62 no. 2	Le serment	3516	1836	trans. dedicated to Géraldy
Lied der Mignon (So laßt mich ...)	62 no. 3	La solitude	3517	1836	
Lied der Mignon (Nur wer die Sehnsucht ...)	62 no. 4	Quand tu me vois souffrir	3518	1836	trans. dedicated to Mlle d'Hennin
An die Laute	81 no. 2	A ma lyre	3520	1836	
Zur guten Nacht	81 no. 3	Bonsoir	3521	1836	trans. dedicated to Géraldy
Der Schäfer und der Reiter	13 no. 1	Le pâtre et le cavalier	3522	1836	
Suleika	14 no. 1	Suleika	3523	1836	
Auf dem Strom	119	Sur le fleuve	3524	1836	
Lied des Orpheus	Nachlass 19 no. 1	Apparition	3525	1836	trans. dedicated to Nourrit
Ritter Toggenburg	Nachlass 19 no. 2	Le chevalier et la châtelaine	3526	1836	trans. dedicated to Nourrit
Um Mitternacht	88 no. 3	A minuit	3527	1836	trans. dedicated to Nourrit
Der blinde Knabe	101 no. 2	Le jeune aveugle	3528	1836	
Im Walde (Ich wandre ...)	93 no. 1	Découragé	3529	1836	
Der Unglückliche	87 no. 1	Un malheureux	3530	1836	
Der Unglückliche	87 no. 2	Espérance	3531	1836	trans. dedicated to Nourrit
Der Jüngling am Bache	87 no. 3	Beau page	3532	1836	trans. dedicated to Nourrit

German title	Opus/Nachlass	French title	Plate	Year	Notes
(An der Quelle saß ...) Der Wallensteiner Lanzknecht beim Trunk	Nachlass 27 no. 1	Le lansquenet de Wallenstein	3547	1836	
Der Kreuzzug	Nachlass 27 no. 2	La croisade	3548	1836	
Des Fischers Liebesglück	Nachlass 27 no. 3	Bonheur d'amour	3549	1836	
Trost in Tränen	Nachlass 25 no. 3	Pourquoi la consoler	3550	1836	trans. dedicated to la comtesse de Sparre
Im Abendrot	Nachlass 20 no. 1	Le coucher du soleil	3551	1836	trans. dedicated to Nourrit
Die Erscheinung (Ich lag auf grünen Matten ...)	108 no. 3 (Richault 108 no. 2)	Souvenir	3552	1836	
Im Haine	56 no. 3	Au bosquet (romance)	3553	1836	Op 56 no. 2 in BM ded. la comtesse Emilien de Nieuwerkerke
Lachen und Weinen	59 no. 4	Les ris et les pleurs	3554	1836	trans. dedicated to M Ed. d'Alembert
Die abgeblühte Linde	7 no. 1	Le rosier dépouillé	3555	1836	trans. dedicated to Mme Dorus Gras
Der Flug der Zeit	7 no. 2	La fuite du temps	3556	1836	trans. dedicated to M Duvilliers
Lob der Tränen	13 no. 2	Eloge des larmes	3557	1836	trans. dedicated to le baron de Stockhausen
Der Wachtelschlag	68	Le chant de la caille	3689	1837	Legouvé's review (in *RGM* Richault's 60 songs by Schubert appeared in Jan. 1837)
Wie Ulfru fischt	21 no. 3	Le pêcheur	3691	1837	

German title	Opus, Nachlass etc	French title	Cotage	Year (est.)	Comments
Jäger, ruhe von der Jagd	52 no. 2	Le chasseur égaré	3692	1837	
from the opera 'Alfonso e Estrella'	opus 42 no. 1	Air d'Alfonso e Estrella	3703	1838	trans. dedicated to Géraldy
from the opera 'Alfonso e Estrella'	opus 42 no. 1	Cavatine d'Alfonso e Estrella	3704	1838	trans. dedicated to Géraldy
Mit dem grünen Lautenbande	25 no13	Le ruban vert	3754	1838	trans. dedicated to Charles Dufort
Die liebe Farbe	25 no. 16	Sa fleur chérie	3755	1838	trans. dedicated to Charles Dufort
Die böse Farbe	25 no. 17	Garde moi souvenir	3756	1838	trans. dedicated to Charles Dufort
Der Neugierige	25 no. 6	Suis-je aimé?	3764	1838	
Ungeduld	25 no. 7	Toute ma vie	3765	1838	
Morgengruß	25 no. 8	Salut du matin	3766	1838	
Des Müllers Blumen	25 no. 9	Ne m'oubliez pas	3767	1838	
Normans Gesang	52 no. 5 (Richault: 52 no. 6)	Au camp	3807	1838	
Lied des gefangenen Jägers	52 no. 7 (Richault: 52 no. 5)	Le prisonnier	3808	1838	
Der Schmetterling	57 no. 1	Le papillon	3809	1838	
Die Berge	57 no. 2	Sur les Alpes	3810	1838	
An den Mond (Geuß, lieber Mond ...)	57 no. 3	Clair de lune	3811	1838	

Title	Opus	No.	Year	French title	Notes
An Emma	58 no. 2	3812	1838	Emma	
Am Feierabend	25 no. 5	3845	1838	Elle ne m'a compris	
Tränenregen	25 no. 10	3846	1838	Fatal présage	
Mein!	25 no. 11	3847	1838	Elle est à moi	
Pause	25 no. 12	3848	1838	Le luth voilé	
Wohin?	25 no. 2	3849	1838	Au bord de la fontaine	
Halt!	25 no. 3	3850	1838	Sa chaumière	
Danksagung an den Bach	25 no. 4	3851	1838	Je vais la voir	
Der Jäger	25 no. 14	3852	1838	Le chasseur	
Eifersucht und Stolz	25 no. 15	3853	1838	Jalousie	
Trockne Blumen	25 no. 18	3854	1838	La fleur fanée	
Der Müller und der Bach	25 no. 19	3855	1838	La voix enchanteresse	
Des Baches Wiegenlied	25 no. 20	3856	1838	L'étranger	
An die Nachtigall (Er liegt und schläft …)	98 no. 1	3857	1838	Rêve d'amour	
Iphigenia	89 no. 3 (Richault: 89 no. 3)	3858	1838	La fille du proscrit	trans. dedicated to Mlle Sophie Bodin
Ständchen	Nachlass 7 no. 4	3859	1838	Roméo	
Lied der Norna	85 no. 2	3860	1838	Norna la sorcière	trans. dedicated to Mme Widemann
Rastlose Liebe	5 no. 1	3861	1838	Toujours	
Nähe des Geliebten	5 no. 2	3862	1838	Je pense à lui	trans. dedicated to Mlle Sophie Bodin
Der Fischer	5 no. 3	3863	1838	La sirène	
Erster Verlust	5 no. 4	3864	1838	Première peine	
Der König in Thule	5 no. 5	3865	1838	Le Roi du Thulé	

German title	Opus, Nachlass etc	French title	Cotage	Year (est.)	Comments
Die Wetterfahne	89 no. 2	Soyez heureux	3866	1838	
Erstarrung	89 no. 4	L'hiver	3867	1838	
Der Lindenbaum	89 no. 5	Le tilleul	3868	1838	
Auf dem Flusse	89 no. 7	Le torrent	3869	1838	
Der greise Kopf	89 no. 14	J'ai cru vieillir	3870	1838	
Letzte Hoffnung	89 no. 16	La dernière feuille	3871	1838	trans. dedicated to Wartel
Der Wegweiser	89 no. 20	Le guide	3873	1838	
Das Wirtshaus	89 no. 21	Point d'asile	3874	1838	
Mut	89 no. 22	Ah laissons pleurer les fous	3875	1838	
Rückblick	89 no. 8	Mois seul j'aimais	3876	1838	
Irrlicht	89 no. 9	Feu follet	3877	1838	
Rast	89 no. 10	Le repos	3878	1838	
Frühlingstraum	89 no. 11	Un rêve	3929	1838	
Einsamkeit	89 no. 12	Solitaire	3930	1838	
Willkommen und Abschied	56 no. 1	Le rendez-vous	3954	1838	
An die Leier	56 no. 2	Eh bien chante l'amour	3955	1838	
Auf der Donau	21 no. 1	Sur le Danube	3956	1838	
Der Alpenjäger (Auf hohem Bergesrücken ...)	13 no. 3	Le chasseur des Alpes	3957	1838	
Gruppe aus dem Tartarus (Horch wie Murmeln ...)	24 no. 1	L'enfer	3958	1838	

Der Sänger	117	Le ménestrel	3983	1839
Pilgerweise	Nachlass 18 no. 1	Le pèlerin	3984	1839
An den Mond in einer Herbstnacht	Nachlass 18 no. 2	Soirée d'automne	3985	1839
Fahrt zum Hades	Nachlass 18 no. 3	Il faut mourir	3986	1839
Der Pilgrim	37 no. 1	Jamais les cieux	3992	1839
Hektor's Abschied	58 no. 1	Le soldat et la fiancée	3994	1839
Auf der Brücke	93 no. 2	On nous attend là-bas	3999	1839
Die Unterscheidung	95 no. 1	La coquette de village	4000	1839
Die Männer sind méchant	95 no. 3	Mais lui, ne m'aime plus	4001	1839
Irdisches Glück	95 no. 4	Chagrins passés	4002	1839
Der Einsame	41	Le coin du feu	4013	1839
Der Musensohn	92 no. 1	Le poète	4014	1839
Totengräber-Weise	Nachlass 13 no. 3	Chant de fossoyeur	4016	1839
Abendlied für die Entfernte	88 no. 1	Tu n'es pas là	4017	1839
An die Musik	88 no. 4	A toi	4018	1839
Auf dem See	92 no. 2	Le lac	4076	1839
Geistes-Gruss	92 no. 3	Le spectre du château	4077	1839
Glaube, Hoffnung und Liebe	97	Aime, crois, espère	4078	1839
Romanze des Richard Löwenherz	86 (no. 1)	Ivanhoë	4079	1839
Die Sterne	96 no. 1	Les étoiles	4093	1839
Jägers Liebeslied	96 no. 2	Je n'ai pu braver l'amour	4094	1839
Fischerweise	96 no. 4	Rendez-le-moi	4095	1839

German title	Opus, Nachlass etc	French title	Cotage	Year (est.)	Comments
Du liebst mich nicht	59 no. 1	Tu n'aimes pas	4114	1839	
Szene aus Faust	Nachlass 20 no. 2	Scène de Faust	4115	1839	
Kennst du das Land	(no. opus number)	Le chant de Mignon	4116	1839	Not in Octavo Edition
Totengräbers Heimweh	Nachlass 24 no. 2	La gloire de la vie	4138	1839	
Des Sängers Habe	Nachlass 7 no. 1	La fortune du poëte	4139	1839	
Hippolits Lied	Nachlass 7 no. 2	Elle	4140	1839	
Abendröte	Nachlass 7 no. 3	La crépuscule	4141	1839	
Orest auf Tauris	Nachlass 11 no. 1	Le maudit	4155	1839	
Der entsühnte Orest	Nachlass 11 no. 2	Le pardon	4156	1839	
Philoktet	Nachlass 11 no. 3	Le naufragé	4157	1839	
Freiwilliges Versinken	Nachlass 11 no. 4	Le soleil à son déclin	4158	1839	
Lebensmut	Nachlass 17 no. 1	Délire	4198	1839	
Der Vater mit dem Kind	Nachlass 17 no. 2	A mon fils	4199	1839	
An den Tod	Nachlass 17 no. 3	La mort d'enfant	4200	1839	
Verklärung	Nachlass 17 no. 4	Mon âme	4201	1839	
Grenzen der Menschheit	Nachlass 14 no. 1	Dieu	4202	1839	
Fragment aus dem Aeschylus	Nachlass 14 no. 2	La justice divine	4203	1839	
An die Freude	111 no. 1	Le plaisir	4279	1839	trans. dedicated to Wartel
Lebensmelodien	111 no. 2	Au bonheur	4280	1839	trans. dedicated to Wartel
Die vier Weltalter	111 no. 3	Dis-le-moi	4281	1839	trans. dedicated to Wartel
Schäfers Klagelied	3 no. 1	Les plaintes de jeune pâtre	4283	1839	trans. dedicated to Wartel

242

Title	No.	French title	Cat.	Year	Notes
Heidenröslein	3 no. 3	Rose sauvage	4284	1839	
An die untergehende Sonne	44	A la chûte du jour	4456	1839	trans. dedicated to Wartel
Drang in die Ferne	71	Adieu ma mère	4457	1839	
Das Echo	130	L'écho	4458	1839	trans. dedicated to Mlle Clotilde Monvoisin
Memnon	6 no. 1	L'Aurore	4465	1839	trans. dedicated to Mlle Clotilde Monvoisin
Antigone und Oedip	6 no. 2	Les proscrits	4466	1839	trans. dedicated to Mlle Clotilde Monvoisin
Am Grabe Anselmos	6 no. 3	Sa tombe	4467	1839	trans. dedicated to Mlle Clotilde Monvoisin
Lied eines Schiffers an die Dioskuren	65 no. 1	Etoile de la mer	4473	1839	trans. dedicated to Wartel
Der Wanderer (Wie deutlich des Mondes …)	65 no. 2	Toujours seul	4474	1839	trans. dedicated to Wartel
Heliopolis I	65 no. 3	Héliotrope	4475	1839	trans. dedicated to Wartel
Wiegenlied (Wie sich der Äuglein …)	105 no. 2	Tu grandiras	4501	1839	trans. dedicated to Mme Emmanuel Garcia
Am Fenster	105 no. 3	Résignation	4502	1839	
Sehnsucht (Die Scheibe friert …)	105 no. 4	Sans toi	4503	1839	trans. dedicated to Wartel
Erlafsee	8 no. 3	Sur ta rive	4513	1839	
Der Vollmond strahlt auf Bergeshöhn	26	Romance de Rosamunde	4513	1839	
Cronnan	Nachlass 2 no. 1	Le spectre de la fiancée	4516	1839	

German title	Opus, Nachlass etc	French title	Cotage	Year (est.)	Comments
Sehnsucht (Der Lerche wolkennahe Lieder)	8 no. 2	Vague désir	4517	1839	
Am Strome	8 no. 4	La vie	4519	1839	trans. dedicated to Wartel
Heimliches Lieben	106 no. 1	Amour secrèt	4523	1839	trans. dedicated to Wartel
Das Weinen	106 no. 2	Laissez-moi pleurer	4524	1839	trans. dedicated to Wartel
Vor meiner Wiege	106 no. 3	Auprès de mon berceau	4525	1839	trans. dedicated to Wartel
An Sylvia	106 no. 4	Jenny	4526	1839	
An Schwager Kronos	19 no. 1	Méphistophélès	4529	1840	trans. dedicated to Géraldy
An Mignon	19 no. 2	Point de trêve à ma douleur	4530	1840	trans. dedicated to Wartel
Ganymed	19 no. 3	La voix d'en haut	4531	1840	trans. dedicated to Wartel
Am Bach im Frühlinge	109 no. 1	Au mois de mai	4556	1840	trans. dedicated to Wartel
Die Liebe hat gelogen	23 no. 1	Amour trahi	4559	1840	trans. dedicated to Wartel
Selige Welt	23 no. 2	Dans mon bateau	4560	1840	trans. dedicated to Wartel
Schwanengesang (Wie klag ich's aus …)	23 no. 3	Chant suprême	4561	1840	
Schatzgräbers Begehr	23 no. 4	Le chercheur des trésors	4562	1840	trans. dedicated to Wartel
Geist der Liebe	118 no. 1	L'amour	4592	1840	trans. dedicated to Wartel
Der Abend (Der Abend blüht …)	118 no. 2	Voici le soir	4593	1840	sung by Wartel, trans. dedicated to Mme Clementine Marchand
Tischlied	118 no. 3	A demain les peines	4594	1840	trans. dedicated to Wartel
Lob des Tokayers	118 no. 4	Eloge du Tokay	4595	1840	

244

German title	Number	French title	Cat. no.	Year	Note
Die Spinnerin	118 no. 6	La fileuse	4597	1840	trans. dedicated to Mlle d'Hennin
Der Mondabend	131 no. 1	Recueillement	4598	1840	trans. dedicated to Wartel
Trinklied (Brüder, unser Erdenwallen …)	131 no. 2	Le joyeux frère	4599	1840	trans. dedicated to Wartel
Klaglied (Meine Ruh' ist dahin …)	131 no. 3	Chant de douleur	4600	1840	trans. dedicated to Wartel
Der zürnenden Diana	36 no. 1	Punis-moi	4604	1840	trans. dedicated to Wartel
Der Kampf	110	Fatalité	4607	1840	trans. dedicated to M Massol de l'Académie Royale de Musique
Der Liedler	38	Edgar (ballade)	4619	1840	trans. dedicated to Mlle d'Hennin
Lied der Delphine	124 no. 1	Delphine	4620	1840	
Lied des Florio	124 no. 2	Paolo	4621	1840	trans. dedicated to Wartel
Viola	123	Ida	4634	1840	trans. dedicated to Wartel
Der Blumenbrief	Nachlass 21 no. 1	Le langage des fleurs	4672	1840	sung by Wartel; trans. dedicated to Mme Stéphanie De La Marche
Vergissmeinnicht	Nachlass 21 no. 2	Le baiser d'un ange	4673	1840	trans. dedicated to Wartel
Der Sieg	Nachlass 22 no. 1	Tu veut que je t'oublie	4682	1840	trans. dedicated to Mme Wartel
Beim Winde	Nachlass 22 no. 3	Le calme de la nuit	4684	1840	
Abendstern	Nachlass 22 no. 4	Etoile du soir	4685	1840	
Gesänge des Harfners (Wer sich …)	12 no. 1	Au terme de tes maux	4689	1840	(trans. by Bélanger). cf 3493

German title	Opus, Nachlass etc	French title	Cotage	Year (est.)	Comments
Gesänge des Harfners (Wer nie sein Brot.)	12 no. 2	L'ange	4690	1840	
Schwestergruss	Nachlass 23 no. 1	Ombre chérie	4693	1840	
Liedesend	Nachlass 23 no. 2	Le barde	4694	1840	
Im Frühling	Nachlass 25 no. 2	Matinée de printemps	4696	1840	
Der Winterabend	Nachlass 26	Soirée d'hiver	4749	1840	
Grablied für die Mutter	Nachlass 30 no. 3	Le tombeau d'une mère	4761	1840	
Die Betende	Nachlass 31 no. 1	La prière	4784	1840	
An Laura	Nachlass 31 no. 3	L'oratoire	4786	1840	
Shilric und Vinvela	Nachlass 4 no. 1	Schilric et Vinvela	4812	1840	
Die Nacht	Nachlass 1 no. 1	Nuit d'orage en Ecosse	4871	1840	
Ellens Gesang (Raste, Krieger …)	52 no. 1	Chant d'Hélène	5730	?	trans. dedicated to Mlle d'Hennin (probably after 1845)

LIST B (The following, together with those in List A, are included in the Octavo Edition, n.d.)

German title	Opus, Nachlass etc.	French title
Jägers Abendlied	3 no. 4	Chant du chasseur
Der Jüngling auf dem Hügel	8 no. 1	Le fiancé (ballade)
Gesänge des Harfners (An die Türen …)	12 no. 3	Le mendiant
Hänflings Liebeswerbung	20 no. 3	Bonheur d'espérance

German title	Opus, Nachlass etc.	French title
Hermann et Thusnelda	Nachlass 28 no. 1	Hermann et Thusnelda
Selma und Selmar	Nachlass 28 no. 2	Pense au retour
Das Rosenband	Nachlass 28 no. 3	La guirlande de roses
Edone	Nachlass 28 no. 4	Pourtant ce n'est pas toi
Die frühen Gräber	Nachlass 28 no. 5	La lune sur les tombeaux
Stimme der Liebe	Nachlass 29 no. 1	La voix de l'amour
Die Mutter Erde	Nachlass 29 no. 2	Peut être?
Gretchens Bitte	Nachlass 29 no. 3	Prière de Marguerite
Abschied von einem Freunde	Nachlass 29 no. 4	A bientôt
Tiefes Leid	Nachlass 30 no. 1	Profonde douleur
Die Liebe (Freudvoll und Leidvoll …)	Nachlass 30 no. 2	Chanson de Claire
Der Geistertanz	Nachlass 31 no. 2	La fête des morts
Einsamkeit	Nachlass 32 no. 1	L'isolement
Der Schiffer	Nachlass 33 no. 1	Le rêve du batelier
Die gefangenen Sänger	Nachlass 33 no. 2	Chant du captif
Auflösung	Nachlass 34 no. 1	Pardon généreux
Blondel zu Marien	Nachlass 34 no. 2	Blondel à Marie
Die erste Liebe	Nachlass 35 no. 1	Premier amour
Lied eines Kriegers	Nachlass 35 no. 2	Chant de guerre
Der Jüngling an der Quelle	Nachlass 36 no. 1	Louise
Lambertine	Nachlass 36 no. 2	Lambertine
Ihr Grab	Nachlass 36 no. 3	Pauvre jeune fille
Aus 'Heliopolis' II	Nachlass 37 no. 1	Les ruines
Sehnsucht	Nachlass 37 no. 2	C'est toujours du bonheur

249

Extracts from *L'Art de chanter les Romances, les Chansonnettes et les Nocturnes et généralement toute la musique de salon ...* par A. Romagnesi (1846)

AVANT-PROPOS

pp. 5–6

Il existe déjà un grand nombre de méthodes de chant; il en est même plusieurs qui jouissent d'une juste réputation et dont je suis le premier à reconnaître le mérite et l'utilité. Mais l'importance et la difficulté d'une partie de ces ouvrages attestent qu'il sont été composés particulièrement en vue des élèves qui se destinent à nos théâtres lyriques ou à nos concerts publics. L'art vocal, considéré sous cet aspect, exige tant d'études et de patience; les voix puissantes et étendues ne s'assouplissent qu'après un travail si persévérant, que dans ce cas on ne saurait trop multiplier les exercices qui tendent à former des talents complets.

Mais si l'on se rend compte de l'extrême différence qui existe entre le chant tel que l'exige l'art dramatique et celui qui convient aux salons, ou, pour autrement dire, entre une voix forte et rebelle et celle plus modeste et plus maniable de la pluralité des amateurs de la société, on se convaincra que, pour ces derniers, les études trop laborieuses ne sont pas de première nécessité; je dirai même qu'elles sont dangereuses, car une voix douce annonce une conformation délicate du larynx. On doit donc, dans ce cas, traiter cet organe avec plus de ménagement que celui qui est plus vigoureusement constitué.

Les personnes, dont la voix naturellement juste et flexible n'a besoin de presque aucune étude de vocalisation, forment la très petite minorité parmi celles qui ont le goût du chant. La plupart, au contraire, ont besoin de rectifier leur organe, d'en adoucir la dureté, de lui donner tout le développement qu'il peut atteindre, ou lui acquérir l'agilité qui lui manque; en un mot, d'en tirer le meilleur parti possible en corrigeant les défauts qui résultent de son inculture.

C'est dans ce but que j'ai rédigé le petit traité que j'offre aux chanteurs de salons. A quelques exercices, qui sont plus ou moins nécessaires pour former la voix selon qu'elle est plus ou moins rétive (ce que le professeur est appelé à juger), j'ai ajouté les règles principales qu'il faut suivre pour l'exécution des œuvres légères qui forment l'une des plus agréables parties des réunions musicales.

J'ai la conviction que les personnes qui auront le courage d'étudier avec zèle tous les enseignements contenus dans ces quelques pages s'apercevront, par leurs succès dans le monde des concerts, de l'avantage qu'il y a de mettre du soin et de la persévérance dans ses études; elles se convaincront que ce n'est qu'en se conformant aux préceptes du goût, de la raison et de l'expérience des maîtres, que l'on arrive à l'exécution parfaite de ces petits opuscules qui paraissent, à ceux qui les écoutent, si simples et si faciles à chanter.

pp. 12–21

DES CONDITIONS A OBSERVER
POUR EXECUTER AVEC SUCCES LA MUSIQUE VOCALE EN GENERAL

Réflexions préparatoires

Tout le mérite d'une composition musicale disparaît si l'exécutant n'est pas pénétré d'abord du sentiment que l'auteur a voulu exprimer.

Une œuvre de musique chantée froidement ou avec une expression exagérée perd entièrement l'effet que le chanteur espérait lui donner, tandis que le même morceau dit simplement, et suivant les intentions indiquées par l'auteur, obtient un succès auquel le chanteur souvent ne s'attendait pas lui-même.

Un chant simple et tendre doit être interprété avec l'âme. Chercher en ce cas à briller par le prestige des ornements ou par la seule beauté de la voix, c'est se montrer privé de goût et de sensibilité.

Les chansonnettes gracieuses, légères, chevaleresques ou même doucement mélancoliques peuvent recevoir quelques agréments passagers; mais on doit en être sobre pour ne pas étouffer l'idée génératrice sous un tissu de détails parasites.

Il est certains sujets tracés dans le dessein d'amener, pour le chanteur, le moyen de faire ressortir la souplesse et la légèreté de sa voix, comme ceux qui rappellent le chant de la fauvette, du rossignol, etc. Assez ordinairement, en pareil cas, les ornements sont écrits par l'auteur, et il est rare qu'on ait besoin d'y rien ajouter.

Moins les œuvres légères semblent avoir d'importance, et plus l'on doit apporter de soins dans leur exécution.

Des paroles d'une composition vocale

Avant d'essayer la musique d'un morceau de ce genre, on doit en examiner les paroles avec soin, en comprendre la pensée générale, en étudier les diverses parties, afin de fixer les éléments à mettre en œuvre pour donner au chant tout l'effet qu'il est susceptible de produire, car, c'est de la coïncidence parfaite de la musique avec les paroles que résulte la bonne exécution d'une composition vocale.

Non-seulement on doit étudier les intentions du poëte, mais il serait à désirer même qu'avant de les chanter, on déclamât à haute voix les paroles d'un morceau, ayant soin de s'arrêter, dans une juste mesure, aux points et aux virgules, d'accentuer avec précision les syllabes longues par opposition aux syllabes brèves, de s'attacher, en un mot, à une prononciation nette et correcte.

De la prononciation

Si je recommande particulièrement aux chanteurs de donner aux paroles d'une œuvre vocale une sérieuse attention, c'est afin qu'ils puissent reporter dans la musique la bonne prononciation qu'ils auront obtenue par ce travail préparatoire.

C'est un fait généralement observé aujourd'hui, que cet étrange défaut de prononciation de la plupart des chanteurs, soit sur nos théâtres, soit dans nos concerts. C'est à ce point que souvent, placé près de l'exécutant, l'auditeur ne peut saisir aucun des mots de la pièce qu'il chante. Je pourrais signaler les causes de ce défaut presque général, mais cela sortirait de mon sujet, et je préfère indiquer ici les moyens de s'en préserver.

Non seulement il faut en chantant s'arrêter convenablement aux repos marqués par les points et les virgules, comme on l'aura fait en déclamant les paroles, non-seulement on devra peser sur les syllabes longues et passer légèrement sur les brèves, mais encore il sera nécessaire d'accentuer tous les mots plus énergiquement qu'on ne le fait en parlant; on devra les articuler comme s'il s'agissait de se faire entendre d'une oreille un peu dure, mais pourtant, en évitant toute affectation et toute grimace.

Par ce moyen (dont je me suis toujours servi pour moi-même), on se fait entendre, quoique avec une voix faible, des auditeurs les plus reculés d'une grande salle.

De la respiration

Le talent de respirer, et de respirer à propos, est encore une des parties essentielles de l'art du chanteur. Écoutez cet artiste habile: c'est à peine si vous l'apercevrez reprendre son haleine; cela vient de ce qu'il s'est longtemps attaché à vaincre cette importante difficulté. Imitez-le: évitez l'aspiration et l'expiration bruyante de l'air; respirez doucement et souvent dans les demi-phrases; absorbez à pleine poitrine, mais sans que cela s'entende, une quantité d'air suffisante pour une longue période; respirez le moins possible au milieu d'une phrase, et jamais au milieu d'un mot; évitez avec soin les contractions du corps et de la figure, et, par votre constante observation de ces préceptes essentiels, vous obtiendrez promptement le prix de vos efforts.

De la tenue du chanteur

La manière dont un chanteur doit se poser près le piano doit être également l'objet de quelques recommandations.

Sans doute il serait de mauvais goût de se placer en face de son auditoire comme un acteur sur le théâtre, Les gestes, les mouvements affectés de la tête et du corps, seraient souvent inconvenants et presque toujours ridicules; mais, pourtant, on ne doit pas oublier qu'une œuvre de musique vocale, si simple qu'elle soit, exprime un sentiment dont le chanteur doit paraître impressionné s'il veut émouvoir son auditoire; que par conséquent son regard, le jeu de sa physionomie, doivent avec le son de sa voix, concourir à l'effet qu'il veut produire. Mais tout cela sans prétention, simplement, avec convenance et bon goût. Le chanteur doit éviter ces regards désespérés, cette sensibilité outrée, cette fausse chaleur, en un mot, qui est à l'art du chant ce qu'un charge difforme est à un beau dessin.

Mais, dira-t-on, comment reconnaître cette nuance qui sépare le vrai du faux en fait d'expression? Où doit s'arrêter celle-ci pour ne pas paraître exagérée? Ici nous entrons dans le domaine du goût, du vrai sentiment musical, que je vais essayer de définir.

Du goût par rapport à la musique

Le goût est une façon d'être impressionné qui paraît d'abord difficile à définir. Ces locutions proverbiales: *Tous les goûts sont dans la nature, il ne faut pas disputer les goûts*, sembleraient partir de ce principe que chaque individu a une façon particulière de percevoir l'impression des objets extérieurs. Cependant pour peu qu'on réfléchisse, on se convaincra qu'il n'y a que deux manières de sentir, la bonne et la mauvaise. En effet, s'il y a deux façons d'apprécier le parfum des fleurs, la beauté du plumage d'un oiseau, la saveur des fruits, et le charme d'un son doux et suave, celui qui à cet égard, ne partagerait pas le sentiment général ne paraîtrait-il pas privé de ce sixième sens qui est la faculté de comprendre les beautés de la nature, autrement dit, la bonne manière de sentir? Oui, c'est dans la nature qu'il faut aller puiser les principes du bon goût. Si les arts d'imagination, tels que la poésie et la musique, ont des formes de convention, particulières à chacun d'eux, ces formes une fois admises, tout ce qui ressort de l'inspiration ne doit avoir pour principe que la nature et la vérité. En effet, quel est le but que le compositeur de musique vocale se propose d'atteindre? N'est-ce pas de rendre avec le plus de vérité possible, mais dans une manière originale qui lui soit propre, le sentiment exprimé par les paroles dont il s'inspire? Son ouvrage terminé, a-t-il atteint son but? C'est le public, dont le tact original, perfectionné par l'habitude d'entendre de la bonne musique, lui suggère instantanément la comparaison du sentiment que le compositeur a voulu peindre avec la phrase musicale dont il s'est servi pour l'exprimer.

Eh bien! c'est de ce jugement, dicté par le sens du beau, par l'appréciation instinctive de l'individualité du compositeur, et par la comparaison de sa composition avec l'objet qu'il a voulu peindre, que se forme le bon goût en musique, autrement dit le véritable sentiment musical.

Maintenant si nous passons d'une composition vocale à son exécution, les devoirs du chanteur dérivent évidemment du principe que nous venons d'établir. Le bon goût l'avertit de ne chercher l'effet que par des moyens naturels et simples; d'éviter la manière et l'exagération; enfin, de conformer les inflexions de sa voix aux sentiments qu'il est appelé à exprimer.

DES ROMANCES EN GENERAL

Les œuvres auxquelles on donne le nom générique de romances peuvent être classées de la manière suivante:

> Les romances sentimentales;
> Les mélodies rêveuses et graves;
> Les chants héroïques et fortement rhythmés;
> Les romances passionnées et dramatiques;

La chansonnette, qui se réserve la gaieté gracieuse, bien différente en cela de la chanson comique qui, jouée plus que chantée, est en dehors des conditions de cette méthode.

Le nocturne, participant à la fois de tous les genres que je viens d'indiquer, se trouve soumis aux règles qui s'y rapportent.

Les romances sentimentales et héroïques sont les véritables romances, eu égard au goût et au caractère français.

Les mélodies rêveuses et graves, dont le style rappelle celui des *lieders* allemands, veulent, ainsi qu'eux, un accompagnement d'une harmonie plus forte et plus travaillée que les autres espèces du genre romance.

Quant aux romances dramatiques, c'est-a-dire celles dont la contexture et les accompagnements rappellent les morceaux qu'on chante au théâtre, elles ont dû prendre naissance dans la nature des études des jeunes compositeurs formés dans nos écoles pour devenir les soutiens de nos scènes lyriques, mais qui, pour la plupart, les trouvant fermées pour eux, à peu près, jettent dans le monde des œuvres recommandables, sans doute, mais qui manquent parfois leur effet pour n'être pas placées à leur véritable point de vue.

APPLICATION DES PRECEPTES GENERAUX INDIQUES PLUS HAUT AU CHANT DES ROMANCES, CHANSONNETTES ET NOCTURNES

Les romances sentimentales

Les romances tendres et mélancoliques sont généralement celles qui trouvent le plus de sympathie dans l'âme des auditeurs. Le chanteur qui fera entendre une de ces mélodies ne réussira à toucher son auditoire que s'il s'est lui-même impressionné de son chant et de l'intention du compositeurs. Qu'il se garde surtout des fiorituras à prétention, ou de ces ports de voix maladroits que quelques-uns prennent pour de l'expression et qui n'en est que la parodie. Qu'il évite encore ces longues tenues sur l'avant-dernière note de la phrase finale que le mauvais goût de quelques chanteurs a mises à la mode.

Les Mélodies rêveuses et graves

Les pièces de ce genre, surtout lorsque l'idéalité du sujet l'emporte sur le sentiment, sont destinées plus particulièrement aux voix graves telles que la basse, le baryton ou le contralto. Elles exigent de l'ampleur dans l'émission de la voix; mais il faut éviter de la donner avec trop de puissance, ce qui arrive à plus d'un chanteur. L'art n'est pas de chanter fort, mais de nuancer son chant conformément à l'expression des paroles.

Cette espèce de romances, à cause de la monotonie des voix graves et de celle des sujets sérieux, peut être ornée de notes d'agrément, mais dans le genre soutenu qui convient surtout à cette spécialité.

Les romances chevaleresques

Ces romances conviennent surtout aux ténors dont la voix est fortement accentuée. Ces chanteurs devront se défier de la vigueur de leur organe et ne pas confondre les cris avec l'expression. Généralement on doit mesurer la vibration de sa voix à l'étendue de la salle où l'on chante. Les romances chevaleresques peuvent être légèrement variées lorsque le sujet le comporte et lorsque la voix du chanteur est suffisamment assouplie; mais s'il n'est pas parvenu à cet égard au degré de perfection qu'il peut atteindre, il devra se borner à chanter la note avec l'expression simple et naturelle dont il faut jamais s'écarter.

Les romances dramatiques

Les romances dramatiques sont du domaine des voix étendues, vibrantes et expressives. Comme pour les précédentes, il ne faut pas confondre les cris avec le sentiment; car on peut montrer beaucoup d'âme en chantant à demi-voix, et l'on n'en fait que mieux ressortir la note qui exprime le déchirement du cœur ou l'explosion de la tendresse.

Mais c'est surtout dans cette espèce de musique théâtrale qu'on doit éviter les contorsions et les grimaces; qu'il faut savoir rester dans une mesure convenable et de bon goût, en ne dépassant pas le but qu'on veut atteindre. Il ne faut pas non plus laisser emporter par la vivacité du mouvement, de manière à ne plus prononcer les mots que d'une façon inintelligible; car c'est en faisant bien comprendre le sujet qu'on interprète qu'on peut faire partager à l'auditoire le sentiment dramatique de la situation.

Les romances et chansonnettes variées

Les pièces de ce genre sont destinées aux voix naturellement légère ou à celles qu'un travail bien dirigé a développées et assouplies. L'auteur de la musique y a le plus souvent marqué les passages qu'il a imaginés pour donner à sa composition plus de charme et de variété. Néanmoins, le chanteur pourra, selon la nature de sa voix et le plus ou moins de perfection de son talent, changer discrètement les traits et les fioritures de l'auteur pour leur en substituer d'autres, mais toujours selon le goût et les intentions de celui-ci.

APPENDIX C 257

Au surplus, dans les chansonnettes, il faut, avant tout, s'attacher à faire ressortir l'esprit et la gaieté des paroles, sans affectation, et avec cette finesse et ce ton de bonne compagnie dont s'écartent quelquefois, dans l'espoir trompeur d'un plus éclatant succès, les chanteurs dont le goût n'est pas assez épuré.

Les nocturnes

Ce que je viens de dire au sujet des divers genres de romances et chansonnettes peut également s'appliquer aux nocturnes. Mais ici la perfection d'exécution est beaucoup plus difficile à obtenir, parce qu'elle exige les soins et l'attention simultanés de deux exécutants qui souvent sont dans l'impossibilité de se réunir autant qu'il est nécessaire de le faire en pareil cas. Aussi ne trouve-t-on presque jamais la perfection dans le chant des nocturnes que chez les personnes qui vivent sous le même toit.

QUELQUES REMARQUES
Sur les fautes contre le goût qui résultent de l'abus qu'on fait de qualités estimables

Une voix étendue et fortement timbrée est certainement un beau don de la nature; mais, ce n'est que la première des conditions nécessaires pour conquérir le talent de chanteur, car celui-ci, 'S'il n'a reçu du ciel l'influence secrète' ne sera jamais qu'un chanteur médiocre.

Privés de cette flamme céleste, les artistes de cette dernière catégorie, qui n'ont à leur service qu'une voix forte et sonore, cherchent leurs succès dans la manifestation de leur puissant organe, et, comme on le dit plaisamment, ils chantent bien fort au lieu de chanter fort bien.

C'est un défaut assez commun chez les basses et les barytons; l'abus qu'ils font d'une qualité essentielle, les prive du succès qu'ils obtiendraient si, même à défaut de l'influence secrète qu'ils n'ont pas reçue, ils se laissaient guider par les principes du goût et de la raison.

Les artistes, vraiment maîtres de leur art, emploient parfois d'heureux artifices vocaux qui, placés convenablement, ajoutent au charme et à l'expression d'une phrase passagère ou d'une cantilène tout entière. De ce nombre est une certaine vibration, un léger tremblement de la voix qui a pour but de rendre plus saisissante l'expression de la douleur. Malheureusement les imitateurs sont là qui se chargent de tout gâter. Ils ont remarqué que ce moyen d'effet a obtenu des applaudissements, et ils s'en servent à tout propos; de telle sorte que leur petit tremblotement perpétuel devient la chose la plus insupportable qui se puisse entendre. Il ne faut donc user de ce moyen que dans les situations assez rares où il peut être employé d'une manière rationnelle.

Les oppositions sont, dans les arts, les plus puissants auxiliaires de l'effet général; mais c'est dans la nature et le raisonnement qu'il faut en chercher les éléments. Cela ne paraît pourtant pas être la manière de voir de quelques-uns de nos chanteurs qui ont imaginé qu'ils pouvaient employer cet artifice sur une même phrase qu'ils disent fort d'abord et, instantanément, *pianissimo* sans qu'il y ait dans les paroles aucun motif à ce contraste. C'est ainsi que les éternelles vérités du bon sens se faussent jusqu'au ridicule lorsqu'elles sont mal comprises par l'ignorance et la présomption.

Je pourrais prolonger mes recherches sur des anomalies analogues de la part des chanteurs; il vaut mieux prévenir contre elles les personnes qui préfèrent travailler à vaincre les nombreuses difficultés de l'art que de se complaire dans une médiocrité trop souvent applaudie par un auditoire qui n'est indulgent qu'en apparence.

FOREWORD

There already exists a large number of singing methods; there are even several which enjoy a justified reputation, their merit and usefulness of which I am the first to give due regard. But the importance and the difficulty of some of these is because they have been written especially for those students who intend to be opera or concert singers. Vocal art, considered from this aspect, demands much study and patience; powerful and resourceful voices are only rendered supple after a course of study that demands such perseverance that it is impossible to give enough exercises that will lead to complete mastery.

But if we consider the big difference between the art of operatic singing and that suited to the salons, or, to put it differently, between a large and intractable voice and the more modest and manageable kind found in the larger number of non-professional musicians, one will be convinced that for the latter, over-laborious studies are not the main requirement. I will even say that they are dangerous, for a soft voice indicates a delicate larynx. This vocal organ must be treated with greater care than the one that is more robust.

Those who, possessing a true and flexible voice, hardly need voice exercises comprise a very tiny minority amongst those who have a taste for singing. The majority, on the contrary, need to correct their voice by softening its hardness, by developing it to the full, or by acquiring the agility that it lacks; in a word, drawing the best from it by correcting the faults that have been acquired through lack of training.

It is with this aim that I have published this little treatise which I offer to salon singers. To a few exercises, which are more or less necessary to form the voice according to whether it is more or less recalcitrant (that which the teacher is called upon to judge), I have added the main rules which must be followed for the performance of light pieces that form one of the most delightful parts of a recital.

I am convinced that those who have the courage to zealously study all the teaching contained in these few pages will see, through their successes in concerts, the advantage of putting care and perseverance into their studies; they will be convinced that it is only when conforming to the principles of the taste, reason and experience of the masters, that one achieves perfection in the performance of these little artistic works, which appear to those who listen to them, to be so simple and so easy to sing.

POINTS TO NOTE IN ORDER TO PERFORM VOCAL MUSIC SUCCESSFULLY

Preliminary considerations

All the merit of a musical composition disappears if the performer has not first of all entered into the expression that the composer wants to convey.

A piece of music sung coldly or with exaggerated expression completely loses the effect that the singer was hoping to give to it, whilst the same piece sung simply and following the composer's indications, achieves a success that the singer himself often did not expect.

A simple and tender song must be interpreted with feeling. In this case, to try to shine through a show of ornamentation or through the beauty of the voice alone demonstrates one's lack of taste and sensitivity.

Chansonnettes that are gracious, light and courtly, or even sweetly sad, may have some tiny embellishments; but they must be used sparingly so as not to stifle the basic idea under a web of parasite-like details.

There are certain subjects that give the singer a lead in how to feature suppleness and lightness in the voice, such as those that suggest the call of the warbler, of the nightingale, etc. Usually in such a case the ornaments are written out by the composer, and it is rare that one has need to add anything.

The less that light pieces seem to be significant, the more care one must have in their performance.

The words

Before trying over the music of a song, it is necessary to examine the words with care, understanding the overall idea and studying the different parts, so as to weigh up the elements of the piece in order to give to the melody all the effect that it is capable of, for it is the perfect union of music and words that produces a good performance.

Not only must one study the poet's intentions, but it would be desirable even before singing the work to declaim the words in a loud voice, taking care to observe closely the fullstops and commas, emphasising through contrast the long and short syllables; in a word, closely attending to clear and correct pronunciation.

Pronunciation

I am specially recommending to singers that they give serious attention to the words of a song, so that they transfer to the music the good pronunciation that has come about through this preliminary work.

Nowadays, this curious fault of (poor) pronunciation is generally noticed amongst most singers, be they in our theatres or in our concerts. Often when placed near a performer, you cannot understand any of the words of the piece they are singing. I could point to the causes of this almost general fault, but that would be going beyond my topic, and I prefer to indicate here the ways of preserving (good) pronunciation.

In singing, not only must one stop appropriately at points of repose, like the comma and full-stop – as will have been done when declaiming the words – and not only must one lean on the long syllables and pass lightly over the short ones, but also it will be necessary to emphasise all the words much more vigorously than in speaking; one has to articulate them as if being heard by a slightly deaf person, but, however, avoiding all affectation and grimacing.

Through this method (which I always use myself) the furthest placed members of the audience in a large room can hear them.

Breathing

The aptitude for breathing – correct breathing – is one of the essential parts of the singer's art. Listen to a fine artist; you will hardly hear him take a breath; this comes though long determination to overcome the problems of breathing. Imitate him: avoid a noisy intake and exhalation of air; breathe softly and often in short phrases; fill the chest, without being heard, with an amount of air sufficient for a long phrase; take a breath as infrequently as possible in the middle of a long phrase, and never in the middle of a word; take care in avoiding contortion of body and face and, through constant attention to these essential precepts, you will win back the price of your efforts.

Posture

The way a singer must place himself near the piano demands consideration.

Without doubt, it would be in bad taste to place oneself in front of an audience like an actor. Gestures, affected movements of head and body would be irritating and almost always ridiculous; but, however, one must not forget that a song, simple as it may be, expresses a mood that the singer must appear to feel if he is to move his listeners; consequently, his face, the movement of his body must, together with his voice, contribute to the effect he wishes to produce. But all this without pretence, simply, with appropriateness and good taste. The singer must avoid desperate looks – that exaggerated sensitivity, that false warmth of expression – in a word, what to the art of singing is distortion in a fine design.

But, one will say, how is one to recognize that nuance that separates the true from the false in the matter of expression. Where must one stop before appearing exaggerated? Here we enter into the area of taste, of true musical feeling, which I will try to define.

Taste in relation to music

Taste is a way of being moved by something, this at first being difficult to define. The old clichés: *All taste being in nature, one must not argue over taste*, would seem to depart from the principle that each individual has his own way of perceiving external objects. However, reflecting on this a little, one is convinced that there are only two ways of sensing: the good and the bad. Indeed, if there are two ways of appreciating the perfume of flowers, the beauty of a bird's plumage, the taste of fruit, and the charm of a sweet and suave sound, the person who thinks this way, would he not share the general belief appearing to be deprived of the 'sixth sense' which is the faculty of understanding the beauties of nature, otherwise known as 'true feeling'. Yes, it is from nature that the principles of good taste are to be drawn. If the arts of imagination, such as poetry and music, have conventional forms, peculiar to each art, once accepted, then everything related to inspiration must have only nature and beauty as its guiding principle. Indeed, what is the goal that songwriter envisages? Is it not to render, with the utmost truth and in an original and appropriate way, the sentiment expressed by the work which inspires him? His song finished, has he achieved his goal? Who is going to judge its worth? It is the public, whose discretion, perfected through the habit of listening to good music, that immediately replies to him through comparing the sentiment that the composer has wanted to paint with the musical phrase that he has used to express it.

Well! it is from this judgement, dictated by the sense of beauty, by the instinctive appreciation of the composer's individuality, and by the comparison of his work with the object he has wished to paint, that is formed good taste in music, otherwise called the true musical sentiment.

Now if we pass from the composition of a musical work to its performance, the responsibilities of the singer derive obviously from the principle that we have just established. Good taste will warn him to search only for those means that are simple and natural; to avoid mannerism and exaggeration; finally, to model his vocal inflections on the sentiments that he is called upon to express.

Of romances in general

Works which have been given the generic name of romances can be classified in the following way:

> Sentimental romances
> Reflective and sombre melodies
> Heroic and strongly rhythmic songs
> Passionate and dramatic romances

The chansonnette, reserved for cheerfulness, yet quite distinct from the comic chanson, which, acted rather than sung, is outside the limits of the present method.

The nocturne, embracing at the same time all the classifications which I have just indicated, is subject to the rules related to them.

Sentimental and heroic romances are true romances in regard to taste and French character.

Reflective and sombre melodies, the style of which recalls that of German *lieder*, need, like the latter, accompaniments with stronger and more highly-wrought harmony than the other kinds of romances.

As for dramatic romances, that is to say, those whose form and accompaniment recall works that are sung in the theatre, these owe their birth to those works from young composers being trained in our schools in writing for opera houses, but which, for the most part, finding them closed to them – or almost – toss into the world some doubtlessly commendable pieces, but which sometimes lose their effect by not being placed in their true context.

APPLICATION OF SOME GENERAL PRECEPTS INDICATED EARLIER TO THE SINGING OF ROMANCES, CHANSONNETTES AND NOCTURNES

Sentimental romances

Tender and sad romances are generally those which are most taken into the hearts of audiences. The singer who wants to have these melodies heard will not touch his listeners unless he himself is moved through his singing and the composer's intention. He must, above all, guard against pretentious flourishes, or against clumsy appoggiaturas [*ports de voix*], which some singers take to be expression but which is only parody. He should avoid those long fermatas on the penultimate note of the phrase that poor taste on the part of several singers has made fashionable.

Reflective and sombre melodies

Works of this kind, above all when the high-flown nature of the text informs the expression, are designed especially for deep voices, such as basses, baritones or contraltos. They demand fullness of voice; but it is necessary to avoid giving too much power as happens to more than one singer. The art is not to sing loudly, but to give nuance to the song in conformity with the expression of the words.

This kind of romance, because of the monotony of deep voices and serious subjects, can be ornamented, but in a subdued way that above all suits this special category.

Heroic romances

These romances suit, above all, the clear tenor voice. These singers must guard against the vigorous nature of their voice and not confuse shouting with expression. Generally, the voice should be matched to the size of the room where one is singing. These romances can be lightly varied when the subject suits this and when the voice is sufficiently supple. But if it has not yet reached this degree of perfection one must be content with singing the notes with a simple and natural expression from which one should not stray.

Dramatic romances

Dramatic romances are the domain of large, vibrant and expressive voices. As with the previous ones, shouting must not be confused with expression; for one can be soulful by singing *sotto voce*, and it is better to express heart-rending emotion or the outflow of tenderness by bringing out the note which expresses the wrenching of the heart or the outburst of tenderness

But, above all, in this kind of theatrical music one must avoid grimaces and contortions; you have to learn how to stay within limits both suitable and in good taste and not going beyond the goal of what one wants to achieve. One must not be carried away by a fast tempo in a way that makes the words unintelligible; for it is by making comprehensible the subject that one is interpreting that one can share with the audience the dramatic sentiment of the situation.

Varied romances and chansonnettes

Pieces of this kind are composed for voices that are light by nature or by training that has been well directed towards vocal development and suppleness. The composer has often marked those passages that he has believed will give more charm and variety to his composition. Nevertheless, the singer can, according to the nature of his voice, and how far he has developed it, discreetly change composer's roulades and embellishments by substituting his own, but always according to the taste and intentions of the former.

In addition, with chansonnettes one must, before everything else, want to bring out the cheerfulness of the words, without affectation and with that finesse and good breeding, which sometimes slips by, in the misplaced hope of success, eluding those singers whose taste is not sufficiently refined.

Nocturnes

What I have just said about the various kinds of romances and chansonnettes can be equally applied to nocturnes. But here a perfect performance is much more difficult to achieve, because it demands the simultaneous care and attention on the part of two performers who are often in the impossible situation of uniting in a way that is necessary to sound as one. Also, one hardly ever finds that perfection in singing nocturnes that one does with singers who live under the same roof.

VARIOUS OBSERVATIONS

About errors of taste resulting in abuse against desirable qualities

A big and rich voice is certainly a beautiful gift of nature; but it is only the first of the conditions needed to exploit the singer's talent, for 'If he has not received from the heaven the secret influence' he will only be a mediocre singer.

Deprived of this heavenly flame, artists in that latter category, who have only a strong and sonorous voice, search for success in the power of their vocal cords, and, as one has neatly put it, sing *bien fort* rather than *fort bien* (very loudly rather than very well). It is a common enough fault amongst basses and baritones; the abuse which they do to an essential quality deprives them of the success they could achieve, even in spite of not receiving the 'secret influence', if they would let themselves be guided by the principles of taste and reason.

Artists, truly masters of their art, sometimes employ useful vocal devices which, appropriately done, add to the charm and expression of the occasional phrase or of an entire passage. Of these devices there is a certain vibration, a light trembling of the voice, the aim of which is to heighten the expression of grief. Unfortunately there are imitators who see to it that they spoil everything. They have noticed that this effect has gained applause, and they use it at will; thus, their incessant little tremelos become the most unbearable thing that one can hear. Therefore this effect must only be employed relatively rarely where it can be used in a rational way.

In the arts contrasts are the most powerful subsidiary elements in the overall effect, but it is in nature and in rationality that one must search for them. That does not appear to be the way that some of our singers see it, who have imagined that they can employ this artifice on the same phrase that they first sing loudly and, instantly *pianissimo*, when no reason exists in the text for making this contrast. Thus it is that the eternal truths of good sense are falsified to the extent of ridicule when they are misunderstood through ignorance and presumption.

I could extend my studies into similar anomalies of the part of singers; it would be better to warn people against them, those who prefer to work so as to vanquish the numerous difficulties of the art, rather than take pleasure in mediocrity too often applauded by a seemingly indulgent audience.

The publication of Monpou's *L'Andalouse* as described in J. Stadler, 'La Première Romance', *L'Echo musical*, 1 September 1839

Il fait bien beau aujourd'hui, et pas un sou en poche! s'écriaient avec dépit, il y a environ douze ans, quatre jeunes gens à la mine éveillée et à l'air jovial, qui, pour le moment flânaient délicieusement pendant une belle matinée d'été sur le boulevard des Italiens. – Et ta romance de *L'Andalouse*, qu'en as-tu fait? – Ne m'en parle pas, mon cher; je l'ai offerte déjà, à plus de dix éditeurs de musique, personne n'en veut; je la trouve pourtant bien jolie. – Vous l'entendez, Messieurs, un père est toujours père; le fait est qu'elle n'est pas mal du tout. – Quand ce serait du Boïldieu tout pur, il n'en est pas plus avancé avec son *Andalouse*, puisqu'elle ne lui fournit pas les moyens de nous payer le plus modeste déjeuner. – Et nos quatre étourdis rirent aux éclats. Si cependant je faisais une dernière tentative? reprit notre jeune musicien. Nous voilà justement devant M Lemoine; c'est le seul, je crois, auquel je n'ai pas présenté mon chef-d'œuvre; attendez-moi; dans cinq minutes, je suis à vous.

Il avait raison. M Lemoine, après avoir examiné attentivement la romance, qu'il trouva assez de son goût, demanda, en souriant, à l'auteur combien il voulait la vendre. "Combien en voulez-vous donner? – Cinquante francs pas davantage." Et déjà le compositeur en herbe tendait la main. Les cinquante francs furent payés. Qui peindra la joie du jeune artiste! Il va rejoindre ses amies, et faisant sonner ses écus, de manière à faire retourner tous les passants: "Victoire! victoire!" s'écrie-t-il du plus loin qu'il les voit. "Nous avons de l'argent." On le félicite, on l'embrasse et l'on remet en route au milieu de la plus bruyante hilarité. "Allons à Belleville!" fut un cri général; "nous y déjeunerons." Ils s'y rendirent, en effet, et y firent un copieux déjeuner qui se prolongea jusqu'à l'heure du dîner. Qui pourra dire toutes les bonnes folies qu'on débita pendant le joyeux festin, tous les plans, les projets, les châteaux en Espagne qu'on y bâtit. Bref, au sortir de table, et après une petite promenade champêtre, nos amis arrivèrent devant la fameuse guinguette de l'Ile d'Amour; c'était un dimanche; on y dansait. Le bruit criard des instruments attira l'attention de nos héros, qui pénétrèrent dans la salle de bal et se mêlèrent à la contredanse. "Quelle enragée musique!" dit l'un d'eux; "les oreilles m'en cuisent." – "Jouons nous-mêmes", reprit un autre; ce sera drôle – "Bravo!" s'écrièrent-ils tous à l'unisson et ils proposèrent au chef d'orchestre et à ses trois musiciens de les remplacer, seulement, ajoutèrent-il, le temps nécessaire pour se rafraîchir. La proposition fut acceptée. Qu'on se figure l'étonnement des auditeurs en entendant une exécution parfaite des contredanses les plus nouvelles! Jamais le bal de l'Ile d'Amour n'avait retenti de sons aussi purs et de coups d'archet aussi précis, aussi vigoureux. L'étonnement redoubla quand dans l'intervalle d'une contredanse à l'autre, nos musiciens improvisés firent entendre plusieurs morceaux d'ensemble, pleins d'harmonie et d'expression; ils captivèrent l'attention générale au point que les plus infatigables danseurs écoutaient en silence, sans songer le moins du monde à recommencer leurs bruyants quadrilles. Les musiciens qui avaient cédé leurs places n'osaient plus de les reprendre; ils étaient l'extase. Le maître de l'établissement survint, et après avoir fait quelques légers reproches à nos exécutants pour avoir envahi l'orchestra sans sa permission, il les engagea, pour prix de leur témérité, à continuer toute la soirée; ce qu'ils firent à la satisfaction générale.

Le lecteur ne sera pas fâché actuellement de connaître les noms de quatre musiciens; c'est peut-être un secret que je trahis, mais ils voudront bien me pardonner mon indiscrétion. Le premier violon, était *Duprez*, admirable ténor de l'Opéra, le second violon, *Wartel*, du même théâtre, le contre-basse, *Renaud*, artiste dramatique à Bruxelles. Enfin, l'alto, *Hippolyte Monpou*, l'auteur de *L'Andalouse*, qui fit aussi l'office de donneur de cachets ... Il n'avait point encore créé ses belles partitions du *Luthier de Vienne*, des *Deux Reines*, du *Piquillo* et du *Planteur*; mais les cinquante francs de sa première romance avaient fait bien des heureux ce soir là.

* * *

'It's lovely weather today, and not a penny in our pockets!' shouted in vexation, about twelve years ago, four young men with lively faces and a jovial air, who were strolling one beautiful summer morning along the Boulevard des Italiens. 'And your romance *L'Andalouse*, what have you done with it?' 'Don't talk to me about it, my friend; I have already offered it to more than ten music publishers, and nobody wants it. But I think it's very pretty.' 'Did you hear him, a father is always a father; the fact is, it's not bad at all.' 'Even if it were pure Boïeldieu, he's no further ahead with his *L'Andalouse*, because it does not give him the means to buy us even the most modest meal.'

And our four giddy friends laughed their heads off. 'But what if I gave it one last try?' our young musician went on. 'Here we are at M Lemoine's; he's the only one, I think, that I haven't offered my masterpiece to; wait for me; I'll be back in five minutes.'

He was right: M Lemoine, after examining closely the romance, which he found quite to his taste, asked the author with a smile how much he wanted to sell it for. 'How much do you want to give me for it?' 'Fifty francs, no more.' And already the budding composer had his hand out. The fifty francs were paid. Who could depict the joy of the young artist! He headed back to his friends and, jingling his coins in a way that made all the passers by turn round, he shouted, as soon as he caught sight of them, 'Victory! Victory! We have some money.' They congratulated him, they hugged him and they continued on their way with boisterous hilarity. 'Let's go to Belleville!' was the common cry; 'We'll eat there.' They did go, and had a hearty meal which lasted until dinner time. Who can tell all the mad schemes that were hatched during the joyous feast, all the plans, the projects, the castles in Spain that were built. In short, on leaving the table, and after a brief walk in the country, our friends arrived at the famous dance hall of the Ile d'Amour; it was a Sunday and people were dancing. The shrill noise of the instruments attracted the attention of our heroes, who went into the ballroom and joined in the dancing. 'What terrible music!' said one of them; 'It's burning my ears.' 'Let's play ourselves!', said another; 'That would be fun.' 'Bravo!' they all shouted together, and they suggested to the conductor and his three musicians that they replace them, just long enough, they added, for them to come back refreshed. The offer was accepted. Imagine the astonishment of the listeners on hearing a perfect performance of the latest dances! Never before had the ball at the Ile d'Amour echoed with sounds so pure, and with bow movements so precise and so vigorous. The astonishment increased when, in the interval between the dances, our temporary musicians played several ensemble pieces, full of harmony and expression: they riveted everyone's attention, to such a point that even the most tireless dancers listened in silence, without thinking in the least of recommencing their boisterous quadrilles. The musicians who had given up their places no longer dared take them back; they were in ecstasy. The proprietor of the establishment arrived, and after mildly reproaching our performers for invading the orchestra without his permission, he engaged them, for their temerity, to continue the whole evening: which they did to the satisfaction of all.

The reader won't object, at this point in time, to learning the names of our four musicians; perhaps I am giving away a secret, but they will be kind enough to forgive my indiscretion; on the first violin was Duprez, the admirable tenor of the Opéra; on the second violin, Wartel of the same theatre;

on the double bass Renard, dramatic artist in Brussels. Finally, on the viola Hippolyte Monpou, the author of *L'Andalouse*, who also filled the role of fee payer. He had not yet composed his beautiful pieces *Le Luthier de Vienne*, *Les Deux Reines*, *Le Piquillo* and *Le Planteur*; but the fifty francs of his first romance had made many people happy that evening.

Extract from Chapter XXI of Jules Janin's *The American in Paris* (London, 1843)

The great delight, the great occupation of the summer, in Paris, is music. As long as the winter lasts, the Parisians play to be applauded, to be admired, but when summer comes, they play for themselves, not for others. If you take pleasure in hearing them sing, or touch their favourite instruments, well and good, they will permit you to be present; but you are perfectly at liberty, if music does not please you, to go and walk in the garden. It must also be confessed, that this great art is admirably cultivated in this city, the progress of which is so rapid in all the arts. Fontenelle, who had so much wit, and who comprehended things so exactly, said in his time Sonata, what would you, from me? If Fontenelle were living now, he would lend an attentive and delighted ear to the skilful melodies of some happy drawing rooms which are justly celebrated throughout Paris. Music is no longer, as in the time of Clementi and the harpsichord, a strumming occupation of the young girl who wishes to be married; it is a complete science, difficult, gravely cultivated even by young scholars, who are trained at an early age, by clever masters. Thus, music is no longer made a frivolous pastime, but is taught as a serious business! I know a certain Parisian house, concealed between the silence of the court and the shadow of the garden, in which, if you have the slightest love for chefs d'oeuvre, you will certainly hear the best and most delightful music. There reign, absolute masters, venerated and admired, Weber and Mozart, Gluck and Beethoven; – all kinds of genius, every great work; the clearest and most beautiful voices, consider it an honour to sing these calm and affectionate melodies. What the master has composed, they sing as he has composed it; nothing more, nothing less. What pleasant evenings are thus passed with the Freischutz [sic], or the Don Juan, or the Adelaïde! Or else, it is some newcomer, who asks aid and protection; it is Schubert for instance, whose ideal reverie makes every mind fall into a thousand happy dreams. To all these great ideas, the most excellent interpreters are not wanted; these fearless singers are encouraged in their noble task by the first composers of the present day, Meyerbeer, if he is at all pleased with these fine voices, will lead the orchestra; Rossini, if he feels himself to be well understood and well rendered, will preside at the piano. How often I have seen Halévy turn the page of the lady who sang! For all the composers of Europe consider as an honour, this musical fraternity, which unites them to the virtuosi of the saloons. They are so happy and so proud to see themselves thus understood, thus sung! At the same time, the best artists ask their part in this long-dreamed popularity. Madame Damoreau, for instance, is never more charming, never more bird-like, than in these friendly réunions, where she can display at her ease, the rare bewitcheries of this inimitable art.

Music! it is the great pleasure of this city, the great occupation of the drawing rooms, which have banished politics, and which have renounced literature, from ennui. Question your recollections, and you will see that this great art of music is exercised by those men and women who occupy the highest position in the world. The Prince de la Moscowa, this spring, had the chefs d'oeuvre of Handel and of Palestrina, sung by the most beautiful voices in the faubourg Saint Germain. Never did the ancient abbey of Longchamps, in the time of its splendour, resound with sweeter voices, or more sacred airs. The intelligence of these happy artists is pushed farther than can easily be told; they bring to the execution of these beautiful works, all the art, all the science, all the poetic genius of primitive times, when the master himself led, in the sweet songs of harmony, his young children of the choir. Happy he who can take his part in these chosen joys of the first drawing rooms in Paris! happy he, who is admitted into these assemblies of artists so well disposed for enthusiasm! For my own part, in this, as in everything else, I have no reason to complain of Parisian hospitality; the stranger is loved in Paris, he is sought, he is protected. Approbation brought from afar, the remembrances which the traveller takes back to his own land, are not without value, even in the eyes of the handsomest women, and the cleverest men. If you arrive with ever so little benevolence and sympathy, you will certainly be welcome. The position of a traveller who knows how to make himself agreeable to these French Athenians, is undoubtedly a position worthy of envy; every house is open to you, every hand is held out to you. You easily pass the first and most difficult preliminaries of friendship. They remember in your favour, past absence and approaching departure; you are in every one's confidence; you are invited to all the soirées; in all the fêtes you have your part, and your good part too; for you and for you only, there are no exactions, no despotism. You visit a house every day. – 'Well!' they say, 'the Englishman is weary and he comes to ask from us, a little friendship and a little chatting.' – You are a whole month without calling; 'Is it because this poor Englishman is so busy seeing, guessing, understanding everything.' – You are at once admitted into the intimacy of these ladies and gentlemen. The ladies do not mistrust you – a bird of passage! The gentlemen have not the least jealousy of you, for, in fact, are you not to leave on the morrow, at latest! Thus you go, you come, you return, you remain, you disappear, you are completely your own master. What a delightful life! But then how sad it is, to know that these Parisians will so soon have forgotten this friend whom they loved so much.

Saloon music has recently sustained a great loss, that of the author of so many popular melodies which are admired throughout Europe; M Monpou; – he who sang so beautifully the ballade of M Alfred de Musset, *Connaissez vous dans Barcelone*; – and all that loving history of the Spanish serenade, dark complexion, autumn paleness, young marchioness with the black mantilla, satin dress which rustles as the lady leans from her balcony, to encourage by a look, the lover who fights for her! This marchioness d'Amaeghi was, for a long time, the rage in Paris. When Monpou died, the fashion in Paris was *le Fou de Tolède*, a Spaniard of M Hugo's, worthy of the Spaniard of M de Musset. Thus each month of the Parisian year brings with it, its novel which succeeds, its vaudeville which is applauded, its romance which is sung; a dozen vaudevilles; a dozen romances, as many novels, and Paris is satisfied. There is a certain romance, *la Folle* for instance, which has been played upon every piano, during a whole year; this is even the only romance which has found favour with his majesty king Louis Philippe, who is an amateur of about the same standing as the emperor Napoleon. Of all known airs, the emperor loved and tolerated only the *Monaco*; with one of these well-received airs, a man's fortune is made in Paris; *la Folle*, for instance, which has traversed the world. *Je vais revoir ma Normandie*, by a Norman poet and a Norman composer, has become the national song of the province; I have found it in all the steam-boats, by the side of every highway, at the door of the inns, everywhere; and the Norman does not tire of it any more than the traveller. And the romances of Mademoiselle Pujet [sic] which I forgot! how ingenious, how copious she is! how she has filled the world with her clearly accented melodies! She is a musical *bel esprit*; they are true dramas which she writes and composes; and by way of rest from her dramas, she produces, from time to time, some lively and beautiful comedy. The fashionable ladies and the most skilful singers, even those of the opera, consider it a pleasure to repeat the compositions of Mademoiselle Pujet. These lines which I write in her praise, are penned to the sound of military music, which plays her finest airs. Is it not strange, an army marching to fight, while music plays in the distance, melodies sprung from the head of a young girl? Certainly, this may be called success!

You understand then all the interest presented by a Parisian saloon thus occupied in this vain passion; there, are boldly produced all the compositions of France, of Italy, of Germany; there, come to exhibit themselves, the rarest talents in Europe; there, you may suddenly see enter the celebrated cosmopolites of the musical art; Ernst, whose violin is filled with such sweet strains; Panofka, who will only play to chosen friends; the inspired Hauman; and the great pianists who make Paris their solemn rendezvous, Doelher, the charming and poetic genius; Thalberg, dreams personified; Hallé, who thoroughly understands the genius of Beethoven; and, finally, Liszt, – Liszt the thundering, Liszt the irresistible, who burns, who crashes, and then suddenly brings you the melodies he has picked up, here and there, in the world. It is a delight to hear them, it is a pleasure to see them, as animated as if for a battle! Each year they wish to know where Paris is, what it is doing, and what it thinks; each year you may therefore see them coming to solicit, – better than their approbation, – to solicit the friendship, of these artistes of the fashionable world, their worthy brethren, impartial and benevolent judges, who accept for themselves all the dangers of the struggle, all the sorrows of defeat, yielding to whoever has the right, the triumph, the popularity, the glory! Happily, in all this triumph or defeat, the pleasure is for all.

The day of which I speak, all the family was assembled in the small music-room; there was no one there but a few intimate friends, of those friends who call at all hours, before whom one thinks aloud, and sings in a low voice. The young lady of the house, who is a true artiste, had just played with the most noble instinct, the overture of Der Freischütz, that formidable composition, to which nothing can be compared; her sister, who is still a child, but an inspired child, had sung the Adelaïde of Beethoven, the most touching and most affectionate complaint which ever sprang from the heart of a lover and a poet. You would have said, that, in order the better to hear these sweet strains, every voice was silent beyond the house. For ourselves, we were entirely absorbed in this near contemplation of old masterpieces sustained by young voices. We said to each other, that assuredly it was a delightful destiny for the poet whose verses are repeated by new generation – for the composer, who can yet hear, from the depth of his tomb, the sweet melodies of his twentieth year. On these conditions, a man cannot die; he is arrested by death, but the idea which urged him, still marches onward; his song expires upon his failing lips, but the interrupted air is immediately taken up by some young and noble singer. This respect for the masterpieces of former music, France has carried to a great extent; there is no music so old and so forgotten, that the French have not restored it to honour. They have found again nearly all the musicians of the sixteenth century; they have searched in the repertories of all the chapels; they have demanded again from the organ of the cathedrals its interrupted chants.

They had a great musician, named Baillot, who played to admiration an Italian air, *la Romanesca*, recovered by a happy accident, beneath the splendid arches of the Genoese palace. It is a melody of irresistible effect; only to hear it tremble beneath the bow, it seems to you, that all this beautiful Italian society of the sixteenth century, these young men, whom Ariosto celebrates, these friends of Medicis, these companions of Doria, are about to re-appear in these magnificent galleries, all filled with the chefs d'oeuvres of painters and sculptors. Assuredly, when young Paolo took you by the hand, lovely and proud Francesca, to dance with you, the orchestra suspended in its marble balcony, did not play a sweeter, a more tender or a more melancholy air. Nothing can equal, for remembrances, some one of these wandering melodies, which centuries have murmured in the days of their youth, by the light of their stars, by the brilliancy of their sun.

And then, the great art of the French virtuosos, is to give a truly poetic expression to the most simple songs of former days. Of all the airs with which their nurses lulled them in their cradles, of the joyous country rounds, of the terrible complaints in which spirits and phantoms are named, these clever people have made so many duets, songs, grave elegies. From an Auvergne dance, they have composed a romance full of art and taste; from the *Clair de la lune, mon ami Pierrot*, they have drawn the most charming of quartetts [sic]. Rossini himself, that great genius, who seizes every light and shade, – did he not write his beautiful finale to the *Comte Ory* from the popular air, *Le Comte Ory disait pour s'égayer*. Following his example, Meyerbeer composed *Les Huguenots* from a psalm of the reformed church; this is what may be called profitably using the smallest parts of the genius of a people. And remember that this passion for music has quickly passed from the drawing rooms of Paris into the streets, and even the crossways. In the summer, if the night is at all fine, if there is anything like silence in the public place, you suddenly hear the sound of all kinds of beautiful voices, which sing ingenious melodies. To hear them, you would fancy yourself in some city of Germany. It is truly noble music, they are real singers; the people slowly follow them, attracted, and as if fascinated, by these unexpected melodies. Whence come they? They proceed from the school of a man named Wilhem, a worthy man, of natural genius good to the poor, devoted to his art, the friend of Béranger the poet, whose most charming songs he has set to music. This Wilhem finding that he was idle, and that the theatre was closed against him as well as the chapel promised himself that he would one day contradict the anti-musical reputation of the good people of France. He would, he said, subdue, to strict time, these bawling voices, these rebellious ears, and replace, by a grave and simple harmony, the indecent song of the alehouse. He wished that in future, whenever the temple needed a thousand singers a thousand singers should at once reply, Here we are! He wished that, on the day when the national hymn was to resound through the cities these young, ardent voices should make of the national hymn a song of glory and not a death cry. ...

Bibliography

Adam, A., *Souvenirs d'un musicien*, Paris, 1857

Ancelot, Mme, *Les salons de Paris, foyers éteints 1824–64*, Paris, 1858

Anon [A. Pougin], *Almanach de la musique*, Paris, 1866

Apponyi, R., *Vingt-cinq ans à Paris 1826–1850*, Paris, 1913

Azevedo, A., *Félicien David: coup d'oeil sur sa vie et son oeuvre*, Paris, 1863

Bachelier, H., 'Hippolyte Monpou', *M*, XC, 1928

Balzac, H. de, *Cousine Bette* (1846), transl. M. A. Crawford, Penguin Classics, 1965

Barbier, A., *Souvenirs personnels et silhouettes contemporaines*, Paris, 1883

Barzun, J., 'Paris in 1830', in *Music in Paris in the Eighteen-Thirties*, ed. Peter Bloom, 1987, New York

Beaumont-Vassy, E.-F., *Les salons de Paris et la société parisienne sous Louis-Philippe I*, Paris, 1866

Becker, H. and G., *Giacomo Meyerbeer – a Life in Letters*, Helm, 1989

Bernac, P., *The Interpretation of French Song*, London, 1970

Berlioz, H., *Mémoires*, trans. David Cairns as *The Memoirs of Hector Berlioz*, 2nd edn, London, 1977

Bishop, L., *The Poetry of Alfred de Musset*, New York, 1987

Boutet de Monvel, E., *Adolphe Nourrit*, Paris, 1903

Bowles, G., *The Defense of Paris*, London, 1871

Brombert, B. A., *Cristina: Portraits of a Princess*, London, 1978

Cairns, D., *Berlioz*, vol. 1: *The Making of an Artist*, London, 1989

Chambrier, J., *La cour et la société de Second Empire*, Paris, 1902

Cooper, M., *French Music from the Death of Berlioz to the Death of Fauré*, London, 1951

Cox, D, 'France', in *A History of Song*, ed. D. Stevens, London, 1960

Curtiss, M., *Bizet and His World*, New York, 1958

Curzon, H. de, *Ernest Reyer, sa vie et ses oeuvres*, Paris, 1924

———— *Léo Delibes – sa vie et ses oeuvres*, Paris, 1926

Dahlaus, C., *Nineteenth-Century Music*, trans. J. Bradford Robinson, Berkeley & Los Angeles, 1989

Daudet, A., *Trente ans de Paris*, Paris, 1888

Daumard, A., *La bourgeoisie parisienne de 1815 à 1848*, Paris, 1963

Dean, W., *Bizet*, London, 1975

Delaborde, H., *Notice sur la vie et les oeuvres de M. Victor Massé*, Paris, 1888

Delaire, J. A., *Histoire de la romance considerée comme oeuvre littéraire et musicale*, Paris, 1845

Deutsch, O., *Franz Schubert Thematisches Verseichnis seiner Werke in chronologischer Folge*, Kassel, 1978

Devriès A. and Lesure F., *Dictionnaire des éditeurs de musique française*, 2 vols, Geneva, 1988

Duprez, G. L., *Souvenirs d'un chanteur*, Paris, 1880

———— *L'art du chant*, Paris, 1882

Ellis, K., *Music Criticism in Nineteenth-Century France*, Oxford, 1995

Escudier, L., *Mes souvenirs*, Paris, 1886

Escudier, Frères, *Dictionnaire de musique*, Paris, 1854

Fauquet, J.-M., 'Alexis de Castillon (1838–1873), sa vie, son oeuvre', thesis for Ecole pratique des Hautes Etudes, Paris 1979

F.-J. Fétis, *Biographie universelle des musiciens*, 2nd edn 1860–65, with suppl., edn A. Pougin, Paris, 1878–80

Fitzlyon, A., *The Price of Genius: a life of Pauline Viardot*, London, 1964

———— *Maria Malibran: diva of the Romantic Age*, London, 1987

François-Sappey, B., 'La vie musicale à Paris à travers les Mémoires d'Eugène Sauzay', *Reveue de musicologie*, LX/1–2, 1974, 159–210

Gautier, T., *L'histoire du romantisme*, Paris, 1874

Girardin, D. de, *Lettres parisiennes*, Paris, 1986

Goncourt, E. and J., *Journal*, Paris, n.d.

Gougelot, H., *La romance française sous la Révolution et l'Empire*, Melun, 1943

Gounod, C. *Mémoires d'un artiste*, Paris, 1896

Gradenwitz, P., 'Félicien David (1810–1876) and French Romantic Orientalism', *MQ*, lxii, 1976, 471–506

Grossir, C., *L'Islam des romantiques 1811–1840*, Paris, 1984

Guichard, L., *Musique et lettres au temps du romantisme*, Paris, 1955

Halévy, F., *Derniers portraits et souvenirs*, Paris, 1863

Harding, J., *Gounod*, London, 1973

———— *Massenet*, London, 1970

Hillairet, J., *Dictionnaire historique des rues de Paris*, 2 vols, Paris, 1963

Horne, A., *The Fall of Paris*, London 1965

Howard, M., *The Franco-Prussian War*, London, 1961

Howat, R., 'Fryderyck Chopin and the Salon, "An accidental home for his music"', *BBC Music Magazine*, October, 1999, 41–3

Imbert, H., *Nouveaux profiles de musiciens*, Paris, 1892.

Irvine, D., *Massenet – a Chronicle of his Life and Times*, Portland, 1994

Janin, J. G., *An American in Paris*, London, 1843 (a translation of the writer's *L'été à Paris and Hiver à Paris,* Paris, 1843)

Jensen, E.F., 'Hippolyte Monpou and French Romanticism', *The Music Review*, xlv/2, 1984, 122–34

Johnson, J. H., *Listening in Paris – a cultural history*, Berkeley, Los Angeles and London, 1995

Julien, A., *Ernest Reyer: sa vie et ses oeuvres* (Paris, 1911)

Laforêt, C., *La vie musicale au temps romantique*, Paris 1929, rept. New York 1977

Laspeyres, I., 'Les salons où l'on chante à la fin du Second Empire', *Revue international de la musique française*, xvii, June, 1985, 57–74

Legouvé, E, *Soixante ans de souvenirs*, Paris, 1894

Lesure, F., (ed.), *La musique à Paris en 1830–31*, Paris, 1988

Liszt, F., 'De la situation des artistes et de leur condition dans la société', *GM*, May–October, 1835

Locke, R. P., *Music, Musicians, and the Saint-Simonians*, Chicago, 1986

Lockspeiser, E., 'The French Songs in the nineteenth century', *Musical Quarterly*, xxvi, 1940, 192–9

Malet, H., *Le Baron Haussmann et la rénovation de Paris*, Paris, 1973

Martin-Fugier, A., *La vie élégante ou la formation du Tout-Paris 1815–1848*, Paris, 1990

Meister, B., *Nineteenth-Century French Song, Fauré, Chausson, Duparc and Debussy*, Bloomington, 1980

Merlin, Countess (Maria de las Mercedes de Jaruco), *Memoirs of Mme Malibran by the Countess Merlin and other intimate friends*, London, 1840

Mongrèdien, J., *La musique en France des lumières au romantisme*, Paris, 1986

Niedermeyer, A., *Louis Niedermeyer, son oeuvre et son école*, Paris, 1867

———— *Vie d'un compositeur moderne*, Paris, 1893

Noske, F., *French Song from Berlioz to Duparc*, trans. Rita Benton, 2nd ed. New York, 1970

Ollivier, D., *Correspondence de Liszt et de la comtesse, 1833–1840*, Paris, 1933–34

Pleasants, H., *The Great Tenor Tragedy: the last days of Adolphe Nourrit as told (mostly) by himself*, Portland, 1995

Pougin, A., *La jeunesse de Mme Desbordes-Valmore*, Paris, 1898

———— *Albert Grisar*, Paris, 1870

———— *Musiciens du XIXe siècle*, Paris, 1911

———— 'Victor Massé', *M*, 6 July 1884

Prod'homme, J.-G. and Dandelot, A., *Gounod – sa vie et ses oeuvres*, Paris, 1911, r. 1973

Querlin, M., *La Princesse Mathilde*, Lausanne, 1966

Quicherat, M.-L., *Adolphe Nourrit, sa vie, son talent, son caractère, sa correspondence*, Paris, 1867

Reed, J., *The Schubert Song Companion*, Manchester, 1985

Rees, B., *Camille Saint-Saëns – A Life*, London, 1999

Reyer, E., *40 ans de musique*, Paris, 1909

———*Notes de musique*, Paris, 1875

———*Notice sur Félicien David*, Paris, 1877

Richardson, J., *Princess Mathilde*, London, 1969

———*La Vie Parisienne*, London, 1971

Ringer, A (ed), *The Early Romantic Era*, New Jersey, 1990

Roger, G., *Le carnet d'un ténor*, Paris, 1880

Romagnesi, A., *L'art de chanter les romances*, Paris, 1846

Rossillion, P., 'Un romantique oublié: "le Berlioz de la ballade": Hippolyte Monpou', *Guide musicale,* iii–iv, 1930

Saint-Saëns, C., *Portraits et souvenirs*, Paris, 1899

———*Harmonie et mélodie*, Paris, 1885

Sardent, M., *La Princesse Mathilde*, Paris, 1928

Scudo, P., *Critiques et littérature musicales*, Paris, n.d., repr 1986

Sheppard, N., *Shut Up in Paris*, London, 1871

Simon, D. R., 'The Life and Songs of Hippolyte Monpou', unpubl. doctoral dissertation, University of Iowa, 1970

Stadler, J., 'La première romance', *EM*, 1 Sept., 1839

Talvart, H. and Place, J., *Bibliographie des auteurs modernes de langue française*, Paris, 1928–76

Thiébault, Général, *Du chant, et particulièrement de la Romance* (1813), in Gougelot (above)

Tiersot, J., *Lettres des musiciens écrites en français XV–XXe siècles*, Paris, 1924

Tunley, D., *Romantic French Song with translations and commentaries*, 6 vols (in facsimile), New York, 1994–95

Vasari, Giorgio, *Delle vite de' più eccellenti pittori, scultori, ed architettori italiani* (1550), transl. George Bull as *Lives of the Artists*, London, 1995

BIBLIOGRAPHY

Chadbourn, W.H., and Danielson, J., *Casanova s Le Icosameron*, Paris, 1974-1975.

Cherpin, M., *La Princesse Mathilde*, Jardins, 1964.

...

Hegel, ..., *The Science, Soul Companion*, Munich ..., 1985-19...

Saint, B., *Confessions*, Livre ... A.E.D., London, 1909.

Marc, ..., *Mémoires nouvelles*, Paris, 1960.

———, *Nouveaux Mémoires*, 1855.

———, *Nouveaux ... Edition Otto*, Paris, 1873.

Robinson, ..., *Giacomo*, ... USA, London, 1960.

———, ... *In Bed*, Paris, nos. 4 and no ...

Rupert, A. (ed.), *The Zorro Romantic Age*, New York, 1969.

Rope, O., *Casanova ... du Livre ...*, Legras, 1882, ... 1889.

Thompson, ..., *Aspects de Casanova ... tome ... .*, Éditions ...

Rosselini, E., *Il vero Casanova, Problème ... Giacomo Casanova, Inédit ... Autographe.*

Mahone, *Chateaubriand*, Berk ... H., 1950.

Saint-André, L., *Portrait d'Casanova*, Paris, 1897.

———, *Casanova et ... siècle*, Paris, ...

Serban, ..., *Le ... et son temps*, Munich, Paris, 1994.

Sorabella, V., *Voyage à un Lieutenant du ...*, Paris, ... 1936, 1984.

Steinberg, N., *Society ... A.M.*, Paris, 1971.

Sam, E. P., *The ... The Saga of Giacomo Casanova ... Memoirs, Impostor, Gangster of Distribution*, Gloucester-ton, 1988, ... p.p.

Starobinski, *La ... transparent ...*, ... XIII Siècle, Paris.

Tamanois, Maurice, Ciano, *L'Italienne, Ascot de nos institutions*, Bruxelles, Pagel ..., Fabre, 1978, 78.

Vincent, Conrad, *Giacomo C. précurseur ... siècle, Révérence* (1917), pp.

Yanès (ed.), (Ed.) ...

Jarnac, Chester, ... *L'Amour Faust ... Vol. Philosophical ... XVIII siècle, F. ...*

Young, ..., ... *Casanova en la vie ... Par ... Lettres ... 1966 ...*

Yuan, ..., *Colour Plates to ... de Venise en son ... Edition Française ... par ...*

Urban ... (1950), *Lettres ... et ... Sex ... Société ... par Vanessa, London, 1936.*

Index